Call Center Supervision

The Complete, Practical Guide to Managing Frontline Staff

By
Penny Reynolds

Contributing Authors:
Maggie Klenke
Pamela Trickey

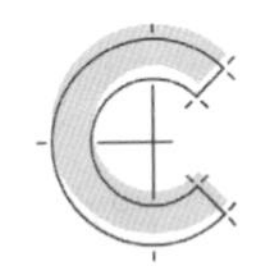

The Call Center School Press
Nashville, TN

Call Center Supervision:
The Complete, Practical Guide to Managing Frontline Staff

Printed in the United States of America by The Call Center School Press
First printing December 2004

Library of Congress Catalog Card Number: 2004195178

ISBN 0-9744179-2-0

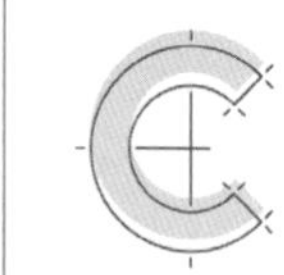

The Call Center School Press is a division of The Call Center School. The Call Center School provides a variety of consulting and educational services to call center professionals. For additional information on The Call Center School products and services, call 615-812-8400 or visit www.thecallcenterschool.com.

TABLE OF CONTENTS

INTRODUCTION

CHAPTER 1: TODAY'S CALL CENTER SUPERVISOR

ASSEMBLING AND PREPARING YOUR TEAM

CHAPTER 2: DEVELOPING A STAFFING PLAN

CHAPTER 3: RECRUITING AND HIRING

CHAPTER 4: TRAINING AND DEVELOPMENT

CHAPTER 5: BUILDING AND MANAGING TEAMS

PERFORMANCE MEASUREMENT AND MANAGEMENT

CHAPTER 6: KEY PERFORMANCE INDICATORS

CHAPTER 7: DEFINING AND MEASURING PERFORMANCE

ANALYSIS AND COACHING

CHAPTER 8: DIAGNOSING PERFORMANCE PROBLEMS

CHAPTER 9: FUNDAMENTALS OF COACHING

MOTIVATION AND RETENTION

CHAPTER 10: MOTIVATING FOR PERFORMANCE

CHAPTER 11: RETENTION STRATEGIES

TOOLS AND TECHNOLOGIES

CHAPTER 12: CALL CENTER TECHNOLOGY OVERVIEW

LEGAL AND PERSONNEL ISSUES

CHAPTER 13: LEGAL AND PERSONNEL ISSUES

Dedication

To Alex, Rachel, and Sarah

Preface

Call Center Supervision: The Complete, Practical Guide to Managing Frontline Staff is a book designed to address the specific knowledge and skills needed by people that manage and support frontline staff in a call center. For many companies, the call center is the main contact point with customers. Therefore, much is riding on the shoulders of the frontline staff and each customer interaction. Ensuring that these staff perform well and are satisfied and happy in the job is the primary role of the supervisor or manager.

This book is designed to help supervisors and managers make the most of their staff's performance. Most of chapters in this book address the unique problems and issues associated with people and performance management. Topics range from recruiting and hiring the right people, to analyzing performance, to coaching and counseling. There are also chapters devoted to the unique aspects of call center operations such as calculating staff requirements, understanding call center technology, and complying with labor regulations.

Every attempt has been made to make the concepts easy to understand, with simple language and real-world scenarios. It is suggested that as you read each chapter, you take some time to look at the examples, and think about how you would apply them in your own call center with your own employees.

Acknowledgments

I would like to thank Maggie Klenke and Pamela Trickey, my fellow founders and partners in The Call Center School for their writing contributions to this book. Maggie is our technology guru and is responsible for much of Chapter 12, while Pam is the expert who provided the content for Chapter 13's labor issues. They both were instrumental in helping to shape and fine-tune the other chapters as well. This book would never have been possible without their advice and support.

In terms of individuals that have shaped my knowledge over the years, the names are too numerous to mention. By rough calculation, I figure I have taught classes to over a thousand call center supervisors and managers, and I have gained a wealth of information from the experiences, problems, and thoughts they've been willing to share. For all you prior students out there, thanks for the information and the ideas!

Finally, I'd like to thank my husband Clint for his understanding and support for the many evening and weekend hours devoted to this project. To my dad, thank you for always believing in whatever new venture I decide to try. To my mom, thanks for instilling the dogged determination to never give up and to get things "just right." And to my children, Alex, Rachel, and Sarah, thanks for the many hours spent in my office keeping me company and always supplying the smiles and laughter to keep me going. I love you all.

About the Author

Penny Reynolds is a founding Partner of The Call Center School, where she heads up curriculum development. She develops and teaches courses on a wide variety of call center topics and speaks at many industry conferences and association meetings. Penny has spent over twenty years in the call center and telecommunications industry, and is known as an industry expert on topics such as workforce management, application of call center technologies, and general call center operations and people management.

Penny writes frequently for industry publications, and has been published in *Call Center, Customer Interaction Solutions, Customer Support Management, Customer Relationship Management, International Customer Service Association Journal, Operations and Fulfillment, Call Center Europe, TeleBusiness International, Business Communications Review,* and others.

In addition to this book, Penny is the author of the book *Call Center Staffing: The Complete, Practical Guide to Workforce Management.* She has also co-authored several other books with Maggie Klenke and Pamela Trickey, including *Business School Essentials for Call Center Leaders, Strategies for Managing Call Center Personnel, Call Center Operations Management I and II, and Call Center Management Overview and Applications.*

Penny served on the inaugural editorial board of *Customer Support Management* magazine, is a member of ICSA (International Customer Support Association) and SOCAP (Society of Consumer Affairs Professionals), and is among the first in the industry to receive CIAC *Call Center Management Consultant* certification. For her contributions to the industry, Penny was awarded *Call Center* magazine's prestigious *Call Center Pioneer Award* in 1996. She is an honors graduate of Vanderbilt University.

Chapter 1 – Today's Call Center Supervisor

Congratulations on your position as a call center supervisor or team manager! While you may not have had lifelong aspirations to be in call center management, you've certainly arrived at an exciting place with much career potential ahead of you.

The call center industry is an exciting place to be in the beginning of the 21st Century. Call centers in the United States alone employ more than four million people, and those people with the skills and knowledge to be successful in call center management have a bright future indeed.

In this chapter, we'll introduce you to this exciting call center industry. You'll read about the roles and responsibilities that you'll have in a call center supervisory role and get a feel for where you fit in the organization.

1. ***What is a call center?***
2. ***What kinds of call centers exist?***
3. ***Where do you fit in the organization?***
4. ***What are your responsibilities as a call center supervisor?***
5. ***What other functions are performed in a call center?***

1. What is a call center?

A call center is defined as: a place where calls are made and received.

The definition of a call center in its simplest form is "a place where calls are made and received." Other definitions increasingly include mention of the handling of various types of interactions in addition to telephone calls, so your organization might use the term "contact center" to refer to the place where your company's transactions take place.

The terms "call center" and "contact center" are used interchangeably, with "call center" being the more commonly used. The term "call center" is more easily understood and for now best represents the proportion of interactions that are indeed carried out by telephone compared to emails or web chats, but may include centers with multiple media contacts. Even with the explosive growth of the Internet and email transactions, telephone calls will continue to be the primary means of customer communications in the first decade of the 21st Century.

In addition to defining a call center as a place for customer interactions, it is important to denote what else makes an entity a call center and not just a place where telephone calls are answered. A call center is typically defined as an operation where more than one person is responding to contacts, and also where the interaction can be handled by anyone within a group. In other words, the call requires a capability and not a specific individual to handle it.

For example, a travel agency where customers call directly into their favorite travel agents would not constitute a call center. In this situation, callers would likely find their agent of choice busy on another call and have to wait or leave a message, while other agents who could just as easily handle the call sat idle. If the agency instead had customers call a number and then directed them to a group of individuals who could address their need, the agency would have a call center. The benefits would be better utilization of their travel agents and a faster response time to customers.

Scope of Business

There are over 80,000 call centers in the United States and over 15,000 in Canada.

Given the far-reaching definition of what makes up a call center, it's hard to pinpoint exactly how many call centers truly exist. Since a two-person office that shares phone responsibilities meets the broad definition of a call center, there could be literally hundreds of thousands of these type operations.

However, since being a call center typically implies having technology to answer and distribute calls, the number of "official" call centers is therefore lower. Using the sale of call center technology as a basis for extrapolation, the following numbers are estimates of the size and scope of the call center industry as of 2005:

- There were approximately 75,000 sites using call center related technologies in the United States in 2000. At current growth rates, it is estimated that there will be over 80,000 by end of 2005.

- It is estimated that Canada has 15,000 call centers in 2005 with forecast growth at over 7% per year.

- There were approximately 13,000 call centers in Europe in 2000 with expectations of 25,000 by the end of 2005.

- Australia is expected to have approximately 4,500 call centers and Latin American countries will have grown to 1,600 call centers by the end of 2005.

- The Asia-Pacific region is the newest region to experience call center growth, with over 5,000 call centers expected to be in place by the end of 2005.

Over 4 million people work in call centers in the United States alone. That's over 3% of the working population.

Labor Force

With such a large number of call centers, the call center profession is obviously one that employs large numbers of employees. Indeed, based on studies from The Call Center School using U.S. Bureau of Labor Statistics, it is estimated that approximately 4 million frontline agent positions are active today.

Approximately 2.6 million of these positions are filled by full-time staff and the remaining 1.4 million positions are shared by part-time staff (about 2.4 million persons). These 5 million persons employed by call centers in 2005 represent approximately 1.8% of the total United States population and about 3.5% of the working population.

The Canadian call center industry employs over 650,000 agents as of 2004, which is over 4% of the working population. In the province of New Brunswick alone, there are over 17,000 agents or 1 in every 20 employed persons.

Economic Impact

Over one trillion dollars of commerce happen in call centers each year.

The call center industry plays an important role in today's economy, not just by employing so many workers, but by enabling trade and commerce. According to a study in the Harvard Business Review, more than 70% of business transactions take place over the telephone and 80% of these transactions occur in a call center setting. There will be an estimated one trillion dollars in products and services sold through a call center in 2005.

2. What kinds of call centers exist?

The present day call center can be defined in a number of ways. It can be defined by the type of contact handled (inbound versus outbound), the type of center (in-house versus outsourced), the primary functions performed (customer service versus sales), and the geographic scope (single versus multi-site). The following outlines the most common definitions of call centers today using these five definitive categories:

Types of Contacts

The types of call center contacts can be categorized into these definitions:

- *Business to Business.* The primary contacts for this call center are other business entities. For example, the call center may take calls from a business that wishes to order company insurance or benefits for its employees. Likewise the center may place outbound calls to sell printer or copier supplies to another business.
- *Business to Consumer.* The primary contacts for this center are individuals. This type of center may take calls from individual customers placing a catalog order or making a hotel reservation, or provide support to someone using the company's products or services. On the outbound side, the center may place calls to individuals to raise funds or sell a specific product aimed at the individual consumer.
- *Internal.* The primary contacts for this center are the company's own employees. The center may be an internal help desk for technical issues or may be a hot-line for employee benefit and compensation issues. All calls are internal communications.

Types of Call Centers

The types of call centers are generally divided into these four categories:

- *Inbound Call Center.* This type of center responds to incoming calls and inquiries related to that organization's customers.
- *Outbound Call Center.* This type of center places outbound calls to its customers or prospects.
- *Blended Call Center.* This type of center takes both incoming calls and places outbound calls. The term "blended call center" also refers to the types of contacts being handled. A blended inbound center might handle contacts that include incoming telephone calls along with emails or web chats. Likewise, a blended outbound center might communicate through outbound calling as well as email or fax communications.

- *Outsourced Center.* An outsourced call center is one that handles calls on behalf of another organization. Its primary business is initiating or receiving other companies' customer or prospect calls.

There are six main functions of call centers: customer service, telesales, technical support, dispatch, collections, and research.

Primary Functions

The primary functions of a call center can generally be categorized into one of the following six categories:

- *Customer Service.* The function of a customer service center is to provide assistance regarding an organization's products or services. Examples include utility customer service, tracking assistance for overnight carriers, consumer hotline for a pharmaceutical company, and credit card service centers.
- *TeleSales.* The function of a sales center is primarily to generate revenue through the sale of the company's goods and services through inbound calls, outbound calls, or both. Examples include hotel reservations, catalog sales, direct television advertising orders, and newspaper classified advertising or subscription centers.
- *Technical Support.* The function of these centers is to provide assistance in using a company's products. Examples may include a computer hardware support, software help desk, or specialized support desks for use of medical technology products.
- *Dispatch.* The function of a dispatch center is to take an inbound call and in turn engage a resource to address the problem or customer need. Examples may include taxi or transportation dispatch, package pickup and delivery, 911 emergency assistance, or vehicle roadside services.
- *Collections.* The function of these centers is to contact customers with the primary purpose of collecting money or funds. Examples include credit card collection centers, mortgage collection, and specialized collection agencies.
- *Research.* The function of a research center is not to sell or support a product, but to conduct research for the company or out side organizations. Examples include market research firms and political polling organizations.

Geographic Scope

Another way to define a call center is by its geographic scope as outlined in the following definitions:

- *Internal.* An in-house center is one that serves only internal customers such as an internal help desk or human resources central hotline.

A call center's coverage may be limited to internal calls or be wide enough in geographic scope to take calls from all over the world.

- *Local.* A local call center may only serve customers in a limited geographic area due to the scope of the business. For example, a local taxi or bus service will likely only take calls from the immediate area where its customer base resides and all calls may be local, not long-distance calls.
- *Regional.* A regional call center may provide a product or service to customers beyond a local area, but limited by regional boundaries. For example, many local telephone companies provide service in a specific regional area and their customer service or sales centers may cover several states with local and long-distance calls coming into the call center.
- *National.* These centers take calls from the entire country, with toll-free services making geography transparent. Examples include reservation centers, catalogs, and various product support centers.
- *International.* These centers take calls that extend beyond national borders in scope. Certainly, with the growth of the Internet, contacts can easily be made with customers all over the world and many of these email and web contacts are handled by the call center.

3. Where do you fit in the organization?

The success of any call center is dependant far more upon its personnel than its technology or processes. Organizational structure is important to any business, but it is particularly critical to a call center operation since the work is so labor-intensive.

Smart organizations recognize the need to be flexible and adaptable to the demands and expectations of callers that include customers, employees, management, and other departments. To provide this flexibility, many call center organizations have abandoned traditional "top down" hierarchical structures in favor of a team structure.

Therefore, it is likely that as a supervisor, you will be responsible for a team of frontline employees. A team structure in the call center typically begins with a functional team of anywhere from ten to fifty frontline agents, with a typical team size being twelve to fifteen.

The official job title of these frontline employees varies widely by company. While the generally accepted term in the industry (and the one we'll use in this book) is "agent," there are many other common titles used in call centers today, such as:

- Agent
- Customer service representative (CSR)
- Telephone service representative (TSR)
- Customer associate
- Customer advocate

Likewise, the title of the person that directly supervises these frontline staff may vary too. Here are a few of the common titles:

- Supervisor
- Team leader
- Team manager
- Team captain

The size of the team and the reporting hierarchy will vary from one organization to another. A sample organizational chart for a call center is shown on the following page.

Sample Organizational Chart

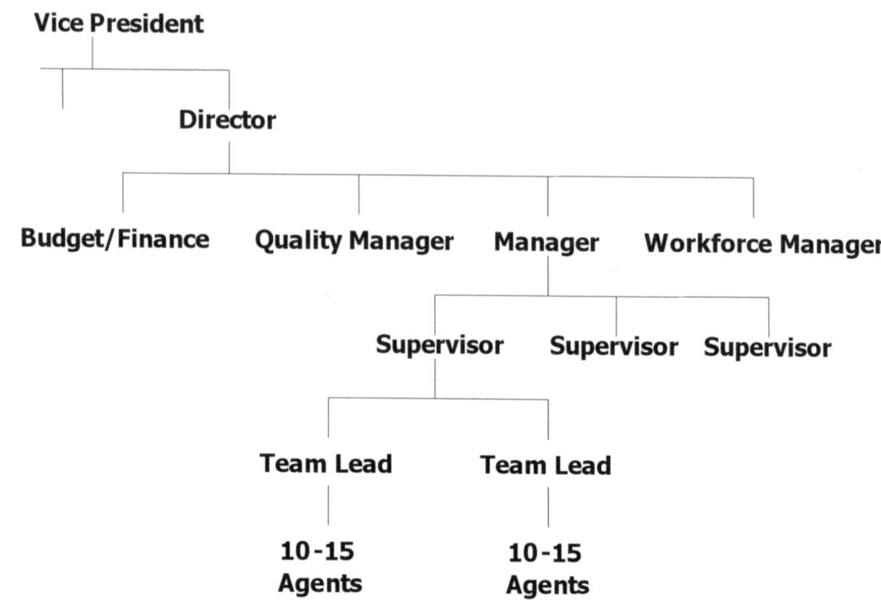

4. What are your responsibilities as a call center supervisor?

Each agent generally reports to a supervisor responsible for several team members. The supervisor is usually responsible for the performance of the members of the team and duties may include the following:

- Address personnel issues of team members
- Monitor calls and coach agents
- Train new staff
- Administer schedules of team members
- Interview agent candidates for hire
- Conduct performance reviews
- Conduct team meetings
- Work on special projects
- Create performance reports for staff and management
- Assist with escalated calls
- Assist with regular calls during busy call times

Standard ratios of agents to supervisors in a call center are 10:1 to 20:1, with supervisors in most call centers having responsibility for 12-15 agents. Where the ratio of agents to supervisors is high (>15:1), the call center may utilize a "team lead" position as an intermediate step between agent and supervisor. This lead position will likely handle calls as well as assist with supervisory duties such as training, coaching, and providing call support.

The supervisor typically reports to a call center manager whose role is to direct the day-to-day operations of the center. The sample job descriptions that follow outline the various lead agent and supervisory roles in a call center.

Sample Job Description

Title of Position: Call Center Lead Agent (or Team Lead)

Reports to: Call Center Supervisor

Position Summary:

This position represents an intermediate role between frontline staff and supervisor and is a stepping-stone to a call center supervisory role. This person will be responsible for assisting the supervisor in managing 14-20 frontline agents in a challenging inbound service industry.

Job Responsibilities and Requirements:

- Assist supervisor with administrative duties to include schedule distribution and management of schedule trades, time-off requests, and schedule exceptions.
- Monitor calls and coach staff based upon performance guidebook.
- Participate in new hire orientation, serving as a mentor for new team members.
- Provide training on specialized call handling techniques and procedures.
- Assist with call handling duties during peak times.
- Provide assistance to frontline agents on escalated calls or problems.
- Assist supervisor in tracking performance results of each team member and communicating results to individual and team.
- Communicate with customers both verbally and in writing where follow-up is required.

Sample Job Description

Title of Position: Customer Service Supervisor
Reports to: Call Center Manager

Position Summary:

This position will manage a group of customer service agents in a fast-paced banking environment. The supervisor will have overall responsibility for direct supervision of staff as well as being tasked with identifying operational issues and areas for process improvements.

Job Responsibilities and Requirements:

- Provide day-to-day supervision to ensure complete and efficient customer interactions.
- Monitor sample calls and coach for improved performance.
- Handle escalated and problem calls.
- Participate in data collection and analysis for performance evaluation, trending, and feedback to other departments.
- Develop motivational programs to keep morale and retention high.
- Participate in recruitment, hiring, and orientation of new staff.
- Coordinate with workforce planning area on scheduling issues.
- Document business policies and procedures.
- Keep records of employee interactions and feedback in disciplinary situations.
- Participate in special projects as needed.
- Conduct weekly pre-shift meetings.

5. What other functions are performed in a call center?

There are many different aspects of running a call center. These operational functions are typically divided into eight categories.

Workforce Management	Quality Management	Human Resources Administration	Technology Management
Forecasting and Staffing	Customer Assessments	Recruiting and Hiring	Selection and Acquisition
Schedule Creation	Performance Assessment	Staff Orientation and Training	Implementation and Upgrades
Daily Service Management	Performance Improvement Process	Compensation and Benefits	Ongoing Management
Reporting and Communications	**Financial Management**	**Facilities Management**	**Risk Management**
Individual Performance	Operating Budgets	Site Selection and Design	Impact Analysis
Call Center Performance	Financial Tracking	Facilities Management	Contingency Planning
Business Intelligence	Financial Assessments	Building Security	Disaster Recovery

Workforce Management

Since an incoming call center is at the mercy of incoming customer calls, the tasks associated with workforce management are among the most important functions of the center. These tasks involve forecasting calls, calculating the optimal number of agents, creating work schedules, and managing daily service levels.

As a supervisor, your role in the process will generally be to communicate scheduling needs to the workforce planning staff. This may include requests for the best times to schedule team meetings or coaching sessions with your staff. Part of your responsibility as a supervisor will also be to ensure that your team members are adhering to their work schedules so that the center can deliver acceptable service to callers.

Human Resources Administration

Because the key component of the call center is people, the functions associated with acquiring and maintaining the workforce are critical to the call center operation. These functions include recruiting, hiring, and training staff, as well as the tasks of ongoing compensation and benefit administration. While many of these functions may be handled exclusively by the corporate human HR department, some or all may also be handled partially within the call center structure.

As a supervisor, you will likely be involved in the interview and hiring process, so it's important to know what to look for and how to effectively interview job candidates. (Note: We'll cover this in Chapter 3 of this book.) Once the new agents are hired, you will likely be responsible for administrative tasks associated with timekeeping, payroll, and time-off administration for each of your team members.

Quality Management

Due to the call center's role as the primary point for customer communications, it is essential that these interactions be handled with utmost quality. The functions associated with quality management include customer surveying, call monitoring, performance assessment, and coaching.

As a supervisor, you will have a significant role in this process. In particular, you will likely be involved in monitoring the calls of your team members, assessing their performance, and coaching them for improved performance. Even if a dedicated quality team exists (as it does in many larger centers), the supervisor will be the one that carries out much of the direct person-to-person coaching. Ongoing performance reviews will also be a part of your responsibility.

Technology Management

The call center today is filled with technology. From the moment the customer picks up the phone to the resolution of the call, many different technologies come into play. A critical function in every call center is the effective management of these technologies including acquisition, implementation, and ongoing maintenance and management. These technologies are generally grouped as call delivery (including telecommunications infrastructure), call handling technologies, and call center management tools.

As a supervisor, you will likely not be involved in the acquisition and implementation of these technologies. However, you'll need to be aware of what they are and how they work in order to make the most use of their capabilities in handling customer contacts and managing the performance of your team. In particular, you'll want to be familiar with the types of reports that each generates to provide you with insight into your team's performance.

Reporting and Communications

One of the components driving the call center operation is information. An effective flow of communications is needed between customers and the center, between the center and other business units, and within the call center itself. Many different types of reports need to be generated every single day to show performance of the center as well as that of individuals. Therefore, reporting and communications is another essential function of call center operations.

As a supervisor, you will likely be generating two kinds of reports: one for management that details how your team is performing and the other for the individual agents to provide feedback to manage performance.

Financial Management

There is an array of costs associated with running a call center operation. And some call centers may be generating revenue of their own as well. The aspects of creating and managing an operating budget and capital budget as well as using financial procedures to evaluate return on investment of proposed technologies or services are part of the financial management function of the call center.

As a supervisor, you may work with the call center manager or director to plan the following period's operation budget. Likewise, you may have a budget for your team to fund training and motivational programs, and it will be your responsibility to manage that budget wisely.

Risk Management

A final function within call center operations is that of disaster recovery and contingency planning. Although not a task that is necessarily performed every day, it is a regular function within the best-run call centers to continually assess risks and potential solutions. This function is referred to in this text as risk management.

As a supervisor, you may be involved on an annual basis in helping to review the disaster plan. It will also be your responsibility as a supervisor to regularly review the plan with your team members so that each person is aware of the steps to take should a disaster happen in your center.

Other Functions

In addition to these primary eight categories of operational functions that apply nearly universally to all call centers, there are others that may apply to specialized environments.

Call centers that operate as outsourcers will have additional functions to perform in their business. For these organizations, the call center is the core business, and therefore additional functions will be required. Specifically, a marketing function will exist that serves to promote the call center's services to others. A specialized accounting function will exist as call center services are billed to other organizations based on contract agreements. And most outsourcers will have a client relations function which serves to manage the relationship with a specific account or accounts.

Likewise, an outbound center will have some additional functions not typically found in an incoming call center environment. In particular, outbound call centers, whether they are related to telemarketing, collections, or some other business, will likely have a campaign management function within the center.

Learning Activities

1. Make a list of all the call centers that are located in your city or region. Note how many people they employ and estimate theirimpact on the local economy.

2. Think about the last three calls you have made to another call center as a customer. Note how these calls were the same as your own call center and how they were different.

3. Think about the geographic scope of a call center's customers. What impact does it have on the call center's operations to have customers who are limited to company employees? What about those centers who serve nationwide audiences? What differences would there be for those serving customers in multiple countries?

4. Describe how your supervisory roles and responsibilities might be different if you worked in a significantly bigger or smaller call center.

Chapter 2 – Developing a Staffing Plan

Since a call center supervisor or team manager's job is to manage frontline staff, the first step in the process is to understand the fundamental components of developing a staffing plan. One of the key considerations in any call center is the calculation of the appropriate number of staff to be on the telephone at any given time, and then scheduling them appropriately to have enough to meet desired service goals.

The process of forecasting workload, calculating staff requirements, creating staff schedules, and managing daily staffing levels and service is referred to as workforce management. This is one of the most critical functions in the call center since three-fourths of a center's operating dollars are typically spent on personnel.

Not only is workforce management one of the most important functions in the call center – it is also one of the most difficult. Simply figuring out how many staff are needed is not an easy calculation, and then getting that number of people in seats at the right times is difficult. This chapter will explain what makes staffing a call center a unique kind of problem and what some of the important staffing tradeoffs are that every supervisor should understand.

This chapter will also explore some various alternatives to staffing that help with getting the right number of people to answer the phones.

6. ***What makes call center staffing unique?***
7. ***How are staff requirements calculated?***
8. ***What difference does one person make?***
9. ***What is staff occupancy and how is it calculated?***
10. ***What are the cost implications of reducing staff?***
11. ***What are the different ways to staff a call center?***
12. ***What is outsourcing and what are its benefits?***

6. What makes call center staffing unique?

Staffing a call center is unlike any other type of staffing scenario for several reasons, each of which has a significant impact on how the center will be staffed:

- Externally generated work
- Random call arrival
- Invisible interactions
- Importance of service

Externally Generated Work

The biggest factor that makes staffing your call center different than staffing other areas of your company is that the call center has no actual control over the amount of work to be done within an hour or a day. Your frontline agents are at the mercy of incoming workload generated by others (either internal or external customers) outside the center. Many different variables affect when your customers will place a call and most of these are outside your control.

Many different variables affect when your customers will place a call and most of these are outside your control.

Random Call Arrival

Another factor that sets the call center apart is the way in which your work arrives. Monthly, weekly, and hourly patterns can generally be determined by analyzing historical call volumes and other business factors. Therefore, your call center management team may have a reasonable prediction of the number of calls expected in an hour or half-hour period.

However, what the call center can't predict is how many of those calls will arrive the first minute, the second, the fifteenth, the twenty-ninth, and so on. In other words, the pattern of calls within the hour or half-hour is *random*. This randomness of work has a significant effect on how call workload is predicted and how many staffing resources you will need.

As an example, let's compare the call center to another part of the organization where a routine task like processing payments received in the mail is being done. If a group of staff has 1000 payments to process between 2:00–3:00pm, and it takes a person 3 minutes to complete each one, that's 3,000 minutes of workload. Divide the 3,000 minutes of workload by 60 minutes within each hour to determine the number of hours of work to do. This results in 50 hours of workload, and if all employees work at 100% efficiency, then 50 people can complete the work. Because this work is sequential, there is a 1:1 ratio of staff hours to workload hours. When a person in the clerical group completes one task, the next one is waiting in line, enabling that person to move from task to task with no "idle" time in between tasks.

Now consider the same 50 hours of work to do in a one-hour period in your call center. Let's assume that all 50 people have headsets on, are logged in, and available to take calls. At 2:05pm, there may be exactly 50 calls in progress. At 2:08pm, there may only be 40 calls arriving, meaning that 40 people will be busy on a call but the other 10 will be "idle" until more calls arrive. Given that there is no work presenting itself at that particular moment, these 10 people cannot operate at 100% efficiency during the hour. If there are periods in which no call workload is arriving, then not everyone can accomplish an entire hour's worth of calls. Therefore, the ratio of staff hours to workload hours will be higher than one. In other words, a call center will always need to have more staff in place than the actual hours of work to do.

A call center must always have more staff in place than the actual hours of work to do because of the random arrival of the work.

An implication of this random workload is that there is often an imbalance of work and staff to handle that work. Either there are few calls arriving and staff sitting idle, or all agents are busy with calls backed up in queue. This type of demand environment requires careful analysis to forecast accurately down to the half-hour increment as well as coordinated effort to manage the fluctuations on a real-time basis as calls arrive. This requirement is one of the critical functions of call center workforce management.

Invisible Interactions

Now let's compare a "retail center" (where the customers arrive and make live contact with employees) to your call center to uncover where another potential challenge might be in call center management. In a live contact environment you would be able to see the number of customers waiting, how long the wait time might be, how many customers give up and walk out the door, and the number of return visits by individual customers.

In your call center, however, there will be instances where a call arrives and there is not a person available to handle it immediately. The call goes into a queue and waits there until one of your staff becomes available. Depending upon the call workload and number of staff available, this delay time could be only a few seconds or could be a significantly longer period of time.

Depending upon the call workload and number of staff available, delay times might be only a few seconds or could be a significantly longer period of time.

Compare the wait in a call center queue to other queue experiences, such as standing in line for a ride at an amusement park. There are several differences in the queue experience:

> ***Visibility upon entry.*** At the amusement park, a customer can see the line ahead and make a conscious decision about whether or not to enter the queue. In addition to viewing the actual line of people, there may even be signs that suggest how long the wait time should be from certain points in line. Based upon this information, the customer can decide to get in line, or proceed on to another activity. In your call center queue, there is typi-

cally no information for arriving callers about how many calls are ahead of them or how long the wait might be. *(Note: There are some technologies that enable an expected wait time to be announced to the caller, but a wait announcement is the exception rather than the norm.)* The caller usually has no information upon which to base a decision about whether to wait in line, try back at another time, or simply go away.

Current status updates. In the amusement park queue, customers can see progress being made as they move along in the queue and get closer to being served. They can constantly observe the speed of movement and make judgments about how soon they will reach the front of the line. If the speed doesn't suit them, they can then make an informed decision to abandon the queue or to stay in line. In your call center, there is typically no progress announcement. In most cases, the callers simply get a repeat of the same delay announcement and have no way to know if their call is the next one up, or if the delay will continue for an extended period.

Satisfaction cycle. An interesting comparison can be made between the cycle of satisfaction levels that a "visible queue" customer experiences versus the "invisible queue" call center customer. Customers in the visible queue may have a low satisfaction level upon entering the queue, but as they move through the queue and see their progress and approach being served, satisfaction levels rise. The exact opposite is true in a call center's invisible queue. Customer satisfaction might not be affected upon initial entry into the queue (as most customers tend to expect a short wait). But as the time in the queue lengthens and customers receive no status information about when they might be served, frustration levels rise and satisfaction with the queue experience drops dramatically.

Your customers' expectations of service will be based on their last, best service experiences, so it's important to staff properly so that service expectations can be met or exceeded.

Importance of Service

The importance of all the unique call center factors discussed here takes on even greater significance when you consider the important role the call center plays within your organization. If you're like most businesses, your call center is the customer's most common way to interact with the business, and for some organizations it may be the only contact mechanism. Therefore it is critical that the call center is designed and operated to respond effectively to customer needs. For the most part, your customers' expectations of service will be based on their last, best service experience. So your call center not only has to benchmark performance against traditional competitors, but also against the "best of class" call centers in the marketplace today.

7. How are staff requirements calculated?

The process of workforce management is all about getting the "just right" number of staff in place every period of the day to meet service levels while minimizing cost. The goal is to have the precise number needed – not too many and not too few – every single half-hour of the day. Having the wrong number of staff in place has serious implications for the call center, both in terms of overstaffing and understaffing.

Overstaffing may happen when your center staffs up to meet peak periods of the day, and then when call volume drops, there are more staff available to take calls than are actually needed. This overstaffing results in lower overall productivity and spending needless dollars for staffing. Overstaffing may also lead to boredom and staff turnover if there are extended periods of time with not enough work to do. The lack of a queue during overstaffed periods may also contribute to escalated customer expectations of service that are difficult to achieve the majority of the time.

The process of workforce management is all about getting the "just right" number of staff in place every period of the day to meet service levels while minimizing cost.

On the other hand, a much more common problem in your call center is understaffing – not having enough agents in place to handle the incoming calls at a given time. The main implication of understaffing is poor service to your callers. Too few staff equates to longer wait times in the queue and dissatisfied customers. If there is revenue associated with your incoming calls, it may be reduced or lost as a result of a long wait.

Therefore, it's important to get exactly the right number of staff in place to handle the call workload – not too many and not too few – every single half-hour of the day. While some call centers settle for overstaffing and understaffing that balance out over the course of the day, most call centers realize the importance of getting the right number in place as many periods of the day as possible to minimize the ill effects that understaffing and overstaffing can cause.

Steps of Workforce Management

The process of workforce management is critical to the success of every call center. The basic steps of the workforce management process are:

1. *Gather and analyze data*. The first step of the workforce management process is gathering a representative sample of historical information that can be analyzed to predict future volumes and patterns. This data typically comes from your automatic call distributor (ACD) and represents numbers of calls offered and handle time information from a representative period of time.

2. *Forecast call workload.* The second step in resource planning involves the application of forecasting models to the historical information in order to predict future workload. The most reliable forecasting model, called time-series analysis, is used to isolate trend rates and seasonal patterns in predicting future months' call volumes, which are then broken down into daily and hourly volumes and patterns.

3. *Calculate staff requirements.* The third step in creating a call center staffing plan is to calculate the number of staff required to handle a given amount of workload in a desired service timeframe. Numerous staffing models exist that take into account call arrival rates and call center queuing scenarios to predict staffing and service levels. Various tradeoffs are evaluated to determine the impact of staffing levels on service, productivity levels, and costs.

4. *Create staff schedules.* The fourth step in the resource planning process is to create a set of workforce schedules that best match your call center workforce to the expected contact workload. Base staff requirements are calculated and then matched up to your potential staffing pool and scheduling constraints to design a schedule plan.

5. *Track and manage daily performance.* The final step in the workforce management process involves tracking actual performance against the staffing and service plan. Your actual call volumes, handle times, and available staff are compared to the forecast to derive net staffing counts and make necessary adjustments to meet service levels.

Sample Staffing Calculation

It was stated earlier that the number of staff required will always be greater than the actual hours of workload to do.

The actual number needed depends upon how fast you wish to answer the calls. What happens with a defined amount of workload and varying numbers of staff is predicted by a mathematical model called Erlang C.

Let's take a look at a sample staffing calculation, where your center is expecting 600 calls to arrive between 2:00–3:00pm and each call takes 300 seconds to handle. This equates to 50 hours of workload, and the table below outlines what service could be expected with anywhere from 51–58 agents in place.

Hourly Call Volume	Average Handle Time	Staff Workload (in erlangs)	Number of Staff	Service Level (in 30 sec)	ASA (in sec)	Agent Occupancy
600	300 sec	50 hours	51	24%	252 sec	98%
600	300 sec	50 hours	52	43%	105 sec	96%
600	300 sec	50 hours	53	57%	58 sec	95%
600	300 sec	50 hours	54	68%	35 sec	93%
600	300 sec	50 hours	55	77%	23 sec	91%
600	300 sec	50 hours	56	83%	15 sec	89%
600	300 sec	50 hours	57	88%	10 sec	88%
600	300 sec	50 hours	58	91%	7 sec	86%

Sample Staffing Table
(generated by Quikstaff software, available at www.thecallcenterschool.com.)

8. What difference does one person make?

Does the following scenario sound familiar?

One of your team members stops by your desk to let you know she'd like to leave early this afternoon. You reply that letting her go would result in understaffing, especially from 2:00–3:00pm. She responds that she doesn't understand what the big deal is. She points out that she's only one person in a call center of 50 staff and asks you how that could possibly be a problem.

The "law of diminishing returns" means that at very good service levels, there is little impact on speed of answer of adding or deleting just one person.

Can you answer her question with facts about the impact her absence would have? The impact that just one person has on service might be insignificant or it might be substantial. It depends on the current staffing levels and your desired service goals for that hour.

In the example on the previous page, let's assume that your call center wanted to have enough staff in place to deliver an average delay of no more than 25 seconds. In order to do that 55 staff would be required. Now let's take a look at what would happen if that number varies by just a person or two.

As each additional agent is added, service improves. Increasing staff from 55 to 56 moves the average speed of answer (ASA) from 23 seconds to 15 seconds, an 8-second improvement. The 57th agent would improve ASA to 10 seconds (a 5-second improvement); the 58th agent would drop ASA to 7 seconds (a 3-second improvement); the 59th agent would improve ASA to 5 seconds (a 2-second improvement). Every time an additional person is added, service improves, but it does so in smaller increments each time. This "law of diminishing returns" means that at very good service levels, there is little impact of adding or deleting just one person.

Service worsens by a greater amount each time a person is subtracted. The incremental change gets larger and larger as the number of agents approaches the hours of work to do.

On the other hand, look at what happens as staff members are subtracted. Decreasing staff from 55 to 54 staff moves ASA from 23 seconds to 35 seconds (a 12-second increase). Dropping to 53 staff would result in a 58-second ASA (a 23-second change); 52 staff would yield a 105-second ASA (a 57-second increase); and dropping to 51 staff would mean ASA would worsen to 252 seconds (a 147-second jump!). Each time an agent is subtracted, service worsens, and it does so by a greater amount each time. The incremental change gets larger and larger as the number of agents approaches the hours of work to do.

A question frequently asked by agents in a call center is "What difference does just one person make on service to customers?" And the answer is … "It depends." If staffing levels are high and delays are very short, then adding or subtracting just one person does not have much effect on service. As evidenced in the table, the difference between 57 staff and 58 staff in this scenario is only 3 seconds – a difference probably not noticeable to callers.

On the other hand, if delays are in the medium to high range already, then taking just one more person off the phones could affect service dramatically. Look at what happens in the table when staff numbers dropped from 52 to 51 staff during the hour – a difference in ASA of 147 seconds! Just one person (in this example, representing only 2% of the group) can have a tremendous effect on service. The good news is that adding a person at this level has a dramatically positive impact. Therefore, call centers delivering long delay times to customers can alter the service picture in a big way by getting just one more person on the phones.

When delays are very long, adding just one person can have a substantial impact on service.

It's important for every single person in the call center to understand this staffing and service relationship. Part of the supervisor's role in the workforce management process is to help agents understand the "power of one" – the role that each person plays in ensuring that service goals are met.

9. What is staff occupancy and how is it calculated?

Another critical number to understand is the relationship between the number of staff on the phones and staff productivity. Adding more staff means that more people will be handling a given workload, so that each individual agent is less busy. As agents are taken off the phones, fewer people are left to accomplish the work, and each person that's left has to work harder.

The measure of how busy the agents are at processing call workload is referred to as staff occupancy or agent occupancy. It is quite simply the workload hours divided by staff hours (or bodies in chairs). In the 50-hour workload scenario, the last column shows the level of agent occupancy associated with varying staffing numbers.

Occupancy is calculated by dividing the workload hours by the number of staff.

With only 52 agents handling 50 hours of workload, the staff will be busy 96% of the time. In other words, there will only be 4% idle time between calls (only 2.4 minutes out of the hour). On the other hand, with 58 people working, the agents would be busy only 86% of the time they are logged in as available with a 14% "breather" between calls.

In staffing a call center, it is important to keep an eye on this occupancy number. With the efficiencies inherent in larger call centers, it's common to have agent occupancy levels at 95% or above. On the other hand, agent occupancy levels in a smaller center may only be at the 70% level, while meeting the same service level goal as the larger center. This difference is illustrated in the table below.

Calls per Hour	Handle Time	Workload (in erlangs)	Number of Staff	Service Level (in 20 sec)	Agent Occupancy
200	180 sec	10 hours	11	39%	90%
200	180 sec	10 hours	12	64%	83%
200	180 sec	10 hours	13	80%	77%
800	180 sec	40 hours	45	80%	89%
800	180 sec	40 hours	46	86%	87%
800	180 sec	40 hours	47	90%	85%
1600	180 sec	80 hours	87	80%	92%
1600	180 sec	80 hours	88	88%	91%
1600	180 sec	80 hours	89	91%	90%

Effect of Group Size on Agent Occupancy Level

First compare the smaller group depicted in the upper portion of the table with the medium-sized group in the middle of the table. In the smaller group that receives 200 calls or 10 hours of workload, 13 agents are required to meet an

80% in 20 seconds service level goal. The resulting agent occupancy is 10/13 or 77%. In the group that receives four times as many calls, or 40 hours of workload, 45 agents are needed to meet the 80% in 20 seconds goal. The resulting level of agent occupancy for this group is 40/45 or 89%. Even though the two groups are staffed to meet the same 80% in 20 seconds service goal, the occupancy levels of the two groups will be different.

If the smaller group's goal was to have an occupancy level equivalent to the larger group, that could be accomplished by reducing the number of staff from 13 to 11. By doing so, a smaller group would be handling the work and each person would be busier. But reducing the number of staff would mean lowering service level, in this case from the 80% goal to only 39% of calls handled within the desired wait time.

As seen in this example, larger groups will enjoy a higher productivity or occupancy level, simply because of the way the work presents itself. With double the calls of the medium-sized group, the larger group depicted in the bottom portion of the table, has an occupancy of 92% when staffed to meet the same 80% in 20 seconds service goal. Care should be taken in staffing larger groups to ensure that productivity levels are not forced too high.

Larger teams will have a higher productivity level simply because of the way the work presents itself. Care should be taken in staffing larger groups to ensure that occupancy doesn't reach dangerously high levels.

Most call centers have found that a reasonable level of agent occupancy is somewhere between 80% and 90%. When occupancy levels go much higher than 90%, there is very little time between incoming calls to take a "breather" and prepare for the next one. If this back-to-back calling continues for any length of time, your agents will begin looking for ways to get a "breather" between calls. They may extend talk time to avoid taking the next call, stay in after-call work mode longer than needed, go into unavailable mode, or make an outbound call – anything to avoid taking the next call. When one agent does this, the reduction in staff simply means that everybody else is just that much busier. Agent occupancy continues to rise and service levels drop, creating a cycle that is difficult to stop past a certain point. Therefore, when calculating staff requirements, it is important to staff so that agent occupancy levels do not exceed reasonable thresholds for more than three or four half-hour periods, or agents will burn out quickly and turnover may be an issue to address in addition to service problems.

10. What are the cost implications of reducing staff?

In determining the "just right" number of staff in the call center, there are many tradeoffs to consider, and cost is certainly one of those. Your business, like many others over the last few years, may have implemented cost-cutting measures to improve the bottom line.

Since about 75% of call center's operating costs are related to staffing, that is generally the first place that senior management might look to reduce costs. It is all too common to think of layoffs and reduction in staff as the simplest way to "tighten your belts." But before you write up the pink slips, make sure you understand the implications of staff reductions.

In our previous staffing example, let's assume that you staff your call center to meet a 35 second delay goal and that 54 staff would be needed. However, three people leave the center, and due to a hiring freeze, the call center is prevented from replacing them. This hiring freeze is intended to save money for the company.

Hourly Call Volume	Average Handle Time	Staff Workload (in erlangs)	Number of Staff	ASA (in sec)	Agent Occupancy
600	300 sec	50 hours	51	252 sec	98%
600	300 sec	50 hours	52	105 sec	96%
600	300 sec	50 hours	53	58 sec	95%
600	300 sec	50 hours	54	35 sec	93%
600	300 sec	50 hours	55	23 sec	91%
600	300 sec	50 hours	56	15 sec	89%

The strategy to decrease staff numbers to reduce costs would impact service directly. The loss of the first person would worsen delays from 35 seconds to 58 seconds. Eliminating another person would increase the wait to 105 seconds, and leaving all three spots open would result in a delay of 252 seconds! So those callers accustomed to waiting for about a half a minute in queue would now be waiting over four minutes!

Unfortunately, service isn't the only thing that suffers. With 33 staff in place to handle the call workload, agent occupancy (the measure of how busy agents are during the period of time they're logged in and available) is already at a borderline high level at 93%. Taking one body away raises occupancy levels to 95%; taking two away results in 96% occupancy; and taking three away means staff would be busy 98% of the time during the hour. In other words, there would be only 2% of the hour (72 seconds during the entire hour!) of "breathing room" between calls. Such a high level of occupancy can't be maintained for long. The likely result will be longer handle times, longer periods spent in after-call work to "catch their breath," burnout, and turnover.

There's even another downside to consider from a cost perspective. The idea was to save money by eliminating staff. Assuming a wage rate of $20 per hour, then eliminating three staff would result in a savings of $60 in wage rates for that hour.

However, if your center is paying the phone bill by providing a toll-free service for callers, the reduction in staff might be outweighed by the increased telephone costs associated with the longer delay times. In this example, with 54 staff in place the average delay is 35 seconds per call. Multiply that by 600 calls per hour and that's 350 minutes of delay time to be billed. If we apply a cost per minute to that usage of $.05 per minute, that's $17.50 for the queue time.

If we reduce the numbers to 51 staff, remember our average delay increases to 252 seconds of delay per call. Multiply that by 600 calls and that's 2520 minutes of delay, priced at $.05 for a total of $126 for the queue time that hour. In other words, by eliminating three staff to save $60, we've just increased our telephone bill by $109 for that hour! In other words, we're paying $50 more per hour rather than saving money! And this doesn't even take into account the likelihood of a longer call given the poorer than expected service levels. Telephone charges would likely increase even further.

So, from three different perspectives – the customer (service delays), the agent (higher occupancy), and senior management (higher telephone costs) -- you can see that a simple staff reduction may not save your call center any money. In fact, it may cost you much more in terms of poor service, productivity, morale, and just the opposite effect on your bottom line than what was intended.

A staff reduction may actually cost your call center in terms of poor service, increased occupancy, higher telephone costs, and poor morale.

11. What are the different ways to staff a call center?

One of the most critical steps in making and receiving customer calls is deciding not just how many staff will be needed, but what type of staffing solution your business will utilize. Since about three-fourths of call center costs are related to labor costs, this decision is fundamental to the operation of your business.

How your business chooses to get people in place to handle its customer interactions will have an impact on every other function within the center, including site selection and facility design, forecasting and scheduling, performance management, technology acquisition and management, facilities management, human resources administration, and risk management.

One option for staffing a call center may be for the organization to make a business decision to not handle all of the calls internally, but rather to outsource some or all of the calls to another organization. This process is called outsourcing, and it is discussed as the next question in this section.

Assuming that your company has decided to handle the calls internally, there are still several options for assembling the frontline staff. In addition to traditional in-house staffing, two options that have become increasingly popular for call center staffing are remote staffing arrangements and contract staffing.

Remote Staffing Alternatives

An increasingly popular option for call centers is to have employees handle customer contacts while working from home or another remote site. The technology exists today to allow agents to log in from home or any other remote site and receive calls in the same way as if they were sitting in your call center. There are many advantages to a telecommuting or remote agent setup, as outlined below.

Schedule Flexibility

The main advantage of using remote workers as all or part of your call center workforce is the flexibility gained in scheduling.

The main advantage of using remote workers as all or part of your call center workforce is the flexibility gained in scheduling. It is very difficult to cover the peaks and valleys of calls throughout the day with traditional staff. Your call center may have a two-hour peak of calls in the morning and another in the afternoon. While the call center can't expect someone to come into the center and work a split shift to handle those periods, it may be reasonable to expect a person working from home to do it. Covering night and weekend hours may also be easier to accomplish with telecommuters. Many people do not like to commute to work at night when crime and traffic risks go up. These same people may be willing to work those hours if they can do so from the comfort of their own home.

Real Estate Savings

Another primary benefit of telecommuting is the space savings accomplished by not needing to house agents in the physical call center. Assuming that an agent occupies 50 square feet of call center space and the lease cost of this space is $20 per square foot per month, the savings per agent would be $1,000 per month or $12,000 per year. And this is just the cost of the space alone. Add to that the one-time and ongoing costs of building and maintaining workstations, furniture, lunchrooms, conference spaces, and other amenities, along with the cost of additional utilities, and that savings could easily double.

Expanded Labor Pool

Another strong reason to consider the utilization of a remote workforce is the potential to attract additional labor sources. This expanded labor pool may include those that are highly qualified workers, but are handicapped or physically challenged and unable to commute daily into the business site. A telecommuting option may also simply bring in a bigger pool of qualified candidates attracted to the prospect of working at home and avoiding the commuting hassles of getting to their job every day. In addition to avoiding the travel time of a long commute, employees can save money on transportation costs, food costs, and a working wardrobe.

Staff Retention

Businesses generally find that their teleworking employees have a much higher job satisfaction and retention rates than traditional in-house employees. In addition to the "hard dollar" employee benefits listed above, the additional time found in their day is a big factor in overall satisfaction and quality of life.

> A telecommuting option may also simply bring in a bigger pool of qualified candidates attracted to the prospect of working at home and avoiding the commuting hassles and expenses of working in a traditional office setting.

Increased Productivity

Many trials of telecommuting workers versus traditional office workers suggest that telecommuters are more productive. The main reason for this higher productivity may be the fact that there are fewer interruptions to distract the employee. Their comfort and increased satisfaction from working at home may also be a contributing factor to the better productivity.

Disaster Recovery

All sorts of disasters and emergencies can happen that disable normal call center functions and having a pool of remote workers can assist your call center in carrying out its work. A flu epidemic or icy road may prevent staff from coming into the center, but work can still be carried out in remote sites. A flood or power outage at the site can damage workstations, but assuming connectivity is still possible to the main switch, agents at home can continue to process calls.

Environmental Impact

Having fewer people driving into the call center every day can certainly reduce auto emissions and pollution. This isn't just a nice benefit, but may help some companies comply with legal regulations. The federal Clean Air Act requires companies with more than 100 employees in high-pollution areas to design and implement programs to reduce air pollution. Setting up a telecommuting program is one option for complying with this rule.

Contract Staffing

Another option for call center staffing is to have staff at your site, but to let an outside agency provide the staff. This scenario, sometimes referred to as "in-sourcing," involves the use of a staffing agency to recruit, screen, hire, and train frontline staff. The contract staffing agency may perform the recruiting, hiring, and training activities at their site, or may reside at your company's location.

While the call center typically pays more for a contract staff person, since the staffing rate includes an "overhead" charge for the contract agency, the added cost comes with many benefits, such as staffing expertise, flexibility, and the capability to try out staff before you hire them as permanent employees.

Staffing Expertise

Despite the slightly higher wage rates, many call centers choose to staff through a contract staffing agency. These agencies have a core competency of recruiting and hiring call center staff, so they may do a better job of it than your own human resources department. These agencies are familiar with labor pools in various communities and most have links to various state or community vocational training programs. They are experts at helping the call center define job requirements, find suitable candidates, and do careful screening to ensure a good match for the job.

> The hourly cost may be higher for agency staff, but this higher cost provides the benefits of hiring expertise, staffing flexibility, and the ability to try before you hire.

Flexibility

Another benefit of "in-sourcing" is the flexibility of procuring exactly the number and type of staff required. Your company can simply inform the contract staffing agency of how many of each type of position it needs to fill and for how long, and the agency can fill the vacancies. This flexibility is particularly useful for what might be a short-term campaign where staff will not be needed for a long period of time.

Trial Staffing

Many contract agencies have a contract with the call center where the center can hire temporary staff to be permanent company employees. This arrangement lets you "try before buy" in terms of adding permanent staff to the payroll. Likewise, if there is a problem with any contract employee, the call center simply has to inform the agency and does not have to go through disciplinary and severance procedures that are likely required with company employees. There are also benefits to the workers who have an opportunity to try out the job tasks and the employer before making the commitment to take a permanent position.

12. What is outsourcing and what are its benefits?

Outsourcing is the practice of contracting out some or all of a business function to a company that specializes in that particular function. In call center outsourcing, businesses contract with other companies to answer or place some or all of its calls or other types of contacts rather than handling those contacts in-house.

The main reason that businesses outsource call center functions is to avoid the resource drain and costs associated with initial set-up and ongoing operation of a function that is typically not the core competency of the business. Developing and running a call center is expensive and many companies find they can accomplish the call handling operation more cost-effectively by outsourcing it than trying to do it in-house.

Call center outsourcing involves contracting with a third party to handle some or all of your telephone contacts rather than handling them in-house.

Outsourcing can be an alternative solution to building a dedicated in-house call center or it can be used to supplement a company's call center operation. It can be a particularly attractive option for start-up companies or for businesses unsure what their call center needs will be. Outsourcing allows the company to buy call center services as needed without investing in expensive equipment, software, facilities, or labor. The benefits are the same for established companies that may choose to focus on their core business and outsource the call handling to the experts, or for companies that have one call center, but do not wish to open another to meet growth requirements.

There are many benefits to be considered in using an outsourcer to handle inbound or outbound calling:

Reduced Costs

While an in-house call center must bear the cost of site selection, building, operating, staffing, and maintaining technologies and facilities, outsourcers can amortize these costs over many clients. The client benefits by paying for only the services directly needed, resulting in cost efficiencies. Outsourcers are also able to reduce labor costs by sharing programs with different companies, so that clients are not paying for idle time. Known as a "shared agent" arrangement, this concept enables companies to benefit from the high occupancy in an outsourced call center, bringing down the staff-to-workload ratios in the center and resulting in a lower cost-per-call that can be passed along to the client.

Flexibility

Inbound calls arrive in peaks and valleys and traditional call centers are therefore by nature inefficient. During periods of low call volumes, agents may be idle and equipment is not utilized. In an outsourced call center, multiple clients' calls tend to smooth out the peaks and valleys meaning a greater utilization of equipment and staffing resources. And given the large size of most outsourcing operations, there are typically more staff and phone lines available to handle even the biggest of spikes in call volume due to marketing or advertising campaigns. An in-house center may have difficulty dealing with unanticipated increases in volume due to insufficient telecommunications capacity or labor resources.

Management Expertise

Running a call center means having a management and supervisory staff with essential knowledge and skills about call center operations. And for larger centers, skilled support staff such as workforce planners and schedulers, quality specialists, trainers, and technology specialists will need to be in place. Many internal call centers find it difficult to hire or to develop this expertise in-house quickly and ensure everyone stays up to speed on the best practices, skills, and knowledge. Outsourcers have these specialists on staff and perform these various functions on a daily basis to keep skills and knowledge finely tuned.

Outsourcers can provide the flexibility to cover peaks and valleys more efficiently, lowering the overall cost per call.

Speed to Market

Outsourcers can get a call-handling function up to speed much faster than an in-house operation. The key to their quickness is in their contractor status. When bidding on a job, the outsourcer has to have the site, labor, and equipment ready to begin delivery on the agreed date. The site and equipment are ready to go and the outsourcer may have staff either immediately available or on-call for the next assignment.

Specialized Expertise

Because many outsourcers specialize in providing services to certain industries only, a company may find a high level of focused expertise with an outsourcer. The outsourcer may bring years of collective experience in a specific industry to a customer that could benefit from a broader perspective and understanding of the competitive environment. For example, a new banking call center may benefit from using an outsourcer who has experience handling the credit card processing for many different banks, perhaps understanding the processing and servicing of accounts better than the bank, where credit card processing is just one of the many functions being handled by an internal center.

State-of-the-Art Technology

Most outsourcers invest in state-of-the-art technology to meet their many customers' demands. Investment in the latest technology is an expensive option for in-house call centers, while outsourcing centers are able to spread the cost of the technology investment across multiple projects and customers. The outsourcer typically has a set of technology specialists on hand whose job is simply to stay on top of the technology and apply it effectively for their customers.

Round-the-Clock Operations

Despite growing customer expectations, many companies cannot afford to operate their call center seven days a week, twenty-four hours a day. The small number of calls that arrive in non-peak hours make it prohibitively expensive to operate at certain hours. Therefore, availability to customers during those times is limited to self-service options for many call centers. An outsourcer can provide this service for a company at a much lower cost per call and help the business maintain round-the-clock availability.

Global Presence

Many outsourcers have centers in multiple countries and specialize in bringing the language and skill sets needed to a customer project. While a company may struggle with setting up operations in a different country, the outsourcer may already have operations and available staff there. Because of their multiple sites in many different countries, many outsourcers can boast of dozens of language capabilities.

Outsourcing Drawbacks

Outsourcers can afford the latest and greatest in technology by spreading the cost of the investment over multiple clients.

While the benefits are many, there are also some drawbacks to outsourcing calls. The primary downside to outsourcing is the loss of control over the staff and perhaps customer information. While many outsourcers provide more functional access to customer information than what an internal call center might have because of its possible CRM expertise, sometimes access to this information is difficult.

Another disadvantage may be the lack of commitment to the end customer. While most outsourcers are focused on providing excellent service, agents are typically held to a set of acceptable standards and behaviors and have no reason to go above and beyond the call of duty to serve a customer, while an internal employee in an in-house center may recognize the value of doing so.

There may also be a lack of incentive for efficiency on the outsourcer's part. Since the outsourcer is paid for the calls it handles, it may have no incentive to provide customers with better numbers to call to get problems solved or questions answered, such as directing calls to a specialized internal group or directing customers to self-service alternatives.

Learning Activities

1. Calculate the staff requirements for each half-hour of an upcoming Monday in your call center. Use one of these sample half-hours and create a chart showing the impact of plus/minus for one, two, and three staff. Create a five-minute presentation for your team on the "power of one" that each agent has on service and team productivity.

2. Review a sample day's service level or ASA statistics by half-hour. In how-many of the half-hours did you meet speed of answer targets? Create a chart that shows how many staff would have been needed for the actual workload each half-hour versus how many were actually in place. Note the under-staffing and over-staffing by period of day and discuss how you might improve.

3. Spend several hours with the person(s) responsible for forecasting calls and creating staff schedules in your call center. How much time is spent each week gathering data, generating forecasts, and planning schedules versus managing the service within the day? What could frontline staff and team managers do to make workforce management more effective?

4. Has your call center investigated the option for some of the staff to take calls from home or from another remote location? What would be the benefits for your call center of implementing a telecommuting program? What are the risks?

Chapter 3 – Recruiting and Hiring

The first step in assembling an effective call center team is to recruit and hire the right staff for the job. Many performance problems and personnel issues down the road can be avoided by simply getting the right people in the positions in the first place. Recruiting and hiring reliable, skilled, and qualified employees is a critical process for any operation, but particularly for the call center where the staff you hire will be the voice of your company.

Securing the best employees is not just the job of the human resources department, but the responsibility of everyone involved in the call center operation. The recruiting team should include personnel experts from human resources, as well as those close to the position being filled, including current employees, supervisors, and call center management staff.

The recruiting and hiring process begins with a needs assessment and job task analysis to evaluate the positions to be staffed. The end product of the job analysis is a job description that will be utilized to create an employee profile.

Once the "ideal agent" profile has been defined, advertising for the open positions begins, followed by a thorough interview and careful hiring process to ensure you have the right people for the job.

This chapter takes you through the step-by-step process of defining various call center roles and positions, creating a job profile, attracting a labor pool, and screening to make the best match possible for the job at hand.

13. ***What kind of people do you need to hire?***
14. ***What does a frontline job description look like?***
15. ***What are the key skills and attributes needed?***
16. ***What else should be included in the job requirements?***
17. ***Where should you look for call center candidates?***
18. ***How should you advertise call center positions?***
19. ***What's the best way to screen candidates?***
20. ***What are the best interview questions?***
21. ***How can you test for skills and motivational fit?***
22. ***How should you make the job offer?***

13. What kind of people do you need to hire?

One of the most important steps in assembling a call center team is to allocate adequate time at the beginning of the hiring process to develop a clear understanding of your staffing needs. Performing a needs assessment is a process that will help your call center management team evaluate the current operating environment and compare it to where the call center needs to be in the future. This needs analysis should take into consideration the short-term and long-term staffing requirements for positions to be staffed and what staffing resources are currently available. If done right, this process will provide you with a clear picture of the types of people and the skills that are needed to accomplish the work now and into the future.

An effective needs analysis will provide a clear picture of the types of people and the skills that are needed to accomplish the work now and well into the future.

It is important for you to get a complete picture of the job at hand from many sources and viewpoints. The first step in the process should be to define required knowledge and skills needed for all types of customer interactions. This review may include interviews with customers, as well as monitoring and tracking the various types of calls and customer segments to define the capabilities needed to handle each and every type of customer contact. This review should also include direct observation of current staff performing the job, as well interviews with frontline staff and supervisors. This review will allow you to examine the core knowledge, skills, and attributes required for the job.

Once all the information has been gathered through the means listed above, the next step of the needs assessment process should be a "gap analysis." The gap analysis involves comparing actual performance against existing standards and objectives of the center. The review will enable your call center management team to identify training needs, examine problems caused by new processes or technologies, and possibly identify opportunities to gain a competitive edge by taking advantage of strengths as opposed to reacting to weaknesses.

Activities and job tasks should be examined in view of their importance to customer needs and organizational goals in order to determine the relative importance of each.

The needs assessment should also examine activities performed by each position and prioritize them along with the importance of each activity. Activities should be examined in view of their importance to customer needs and organizational goals in order to determine the relative importance of each.

After the needs analysis for the overall call center has been completed, a job task analysis for each call center staffing position will be created utilizing much of the data gathered during the needs assessment process.

14. What does a frontline job description look like?

Like it or not, every unique position in your call center should have a job description. Nobody likes writing these or updating these documents, but a comprehensive job description or position description is a necessary element in both the recruiting process as well as for ongoing performance evaluation and management.

> A comprehensive position description is necessary for both the recruiting process as well as ongoing performance management.

To develop a comprehensive job or position description, you will want to review what the employee needs to accomplish, the activities or behaviors required to perform the job, equipment the employee uses to perform the job, the work environment in which the job is performed, and the job specifications needed to perform the minimum requirements of the position. A comprehensive position description is essential to formally analyze and define what is expected of each call center staff position.

The duties and tasks in the position description define the required activities to perform the job and may include frequency, duration, effort, skill, complexity, equipment, standards, and any other job requirement. The environment may have a significant impact on the physical requirements to be able to perform a job and should also be included in the description. Environmental factors in the call center may include conditions such as stress, repetitive tasks, and confined workspace.

Job descriptions don't just add focus to the recruitment and selection processes. They can also form the basis of an advertising campaign, be helpful in evaluating whether a full-time or part-time employee is required, and can play a part in evaluating whether a candidate meets or exceeds the guidelines required for each position. Finally, well-written job descriptions can help you justify pay decisions, promotions, and disciplinary actions after the employee is hired.

Job descriptions should be considered works in progress since they should be altered in response to the changes that occur in the workplace. Once the job descriptions are finalized, copies should be given to each employee along with a signature form to return to indicate awareness of job expectations.

> Job descriptions should be considered works in progress since they should be altered in response to the changes that occur in the workplace.

An example of a job description is provided on the following page. It outlines the overall purpose of the job, its basic roles and responsibilities, required knowledge and skills, and competencies associated with the job.

Sample Job Description for Customer Service Associate

Position Title: Customer Service Associate (CSA)
Department: Order Inquiries

Reports to: CS Supervisor
Division: Customer Service
Updated: January 1, 2005

PURPOSE OF POSITION

Answer continuous volume of phone calls from a variety of customers regarding catalog orders. Responsible for providing answers to questions from customers regarding availability and pricing for catalog items. Working on Windows-based computer system for all inquiries, CSA will provide one-call resolution for problems identified by customers and will provide feedback to company as to ways to improve efficiency and customer service.

BASIC DUTIES / RESPONSIBILITIES

- Handle multiple tasks (i.e., talking with customers while accessing information in computer).
- Encourage the customer to place an order.
- Offer alternatives and options to overcome objections and pursue the sale.
- Cross-sell and up-sell associated catalog items.
- Adapt to the needs of individual callers.
- Adhere to shift assignments based on seniority in a 24-hour / 7 day operation.
- Accept repetitive work tasks performed in a confined work area.
- Adjust to changing work schedules with rotating days off.
- Provide timely and accurate information reflecting a customer-oriented image for the enterprise.
- Maintain a courteous and pleasant demeanor while speaking with external and internal customers.

REQUIRED SKILLS AND COMPETENCIES

- Typing speed of >25wpm
- Excellent verbal and written communication skills
- Strong computer skills
- Strong problem solving skills
- Basic sales skills
- Telephone etiquette

ESSENTIAL ATTRIBUTES

- Customer service awareness
- Tolerance for stress
- Adaptability/flexibility
- Interpersonal/communication skills
- Team player
- Detail oriented

15. What are the key skills and attributes needed?

Part of a position description will include the necessary knowledge, skills, and attributes needed for the job. The definition of these knowledge, skills, and attributes (often referred to as KSAs) will vary, depending on the type of position. For example, if you were supervising staff in a sales environment, you'd be looking for a different set than those that would be required for employees in a technical support environment.

Types of knowledge requirements may include such things as basic telephone etiquette, customer service experience, sales experience, Internet experience, product knowledge, knowledge of the company, and industry knowledge.

Skills for call center staff are typically divided into four categories: technical, interpersonal, verbal, and written. Some of these potential skills are listed in the table below.

Technical	Interpersonal	Verbal	Written
Computer navigation	Conflict resolution	Information assimilation	Expression of ideas
Word processing	Problem solving	Summarization	Organizational skills
Math skills	Empathy display	Grammar, diction	Document structure
Mechanical skills	Phone etiquette	Vocabulary range	Grammar/punctuation

Personality attributes are also an important factor in defining the ideal person for a position. Unlike knowledge or skills that can be acquired, attributes are elements of a person's personality that are innate or developed over a long period of time and not likely to be as easily shaped or changed. Some of the personality attributes desirable in a call center role are stress tolerance, adaptability, assertiveness, attention to detail, warmth, and friendliness.

The table on the following page lists sample knowledge, skills, and attributes for a frontline customer service position. This particular set is provided as a guideline and is not intended to be all-inclusive as each call center will have its own unique set of requirements.

Sample Attributes for Frontline Customer Service Success		
Knowledge	**Skills**	**Attributes**
Customer service experience General computer literacy Microsoft Office background Call center industry knowledge Specific product knowledge Vertical market knowledge (ex: transportation, banking, telecommunications, insurance, travel, etc.)	Clear, concise writing skills Effective listening skills Fast, accurate typing skills Organizational ability Telephone system navigation Use of proper grammar and sentence structure Vocal skills (pitch, inflection, tone, tempo, rhythm, placement) Ability to build rapport	Adaptability Assertiveness Attention to detail Courtesy and helpful demeanor Customer focus Flexibility Patience Punctuality Selflessness/Team player

Use the space below to list the unique knowledge, skills, and attributes required for frontline staff in your call center.

Your Call Center Requirements		
Knowledge	**Skills**	**Attributes**

16. What else should be included in the job requirements?

In addition to defining the knowledge, skills, and attributes that make up the ideal call center employee, another important consideration in assessing the job is to define the unique working environment of your call center.

In particular, you'll want to identify aspects of the job and the environment that may be less than desirable and assess candidates' motivation to accept these conditions. Some examples include the following:

Identify aspects of the job and the environment that may be less than desirable and assess candidates' motivation to accept these conditions.

Confined space. Is the workstation space in your call center limited? Some people will feel uncomfortably confined in a small cubicle workspace.

Repetitive tasks. Is there variety in the type of work your agents do, or are the tasks fairly repetitive in nature? While some people like the predictability of call center work, others need more variety and challenge on an ongoing basis.

Solo work. Will the employee get to interact with others in the center? While you may be looking for a "people person" when making a hiring decision, it is important to recognize that a call center employee may have limited opportunity to actually interact face-to-face with peers and others in the workplace.

Frequent monitoring. Can you think of any other place where an employee is monitored so carefully? You probably record calls to ensure quality and review statistics that indicate an agent's work state every single second of the day. Some of your potential candidates will view this lack of privacy as a negative working condition.

Inflexible schedules. How much flexibility can you provide in the work schedule? While many other departments of your company may have a flex-time policy in which staff may start at any time as long as a set number of hours are worked, the call center is at the mercy of incoming call demand. Therefore, there's probably little to no flexibility in a person's work schedule to accommodate personal needs.

While the "can do" elements of knowledge and skills are certainly important, the "will do" elements of personality attributes and environmental fit are even more closely correlated with retention and employee satisfaction in the long run.

Finding a person with the skills and attributes who will also be happy with these unique work environment conditions is one of the biggest predictors of long-term retention and job success. Therefore, all work conditions – both positive and negative – should be included in the position description form. Defining these unique characteristics as part of developing the position description will help to identify personnel during the selection process that are the best possible fit for the call center environment.

While the "can do" elements of knowledge and skills are certainly important to make sure a candidate has the basic capabilities to do the work, the "will do" elements of personality attributes and environmental fit are even more closely correlated with retention and employee satisfaction in the long run.

17. Where should you look for call center candidates?

Once you've defined your unique requirements, the next step is to identify potential labor pools based on your specific needs. Your human resources department may have information about the demographics of your city or region, wage and salary expectations, and labor saturation statistics for the particular types of employees being sought. This type of information is critical to the recruiting process to determine where best to focus advertising efforts as well as how to set wage rates to be competitive for each type of position.

Sources of labor are generally divided into internal and external sources. Recruiting internally involves looking for staff within the company to fill open positions. If you can find candidates that are already employed by your company, you have the benefit of lower recruitment costs and a shorter ramp-up time since the employee will already be familiar with company products, procedures, and culture.

To ensure internal resources are made aware of your job openings, be creative about keeping employees informed about call center opportunities. Use bulletin boards, internal newsletters, cafeteria postings, and email. For internal recruiting, a copy of the job description should be posted either in the department, in the human resources department, on the intranet, or all three.

> If a workforce analysis reveals a high turnover rate, unqualified candidates in the job, or positions that remain open for long periods of time, then perhaps it's time to think about a new recruiting approach.

If your call center is like most, you will more than likely need to search outside your company to fill the seats in your call center. Your labor pool may be right in your back door with a ready supply of current employees' friends and family, or you may have to search a little harder. Expanding your search might include exploring temporary staffing agencies or contractors, school internships, professional associations, public employment services or outplacement programs, retirement agencies, other call centers in the area, and the general market of job-seekers.

The call center, in conjunction with the human resources department, should be constantly evaluating ways to improve efficiency and effectiveness of the recruiting process. If the analysis reveals a high turnover rate in candidates, unqualified candidates, or positions that remain open for long periods of time, then perhaps it's time to implement a new recruiting approach.

As a final thought on labor sources, it is important not to limit the definition of the potential labor force to those individuals who are currently seeking employment. Some of the best candidates may be those people that are currently employed elsewhere and satisfied with their current position. It may take some extra effort to get the attention of these candidates, but the extra work can pay off to find the "just right" fit of capabilities for the positions to be filled.

Given the ever-increasing competition for qualified call center staff, many call centers are turning to non-traditional pools of labor from which to recruit candidates.

Retirees or Seniors

If life experience, patience, good judgment, strong work ethic, punctuality, and low turnover are attributes you are looking for in your call center employees, then you may want to consider actively recruiting a more mature workforce. Many call centers actively seek to hire older, experienced workers. Information on hiring this workforce segment can be found at: www.aarp.com, www.seniorsearch.com, and www.seniorjobbank.com.

If patience and punctuality are important traits in your hiring criteria, then you may want to consider seniors in your labor candidates.

Disabled or Handicapped

Disabled individuals represent an excellent source of labor for many call centers. There are many individuals with disabilities that may prevent them from doing other types of work, but who are nonetheless well suited to the work of a call center. Many call center managers who employ these types of individuals find them to be the most reliable and devoted workers in the center. Another plus may be the tax benefits of hiring disabled workers. Information about hiring workers with disabilities can be found through the Equal Employment Opportunity Commission (www.eeoc.gov) and the Office of Disability Employment Policy (www. dol.gov/odep).

Students

While call centers have long since realized the benefits of a part-time college student workforce, some are taking the student definition one step further and considering the use of high school students as part-time staff. Many call centers have found that some high school students have the personality, service outlook, and computer skills to make them good entry-level employees.

Many call centers find their disabled or handicapped workers to be their most loyal and devoted performers.

18. How should you advertise call center positions?

While the most common way to advertise for call center positions is the traditional classified newspaper advertisement, you'll be smart to expand your advertising beyond this fairly limited approach. Some possibilities include:

Job fairs

Many call centers participate at job fairs hosted by professional associations and community organizations. Job fairs can be used to acquaint the community with the call center operation and to provide an overview of the open positions and benefits of working for the call center. Since these events tend to attract multiple companies from the local area, keep in mind that you may be competing with others for qualified candidates. The other option is to hold your own event where you'll have exclusive time with the candidates and the opportunity to show off your facility and benefits.

School placement programs

College recruiting is typically coordinated through a local college placement office with students invited to submit resumes and schedule interviews with the call center recruiters during a campus visit. When recruiting students, be sure to promote the students' ability to grow and learn at the call center with potential for an advanced position in the center upon graduation.

Web postings

Posting on the Internet may be a good match since online job seekers tend to be more technologically literate and generally have at least moderate computer skills. Also, job seekers can submit resumes instantly at anytime day or night, seven days a week. The postings may also be much cheaper than placing a classified ad.

Employee referral program

Employee referrals probably represent one of the most reliable recruiting resources for your business. Employee referrals are generally successful since employees are much more likely to recommend a qualified candidate than one that would be likely to be a source of embarrassment for them. Employee referral programs usually include some type of reward or incentive for employees who recommend potential candidates, typically matched to candidates who are hired and stay with the company for a specified period of time. When an employee is rewarded for making a referral, a notice should be sent out to make sure others are made aware of the success of the program.

Outside recruiters

Depending on the position level of the call center employee, search firms or "head hunters," employment agencies, and outside recruiters may also be utilized to recruit a qualified pool of candidates. These outside recruiting agencies fulfill the same basic functions as internal recruiters, with the exception that they recruit candidates for a fee.

An important factor to keep in mind when advertising for call center positions is that the best candidates for your center may be people that already have jobs and may not be reading the classifieds or attending job fairs. Part of an effective advertising program will include methods that get in front of qualified candidates currently working elsewhere. Some of these options may include:

Radio and television ads

Although more expensive than print advertising, radio and television spots can be very effective in getting the word out about available positions. Hearing a radio advertisement while driving to work, or seeing a television ad during the evening news will get the message in front of many people who aren't actively searching.

Billboards and buildings

When trying to attract candidates that live in the area within a fairly close radius of the call center, billboard advertising can be very effective. And there are a variety of media that can serve as a billboard in addition to the traditional big signs along roadways. Message space can be rented on a bus, a city bench, the back of restaurant restroom doors, and so on. Many companies hang huge banners on their buildings announcing open positions.

Handbills and flyers

If trying to attract people that live and work in the neighborhood, then handbill advertising may work well. Putting handbills on cars at a mall or grocery store can get the message out to a large audience. (Just be sure to legal clearance from city or property owners.)

Event advertising

Companies that want to reach thousands of candidates in one attempt have found advertising at large sporting events to be effective, in the form of an ad in the game program or on the display board at half-time. Video advertising in the local movie theatre can be effective as well to get a message across to a captive audience.

Local community meetings

Depending upon the pool of candidates the call center is trying to attract, there may be other choices for advertising as well. For example, if the center is looking for part-time personnel, advertising at local PTA meetings or other community meetings may be an alternative.

19. What's the best way to screen candidates?

Once the position has been advertised and you begin to receive responses, you'll need an effective screening process that weeds out undesirable candidates immediately. Many companies use telephone screening as this first step to gauge the candidate's voice and overall telephone skills.

This telephone screening is essential since it most closely reflects the applicant's ability to communicate over the telephone. Many call centers miss this opportunity by focusing on a written application as the first screening gate, but the smart recruiting team will focus on either live calls or at least a voice mailbox to weed out unsuitable candidates before taking time with a resume/application review.

Telephone screening is probably the best initial test since it most closely reflects the applicant's ability to communicate effectively on the job.

There are clear advantages to using telephone screening. Telephone screening identifies if a candidate has a basic understanding of telephone etiquette and the required communications and listening skills. This screening will determine if the applicant has the minimum skill set required and helps to establish if an on-site or face-to-face interview will be scheduled. The drawbacks of using telephone screening include the fact that no visual observation of the applicant is made and it can also inadvertently "screen out" qualified candidates.

To ensure that telephone interviews are consistent and objective, it's useful to have a telephone interview form, perhaps along with a script for multiple interviewers to ensure each candidate is being reviewed in the exact same manner. A sample telephone interview form is provided on the following page.

Screening for potential success in the call center can also be done using an automated IVR process or via an interactive web tool. These web-based and IVR-based tools often use branching technologies to take the candidates down a path of questions that vary depending on the answers given as they go along. Reporting on the results is provided so that the most viable candidates are moved to the next step in the process and those who appear to be a poor match to the center's requirements can be screened out or given lower priority. The IVR format will limit the answers to yes/no or some numeric entry, but more current models using speech recognition can solicit more free-form answers.

Sample Telephone Interview Form

Applicant Name ____________________ Date ____________________
Interviewer ____________________ Report to: ____________________

Application on file: Yes No Referred by: ____________________

1. How did you hear about this position?

   Radio Station: Newspaper Name: Flyer Location: Other Identify:

2. Have you received a job description for this position?

   Yes If yes, proceed to question 3.
   No If no, describe the purpose of position from Job Description form.

3. Does this sound like a job you may be interested in? Why?

4. Have you been in customer service/sales/telemarketing? Yes No
   Please tell me about your experience in that position.

5. Do you have a college degree? Yes O No O High school diploma? Yes No
   Additional education, related degrees or experience:

6. This job requires typing on a keyboard using a computer. Tell me about your computer experience and the rate of your typing.

7. This job may require you to work on different shifts, such as 7:00 a.m. to 3:00 p.m., 3:00 p.m. to 11:00 p.m., and 11:00 p.m. to 7:00 a.m. It may include weekend work. Would you be available for all shifts and weekends? If not, which shifts would you be available?

8. This job requires a courteous attitude even when dealing with difficult customers. It is also in a fast-paced environment. Have you worked in an environment like this before? Tell me about your experience. (If no experience, ask them to tell about experiences working with difficult people in a previous job.)

9. Explain the pay rate/pay range. (Include training wage and pay for experience.)

10. Explain relevant company policies such as dress code, smoking, etc. Confirm agreement with each.

11. If you were selected for this position, when would you be able to start work?

12. If satisfactory, schedule for a face-to-face interview.

20. What are the best interview questions?

Conducting an effective interview is critical to making a good hiring decision. You should plan interview questions in advance and ask them consistently of all candidates rather than just letting the interview flow freely.

> Create interview questions that are related to the job description and probe for job-related skills.

Asking the wrong questions can result in a poor choice of employees and can be legally troublesome as well. In preparing for the interview process, interview questions should be carefully created to ensure they are related to the job analysis and description, that they probe for job-related skills, and that all interview information is related to job requirements.

One of the key factors in creating an effective interview guide is to employ the concept of behavior-based interviewing. With the assumption that past experiences are the most accurate predictors of future actions, asking a candidate about past behaviors in a particular circumstance will help you determine if the applicant has the ability and motivation to perform certain roles and tasks.

The most successful interviewers use behavior-based interview questions due to the structure and positive results gained from the process. Where traditional interview questions tend to be subjective, closed-ended, and may telegraph the desired response, behavior-based questions are more objective, open-ended, have a job-specific focus, and seek examples of behaviors that predict performance.

> Asking a candidate about past behaviors in a particular scenario will help you predict what they may do when faced with a similar situation.

An example of a traditional interview question might be, "How would you assist an angry customer?" This question gives the candidate the opportunity to give the type of answer an interviewer is seeking. A corresponding behavior-based question might be, "Tell me about a specific time where you were presented with an angry customer. What were the specifics of the situation and what steps did you take to resolve the situation?" This question relates back to an actual experience and the behaviors or actions of that person in that situation. You can look for characteristics and skills that you need in the candidate's response.

During the interview process, the candidates should be able to relate their answers back to specific work-related examples and their answers should reflect the characteristics and skills the call center requires for the position.

Look for the candidates who display confidence when responding to questions. Listen for quality answers – not quantity or length. Remember that long answers do not necessarily mean quality responses.

It's important for you to get as many behavioral examples as possible in order to rate the person's skills for the specific job in question. Some sample interview questions might be:

- Describe a time when you were faced with problems at work that tested your coping skills. What did you do?

- Tell me about a time when you had to use your oral communication skills to get a point across that was important to you.
- Tell me about a specific occasion when you conformed to a policy, even though you did not agree with it.
- Give an example of a time when you used your fact-finding skills to gain information needed to solve a problem. Tell me how you analyzed the problem and came to a decision.
- Give an example of an important goal you had to set, and tell me about your progress in reaching that goal.
- Describe someone that you found hard to communicate with. What were the major obstacles? How did you overcome them?

In addition to several behavior-based questions, there are several other questions that can help pinpoint qualities and characteristics you may find desirable. Other questions that you might pose to a potential candidate include:

- Tell me what you know about our product/service.
- What management style do you prefer?
- How would your last supervisor describe you?
- What motivates you?
- What are your strengths?
- What is your biggest weakness related to this position?
- What would you like to continue to develop?

Perhaps the best approach to developing an interview guide and set of questions is to have a brainstorming session with your manager, other supervisors, and perhaps some of your star performers. Remember to prioritize the traits and characteristics you're looking for related to the job and create questions that best uncover these in the interview process.

Be careful asking questions that are not related directly to the job, or ones that can be viewed as discriminatory in nature. The table on the next page is designed to help you distinguish appropriate versus potentially illegal questions. When in doubt, review all your potential interview questions with your human resources or legal department to ensure they're legally safe and within company guidelines.

Subject	Do Not Ask	Permissible to Ask
Sex	Are you male or female? What are the names and relationships of people living with you?	None
Residence	Do you own or rent? Give the names and relationships of persons living with you.	What is your present address?
Race/Color	What is your race? What color are your hair, eyes, or skin?	None
Age	What is your date of birth? How old are you?	If hired, can you provide proof that you are at least 18 years of age?
National Origin	What is your ancestry, national origin, descent, ancestry, parentage, or nationality? What is your native language? What is the nationality of your parents or spouse?	We have a need for personnel who speak 'x' language. Do you speak or write 'x' fluently? (Do not ask unless strictly job-related.)
Marital or Family Status	What is your martial status? What is your spouse's name? What was your maiden name? How many children do you have? Are you pregnant? Do you plan to have children? What day-care provisions have you made for your children?	None. (An employer may ask if candidates have any commitments or responsibilities that might prevent them from meeting attendance requirements or if they anticipate lengthy work absences. If used at all, it should be asked of all applicants.)
Arrests and Convictions	Have you ever been arrested? Have you ever been charged with any crime?	Have you been convicted of any crime? (If the application form asks for information on convictions, the employer should indicate that a conviction itself does not constitute an automatic bar to employment and will be considered as it relates to fitness to perform the job in question.)
Religion	What is your religious affiliation or denomination? What church do you belong to? What is the name of your pastor, minister, or rabbi? What religious holidays do you observe?	None. (If you wish to know if an applicant is available to work Saturday or Sunday shifts, ask: "Are you available to work on Saturdays or Sundays if needed?" and ensure the question is asked of all applicants.)
Disabilities	Are you disabled?	Are you capable of performing the essential functions of this position, with or without reasonable accommodation?
Citizenship	From what country are you a citizen? Are you or other members of your family naturalized citizens? If so, when did you or they become a U.S. citizen? Attach a copy of your naturalization papers to your application form.	Are you a citizen of the United States? If hired, are you able to prove eligibility to work in the United States?

21. How can you test for skills and motivational fit?

To ensure your candidate is a good fit for the job and working conditions, you may want to consider doing some aptitude testing. This testing could screen for basic skills or could be more intricate to test for more advanced skills. Simple aptitude tests can be accessed via the Internet, or done at your company's site during the interview process.

For example, if navigating on the computer and typing quickly and accurately are needed skills, testing for these up front will help you identify the right candidates for the job, as well as help pinpoint initial and future training needs.

Personality profiles are being increasingly used in call centers to test important traits like team orientation, communications styles, and more.

In addition to aptitude or skills testing, personality profiles are often used in selecting personnel in the call center. These profiles measure such traits as results-oriented drive, motivation to learn, and team orientation. There are also psychometric instruments that can be matched to the call center's requirements (including questions about character traits, communications style, stress management and dealing with conflict).

As part of the screening and assessment phase, some call centers provide a means for a candidate to "test drive" the call center job through simulation testing. Simulation is used to set up a situation for the prospective employees to work through that replicate the type of work that they may be asked to perform on the job.

The idea is not to see how much product knowledge the candidate has, but to see how well the person handles the flow and pressure of the job including focus on customer service, handling anger, solving problems, building relationships, and navigating through the computer and telephone system. The simulation may have the candidate hear caller contact information such as name, address, and phone number and must enter the data as quickly and accurately as possible. Or the candidate may be presented with several sample comments from a customer and asked to select appropriate contextual responses.

Simulation testing can replicate job task scenarios to see how a potential candidate might respond to a sample situations or obstacles.

Many call centers today use these tools not only to screen candidates up front, but also during the orientation and training process and for ongoing skill development. The tools can be used to assist in developing a career path for the individual and managing the progress along that path.

22. How should you make the job offer?

Once you have narrowed your choice of candidates, it's time to review all the possibilities, make a decision, and then extend the offer. All of the people in your center that interviewed the candidate should discuss the advantages and disadvantages of each candidate. The evaluation process should stay focused on job skills. If there is an even match between candidates, the evaluation team might consider each candidate's enthusiasm and willingness to learn skills as the potential "tie-breaker." The evaluation team should also compare all finalists against each other and against the standards set prior to the interview.

Once a decision has been made, extend the offer immediately so the candidate isn't lost to another competing job offer.

Upon reaching a final decision, it's time to extend the job offer. The timing of the offer should be immediately following the decision to hire so the candidate isn't lost to another job opening.

In making the offer, it's important to sell the candidate on all the high points of the job, as well as the benefits of working for your particular organization. In addition, you'll want to communicate what might be viewed as a downside to the job as well as the many benefits.

It's important that you define all aspects of the job in the offer letter, and it's particularly critical to spell out in clear language anything that may become an issue later in the person's employment.

Explain policies like schedule expectations clearly to prevent misunderstandings later in the employment cycle.

You may wish to include explanations of the candidate's work schedule and attendance/schedule adherence expectations, monitoring policies, performance measurement practices, training schedule, and so on. If you make these things clear in the offer letter, you can prevent misunderstandings and help reduce or eliminate turnover several weeks or months into the job.

Most job offers are typically made in writing, and should include a description of the position, the rate of pay, starting date, schedule hours, and performance expectations. A sample job offer letter is illustrated on the following page.

Sample Job Offer Letter

January 5, 2005

Ms. Jane Doe
123 Anystreet
Anytown, TN 37204 USA

Dear Jane:

It is our pleasure to extend an offer of employment to you for the position of an entry level Customer Service Representative (CSR1).

As a CSR1, your job responsibilities include, but are not limited to answering a continuous volume of phone calls from a variety of customers regarding catalog orders. You will be responsible for providing answers regarding the availability and pricing for catalog items.

You will be employed at a rate of $12.00 per hour initially, with a salary review after six months of employment. In addition, you will receive one week of paid vacation for each full six months of employment. Your benefits will include full medical insurance for yourself (with an option to purchase for your dependents.) We also offer optional dental and vision plans for a nominal fee.

You will be working a 7 1/2-hour shift with two 15-minute assigned breaks and a 30-minute assigned lunch. Your start time will initially be 11:00 a.m., but that start time may vary by two hours earlier or later on an as-needed basis.

Your immediate supervisor will be John Smith. In your role as a CSR1, your supervisor will monitor your performance using side-by-side and recorded monitoring. You will have a minimum of five calls per month that are recorded for review on a random basis.

Your first day of work will be on January 10th. If these terms are agreeable to you, please sign and date this letter below and return it to our Human Resources department.

We are very pleased that you are joining the company and we look forward to having you on our team.

Sincerely,

Call Center Anywhere
Ms. Call Center Director

Agreed and Accepted:

Employee Signature ____________________________________

Date ____________________________________

Learning Activities

1. Write a detailed job description for an intermediate position between entrylevel agent and supervisor within your call center (team lead, senior rep, etc.). Begin with what you believe their roles and responsibilities are, observe their daily job routine, then interview them to fine-tune your list. Finally, compare this description to the one on record in the human resources area. Note any changes needed.

2. Interview one of the human resources specialists in your company that is responsible for recruiting and hiring staff for the call center. Discuss how the company's recruiting and hiring procedures and policies are structured to conform to various human resource regulations and laws?

3. Gather the past few advertisements and marketing plans that have been used to recruit call center staff. Compare this with other advertisements for call center staff in your local/regional area. Evaluate how your recruiting efforts compare to others and how your call center might improve the next recruiting effort.

4. Assume that your call center has been experiencing high rates of staff turnover in the last six months. Your wage rates are equal or above other centers in your area, so compensation does not appear to be the reason for attrition. Design three behavioral-based interview questions that are designed to ascertain whether someone might have the right motivational attributes to be successful and satisfied working in the call center on a long-term basis.

Chapter 4 – Training and Development

It's critical to equip each of your frontline staff with the skills and knowledge to confidently handle customer contacts. To remain competitive in today's evolving call center environment, it's important not just to train employees on product knowledge and soft skills, but also to provide the knowledge and skills that will help them to cope with the increasing demands and pressures of the marketplace.

Your training program should include new-hire training programs, training to introduce a new policy, procedure, or a new technology, or bring an employee up to the expected level of performance in a certain area. Care should also be taken to address the ongoing personal development and professional growth of each employee.

Your call center should have a training program in place that supports customer and employee satisfaction, optimal performance, and realization of each employee's potential. This chapter will focus on the value of training to the organization, and examine the components of a successful training program including the needs analysis, types of training, and the various training delivery methods.

23. What can you do to prepare for new employees?
24. What should be included in new-hire orientation?
25. What should be included in regular and ongoing training?
26. How do you assess ongoing training requirements?
27. How do you assess and support ongoing career development?
28. What kind of training will you need as a supervisor?
29. What kinds of training techniques are most effective?
30. Which is more effective – classroom training or e-learning?
31. How do you know if the training is working?
32. How can you create a learning environment?

23. What can you do to prepare for new employees?

One of the critical steps of the new agent orientation program is to prepare for the agent before the first day. There are many different administrative, technical, and organizational tasks that need to be done to prepare for a new employee's arrival. A sample pre-orientation checklist can be found on the following page.

New employees may feel anxious and overwhelmed as they arrive for their first day of work, and it's your job to simply make them feel welcome and orient them to the new environment with a minimum of hassle and stress.

One of the easiest ways to address the anxiety and confusion the new employee may have is to answer the basic questions of Who, What, When, Where, Why, and How:

Who?

This question should identify the resources the agents can utilize. They should be welcomed by you, the direct supervisor first, and then introduced to the senior manager, their mentor or "buddy" if one is assigned, and their peers.

What?

This question should provide immediate responses to the job requirements, performance standards, policies and procedures, and department expectations.

When?

This question will probably be about their specific work schedule, and should outline start/stop times, as well as lunch and break times. You'll also want to include when they will be paid and how often their performance will be reviewed.

Where?

This question should be designed to point out the location of the agent's workstation, restrooms, lunch/break area, copy/fax machine, parking, supervisor's office, human resources, and so on.

Why?

This question should primarily address what role the agent will play and why this customer interaction role is so critical to the success of the business. There will be many more "whys" to answer later in terms of the reasons for various procedures or tasks, but the orientation should primarily focus on their critical role in the business.

How?

This question will begin to address some of the important basic instructions of their job and may include how to log in to the computer system and phone system.

Pre-Orientation Checklist

- ○ Coordinate call center program with HR orientation program.
- ○ Send "welcome" materials to agent prior to first day arrival.
- ○ Contact telecom department and request user ids and passwords for phone.
- ○ Assign to appropriate queue.
- ○ Contact IT department to set up computer and install any necessary applications.
- ○ Request network user ID and email account from IT department.
- ○ Notify workforce team of new arrival to obtain individual work schedule.
- ○ Notify quality assurance team of new arrival.
- ○ Notify security of new hire start date and make arrangements for security/ID cards.
- ○ Prepare the individual desktop and work areas.
- ○ Order nameplates and other needed supplies.
- ○ Send a memo to the call center staff with new agents' names, start date, schedules, and responsibilities.
- ○ Assign a "buddy" to each agent and coordinate work schedules.
- ○ Assemble materials to give to new staff on first day:

- Welcome letter from call center manager
- Organizational chart
- Map of the facility
- Products and services description
- Terms and acronyms unique to industry
- Call center department and team metrics
- Individual performance metrics form
- Frequently asked questions document
- Schedule (confirm first day details)
- Contact information for "buddy"
- Training agenda
- 1-week, 2-week, 30-day checklists
- List/location of resources
- Job description

24. What should be included in new-hire orientation?

Your new-hire orientation program should be designed to provide an introduction to your company, the call center, and the industry. The goal of the new agent orientation program should be to make new agents feel welcome, quickly integrate them into the call center team, and create a positive impression of the call center.

The goal of orientation is to make the new staff feel welcome and quickly integrate them into the team.

The orientation program is your new employee's first real exposure to the organization and it should be an enjoyable and memorable experience. The orientation program is the perfect opportunity for new staff to understand how they fit into the big picture and to recognize the important role they play in the interaction with your customers.

Many different people will play a role in the orientation process. As a supervisor, you may also conduct a tour of call center and introduce the agent to the staff and to their co-workers. During the first week, you will probably meet with the agent to review the department's organization chart, provide an explanation of where and how to get support, review the job description and work schedule (hours/days, breaks, lunch, overtime), and discuss the department's attendance policy and performance expectations. Additional discussions will include the products/services the agent is expected to support and any job assignments and training plans.

The call center manager or director should also be involved in this orientation process. It is probably the manager's role to ensure at a higher level that department orientation links appropriately with the orientation components that the human resources department will provide. The manager should also take time to visit with agents for a few minutes at the beginning of orientation to welcome them, as well as at the end of the process to see how the overview went and to answer any questions.

Plan with senior management what their role will be in the orientation process beyond a welcome message.

Many call centers use a "buddy system" to help orient new staff to the workplace. Each buddy or mentor should be assigned as soon as possible to ensure each agent has a readily available resource for logistical questions and for "hand-holding" during the first week. A buddy or mentor is the person assigned to act as the information source for policies, procedures, and work rules, to act as a tour guide and lunch companion, and to provide feedback and encouragement. The buddy will also help to identify resources, clarify assignments, provide introductions to other departments, and to act as a "social director" to include the new agent in social activities. The buddy or mentor may also assist with training and help the agent sort out priorities in the early stages of the job.

While every call center is different in terms of what is covered in the early orientation phase, some of the common items that are typically included at this stage are included in the checklist on the following page.

Orientation Checklist

Organization

Origin and history

Organization's mission and goals

Call center mission and goals

Core operating values

Organizational structure

Customers

Products and services

Headquarters, other sites

Compensation

Pay schedule

Timekeeping

Overtime policy

Payroll deductions

Benefits

Medical, dental, vision, life plans

Investment opportunities

Incentive programs

Employee purchases

Tuition reimbursement

Training and development

Service and recognition awards

Employee-assistance program

Wellness program

Attendance

Call center schedule

Holidays

Leave policy

Vacation

Facilities

Cafeteria/break facilities

Fax/copy room

Restroom locations

Parking

Security

Security procedures

Restricted areas

Confidentiality and privacy issues

Company identification

After-hours procedures

Network security

ACD login

Email ID/login

Performance

Overall expectations

Performance measures

Monitoring practices

Coaching expectations

Ethical standards

Conflict of interest

Probationary period

Dress code

Telephone etiquette

Email policies

Personal calls and visits

Performance reviews

Disciplinary process

Causes for termination

25. What should be included in regular and ongoing training?

After the new-hire orientation has been completed, the next phase is considered initial training and often includes training related to the company's products and services, as well as various types of "soft skills" training.

Your company will probably include general customer service training programs as part of the initial training program. This general service training might include such topics as conversation control, tips for handling an angry caller, telephone etiquette, and so on. For agents who are in a sales role, topics such as assertive selling or overcoming objections could also be included.

Training in general service skills like conversation control, telephone etiquette, and handling a difficult caller should be a part of every call center curriculum.

Large organizations will likely have a dedicated training function with specialists that can develop and deliver the training. However, in small and medium-sized centers, the development and delivery of training is often left to the supervisor. Whoever is developing the training program and materials should ask the following questions:

- What are the steps of the task to be accomplished?
- What are the expected results – in other words, how will you recognize that the task is being done correctly?
- How will you ensure the student can identify the critical steps of the task and perform them in the proper sequence?

For any new task or skill to be learned, the student should be able to observe the required steps or behaviors. Then you should be able to track whether the student has completed the task correctly and in the proper sequence. One way to do this is to create task-based modular training components.

For example, you might have a new employees observe a task several times and then demonstrate the same procedure. After observing several satisfactory demonstrations, you may ask the student to summarize or flowchart the steps for how to complete a particular task and then compare what they've done to the standard you have provided. If there are discrepancies, you have the immediate opportunity to provide coaching to correct any errors or misconceptions.

For any new skill to be learned, the student should be able to observe the required steps and then have the chance to demonstrate the steps correctly and in the proper sequence.

Classroom training should be supplemented regularly with on-the-job training. This is often accomplished by teaming the new agent with experienced staff to observe the step-by-step process of certain tasks. You'll want to do this as early as possible in the training process so that the new agent gets a true flavor of the work to be done.

There can be many variations of this partnering arrangement. In some cases the agent may observe by watching the keyboard/screen activity while listening to an experienced employee handle the call. The next step might be for the agent to do the keyboard work while the senior agent handles the conversation with the caller, or conversely to have the senior agent handle the computer part of the call and navigate through menus while the new agent talks with the customer (with the senior agent listening in for back-up). There are many different variations of how this side-by-side activity may occur, and each call center must determine when it is optimal to introduce it in the training process.

As new agents are introduced to the call center, the call center training program needs to spend adequate time discussing the use of the automatic call distributor (ACD) telephone set (or soft phone), especially use of the proper buttons for various states and activities. Proper button usage is essential for the call center management team to retrieve accurate statistics from the ACD system.

One "missing link" in most new agent training programs is a basic frame of reference about the overall operations of the center. There are basics of call center operations that all staff need to know. These basics may include how call center performance is measured and why, how overall call center goals translate to individual goals and how performance will be monitored and measured. It is useful for all staff to know how staffing levels are determined and the impact of one person being out of place and what technologies are at work to deliver a call to the desktop. The table below provides a partial listing of the components to be considered in an overview of call center operations.

Topic Area	Content
Call center industry	Call center terms and acronyms Types of centers and business functions Call center's role in the business
Performance measurement	Service and quality measures Efficiency measures Individual agent performance measures
Customer service basics	Telephone etiquette Scripting and phrasing Handling difficult calls
Staffing and scheduling	Forecasting and scheduling process Impact of one person on service Importance of schedule adherence
Call center technology	Call delivery technologies Performance management tools Agent desktop tools
Customer relationships	Value of the customer Cost of customer attrition Customer's view of quality

26. How do you assess ongoing training requirements?

Training for the agent shouldn't stop after the new-hire orientation and initial training period is completed. Training is an ongoing evolutionary process. The goal of your call center's ongoing training program is to provide training for the skills necessary to perform the job, plus training for the skills necessary to enhance ongoing performance.

Common assessment milestones are at 30, 60, 90, and 120 days on the job.

In developing your ongoing training program, it is useful to define what employees need to know and be able to do at defined job anniversaries. Common milestones are at 30 days, 60 days, 90 days, and 120 days. For each of these timeframes, a checklist should be developed that outlines critical knowledge and skills so training gaps and performance issues can be identified.

Some typical questions you might ask at each of these stages are:

- What additional things does the agent need to know?
- What policies and procedures could affect job performance?
- What behaviors should be reinforced?
- What specific tasks can be assigned to allow for growth?
- Is it time to expand level of authority and empowerment?
- What feedback is needed on each agent's performance?
- What training objectives have been met or not met?

At some point your staff will move from an "initiation" phase to a "competency" phase. This transition occurs at different points for different companies. Some organizations may have a 90-day training followed by another 90-day initiation phase. Agents in other call centers may only receive a two-week training period and then be fully competent in their call-handling capabilities after another few weeks. Regardless of how long it takes, there is some point at which the agents discover how things really work and have developed all the competencies needed for the job. At this point, they can work productively most of the time. During this phase, agents also begin to offer suggestions on how their performance can be improved or possible improvements to policies or procedures.

Even after agents move into the competency phase, there still needs to be ongoing training for specialized skills based on their job function(s) or for areas where they've indicated career interest.

Even after agents move into the competency phase, there still needs to be ongoing training for specialized skills based on their job function(s). For example, agents responsible for selling may benefit from advanced training on consultative selling or advanced closing techniques. Also, in addition to expanding abilities in their current role, there may also be opportunities to learn new skills or enhance general skills like time management, stress management, telephone and email best practices, vocal skills, written communications skills, and so on.

27. How do you assess and support ongoing career development?

After your staff have completed the initial and secondary training programs and are functioning at a satisfactory level in their job, they still need to have opportunities for ongoing training and development. These opportunities may be related to career advancement within their current role as outlined earlier, or may be programs to prepare them for other roles, such as a promotion to lead agent or supervisor position, or to a support role such as workforce planning, quality assurance, or training.

One of the most important components of developing a career development plan and associated training program is to first determine the people that are best suited to a particular role. It's important to consider that the best agents in a call center may not make the best team leaders or supervisors or technical specialists. Some of the best agents have a high need for individual achievement, but don't enjoy interacting with or supervising other people or compiling numbers or reports.

> Career opportunities may be advancement within a current role, to a supervisory role, or a different support role within the call center.

The best way to find the right candidate for any "next step" position is no different than the procedure to find the right frontline staff for the job. Potential team leaders or supervisor candidates should be interviewed for the position. They also should take part in situational role-plays and problem-solving tests. Another tool that can provide valuable feedback is the use of a 360-degree instrument. With a 360-degree tool, the goal is to gather feedback from subordinates, peers, superiors, and self-evaluation to determine the strengths and weaknesses of the potential candidate being considered for a new type of role.

Many organizations use a career development profile to determine which candidates are best suited to various future roles based on an interest and capability inventory. A partial career development profile is included on the following page and can be used as a screening device to identify the potential roles for various employees.

Once the profile has been completed, the results can be "plotted" using a graph with interest scores on the x-axis and capability scores on the y-axis. The graph will consist of four quadrants: Q1, Q2, Q3, and Q4, as illustrated below.

CAREER development profile CHART

Interest		
	Q1	**Q2**
	Q3	**Q4**
	Capability	

An area that falls into the Q1 quadrant indicates an area in which the employee has the interest but not the capability in a certain area. The Q2 quadrant indicates both interest and capability in the area. The Q3 quadrant indicates no interest or ability for the job, while Q4 areas show high capability but limited interest. In short, if the responses fall into the high interest/high capability quadrant or the high interest/low capability quadrant, these are the areas for concentration when creating a training plan.

Career Development Profile Form

	Capability	Interest
Analytical Capability Using logic to break information into smaller units for analysis and comparison of similarities/differences to solve problems		
Decision Making Analyzing details by considering all the facts and alternatives to make informed decisions		
Information Gathering Gathering relevant information from written sources, observation, or through interviews in order to analyze issues from a different perspective		
Leadership Providing a sense of direction. Ability to develop a group of individuals into an effective team by providing a clear sense of direction to other people to enable them to carry out tasks and achieve goals		
Listening Extracting information and details from verbal communication		
Mathematical Analyzing, process and present numerical data		
Motivation Energizing others and building enthusiasm both with individuals and teams		
Organization Creating a systematic course of action by prioritizing, scheduling, coordinating, and monitoring performance against objectives to achieve a task or objective effectively and efficiently.		
Planning Planning activities, projects, productions or systems, or different phases of work to achieve a goal		
Problem Solving Analyzing situations, seeking relevant data, diagnosing possible causes and generating alternative solutions to find the best solution		
Strategic Thinking Knowing how to create a clear vision of the long term future after considering a wide range of possibilities and options		
Verbal Presentation Expressing verbally in a manner which is clear, concise, accurate, and to the point in order to capture the attention of the audience		
Written Communication Using the written word to clearly express ideas in a manner which is readily understood by the recipient		

High Interest - Low Capability. If an area falls into this category, your employee may have interest in that area, but no current capabilities. Experience and exposure to suitable tasks may help develop these competencies. There may be an opportunity to look for projects, assignments, and development opportunities that will allow the employee to exercise and develop these competencies further. Questions to ask include:

- What development opportunities exist that would allow the employee to develop skills and knowledge in the areas of interest?
- Who can help the employee develop these competencies?
- What resources are available to help the employee develop these resources?
- Are there low risk opportunities to develop these competencies?

High Interest - High Capability. These competencies form the profile of the employee's ideal job. You should look for opportunities to exercise these competencies and interests either in a new job or role, or by seeking projects or assignments where these competencies can be utilized. Questions to ask include:

- Does the employee's existing job provide enough of these to sustain the employee?
- What key projects or assignments require or benefit from these competencies?
- What sort of jobs or roles would match these competencies?
- How can these competencies be used to maximize organizational benefits?
- Is the employee's supervisor aware that these competencies and interests exist?
- What development opportunities exist to maximize these competencies?

Low Interest - High Capability. For employees in this category, even though they have mastered these skills, they are not interested in them. Questions to ask include:

- How can these tasks be reduced without impacting company performance?
- How can you free up the employee to do different things if current skills are needed and valued?
- What changes can be made to motivate the employee to use these competencies?
- Are there opportunities for the employee to mentor others whose competencies are not as strong in this area so that they can take responsibilities for some of these activities / tasks?

Low Interest - Low Capability. This area identifies skills that the employee does not want to use. If the employee's existing job requires using a high proportion of these competencies, the employee is likely to be unhappy. Questions to ask include:

- Are these competencies important for the successful execution of the employee's job?
- Are there other jobs that require fewer competencies?

28. What kind of training will you need as a supervisor?

If you are like most call center supervisors, you may have "come up through the ranks" from a frontline position. You may have been promoted to your current role because you performed exceptionally well as a frontline agent and possessed good customer service skills. However, you may have grown into this position without the needed knowledge about what it takes to supervise and manage in a call center environment. Successful call centers have a formal management succession plan and career development program in place to make supervisory staff successful in their people management roles.

Most call center supervisors are promoted from frontline positions and many are not equipped with all the skills and knowledge to be a successful supervisor.

Supervisory knowledge and skills typically fall into the broad category of people management. People management encompasses all of the following competencies:

Recruiting and Hiring

Supervisors in some centers are more involved in this process than in other centers. But even with a specialized team of recruiters and staff to do screening, you will be involved in at least the interview process. It's important for you to have the necessary interviewing skills to ask the right questions and read responses to find the best match for the job.

Motivational Techniques

There are seven main types of strategies for keeping staff motivated and happy on the job, and you should understand basic motivational theory and how to select the motivational techniques that are best suited for your unique staff and working conditions. Understanding which techniques work best in the unique world of call centers is critical to performance success.

Most of the skills and knowledge needed by supervisors falls into the category of people management.

Retention Strategies

While compensation and job fit are important factors in why people leave or stay with the company, some of the biggest drivers of retention are under your direct control as a supervisor. You must understand what the key drivers are to team and individual satisfaction and strive to meet them.

Defining Performance Standards

Defining realistic goals and expectations and measuring their attainment are critical to every call center's success. You need to be able to define these goals with corporate and call center objectives in mind and then communicate the individual behaviors that you want to see demonstrated by your frontline staff.

Diagnosing Performance Problems

Once you have defined goals and standards of performance, you must be well-versed in comparing actual performance to the goals to identify performance gaps. You should be able to diagnose the root cause of performance issues unique to the call center environment.

Coaching and Counseling

One of the most fundamental skills you'll need is the ability to coach and motivate employees. There are many things about working in a call center that make it unique, and the coaching skills that work in another environment may need to be fine-tuned to be successfully applied to call center issues.

Human Resources Issues

While some of the human resource issues will be the same from one department to another, there are some elements of call center operations that generate additional personnel issues and potential legal problems. It's imperative that you are aware of these from an interviewing, monitoring, coaching, and discipline perspective.

Staffing and Scheduling

Given that call center staff are at the mercy of incoming customer calls, the issue of staffing and scheduling staff is one that every supervisor will have to address. While you don't need to be able to forecast workload and create staff schedules, you will need to understand the basic concepts of call center staffing and the tradeoffs with cost, service, and productivity so you can communicate them to your staff.

In addition to people management skills, you will also need to be competent in various areas of call center operations management, including the following:

Call Center Math

Managing in today's call center means managing by the numbers. There is a vast array of numbers available from today's call center systems and you will need to understand how to assimilate the statistics to isolate performance trends and exceptions. You will be reviewing overall call center statistics, team performance numbers, and individual scores.

Call Center Technology

While you probably don't need to be able to trouble-shoot network routing problems or program the ACD, it is important for you to have at least a basic understanding of the technologies at work in your call center. You should understand the basic concepts of call routing and delivery and be able to explain how each technology is used to support your customers' interactions.

Performance Measurement

Every supervisor should understand the top twenty performance indicators that cover the areas of service, quality, efficiency, and profitability in your call center. You should know what these measures are and how your team and each individual agent affects the overall call center's performance success in each of these categories.

29. What kinds of training techniques are most effective?

Did you ever wonder why some of your employees come out of a training program and just simply don't seem to get it? Do some of the trainees seem to assimilate all the information just fine, but others seem like they were never even in the class?

The problem may not be in the intelligence levels or the classroom efforts of the trainees, but in the way the training is designed and presented. It's important that your training programs are designed to engage and stimulate all types of students and learning styles.

> Training programs should be designed to engage and stimulate all types of students and learning styles.

An important consideration in developing call center training programs is to understand how adults learn. The concept of adult learning theory that emerged in the 1970s suggests that we learn differently as adults than we did as children in school. Some characteristics of adult learners are:

- Adults need to be able to integrate new ideas with what they already know.
- Adults need to practice what they have learned on relevant problems.
- Adults learn better in a friendly and informal climate.
- Adults usually require more than one medium for learning.
- The medium that works best will vary and depend upon the preferred communications and learning style of the individual.

Studies have shown that adult educational programs are more successful when modular pieces of content are delivered in small blocks of time. These adult learning blocks are:

> Adults learn better when pieces of content are delivered in small blocks of time.

- Tell them.
- Show them.
- Let them try.
- Monitor and provide feedback.
- Let them try again.
- Reinforce.

It's also important to understand that adults have different learning and communications styles. A learning or communications style refers to the way in which a person understands, gathers, collects, and recovers information. Adults use a combination of learning styles, but each person will gravitate towards one of these styles: visual, auditory, or kinesthetic. These styles are explained further in the table on the following page.

Learning Style	Indications	Training Implications
Visual	Prefers to obtain information through sight Learns by visual aspects Learns from body language and visual cues as well as words	Use reading assignments Write on the whiteboard Have students take notes
Auditory	Prefers to learn through listening Likes to talk things through Uses voice tone, pitch, speed to interpret content	Have students read aloud Include verbal lectures Provide audio tapes of written materials
Kinesthetic	Prefers to learn by doing or touching Explores physical aspects of lesson Distracted easily without activity	Include hands-on activities Incorporate physical activity Use on-the-job training to demonstrate tasks

Since adults learn through a variety of means, no one learning mode is right or even better than another. The point is that each person learns differently, and a successful training program should be designed to accommodate such style differences.

It's also important to avoid teaching others using just the style that is most comfortable for you. All styles should be accommodated if all trainees are to successfully complete the call center training curriculum.

Each person learns differently, and your training program should accommodate all three learning styles.

30. Which is more effective – classroom training or e-learning?

One of the decisions to be made in your overall training strategy is the medium used to deliver training – traditional classroom training or computer-based e-learning?

> Most call centers use traditional, classroom training for the majority of their training programs.

Most call centers still rely on doing training the old-fashioned way – traditional, classroom training with a live instructor. This is referred to as ILT, or instructor-led training. It's worked for years and still is the most popular approach for most centers. Training can be developed and delivered by in-house staff or professional training organizations.

Much of its success depends upon development of good courseware, with the most successful programs being built upon adult learning principles. A knowledgeable instructor who's adept at facilitation is also key to successful knowledge transfer and learning. If both courseware and facilitation are good, then ILT programs are very effective. And they have the benefit of immediate question/answer, interaction with an instructor and other students, and the leveraging of class questions for further learning.

Classroom training does have its drawbacks however. It's the most expensive type of training and can be quite costly for one-to-few training. Training often happens too late or too soon, with training happening based upon a calendar or schedule plan, instead of a student's immediate needs.

It's best when you have multiple students at a single location at a similar skill level. Classroom training is the top choice when learning needs to involve highly interactive knowledge sharing, or where new skills need to be practiced and observed with feedback.

> Classroom training is the best choice when learning needs to be interactive or new skills need to be practiced and observed with immediate feedback.

The other option is to utilize e-learning. This is the type of training that is delivered via an electronic medium – typically from either CD, from a training program residing on an internal server or intranet, or via the web. Online learning offers an obvious range of benefits, such as self-paced learning, consistency of delivery, approved content, speed of delivery, and 24 x 7 accessibility. Depending upon how it's developed and delivered, e-learning can also be quite cost-effective when compared to traditional ILT programs.

However, e-learning has its drawbacks. E-learning requires some level of self-directed motivation which can be problematic for many employees. And the collaboration and interaction with a teacher and other students in a traditional classroom environment is often difficult to replicate in an online learning experience.

It's perhaps best utilized in a "basic training" mode where it's necessary to "teach" certain knowledge. And it's also an obvious choice when there are many students that need to participate stretched over multiple locations.

There's one other solution that manages to combine the best of both training worlds into one solution. Synchronous, or real-time, training via the web (or intranet) is a nice "in between" choice for many training applications. It combines the live instruction from the classroom with the cost benefits of the online training where students may be scattered among multiple sites.

E-learning is perhaps best utilized to teach basic knowledge components.

Thankfully, it's not an "either/or" decision between these three choices. The use of a wide range of training methods and media – a blended learning solution – can enhance and maximize learning opportunities. If you look at the three different areas of knowledge and skills needed by your frontline staff, you will see that a blended approach may be ideal.

Product Knowledge

Since much product information will be basic content that is simply a "data dump," and some students will absorb this information faster than others, this type of training is probably a good place to use e-learning solutions. You can have new agents go through the basics with e-learning, and save your instructors to present the more advanced material and to facilitate interaction as students fine-tune and test out their new knowledge about the company and products.

Soft Skills

There are some basic rules of telephone etiquette and some communications skills that can be "e-learned" – no doubt about it. But while it may be easy to master the basic concepts, it's actually much harder than it looks to perform the skills on a live call. To get it right, your staff will need a lot of practice. Ideally, this practice should be in a social context, since what they're learning is a social skill. There's a big difference in learning the concepts (which may be done through e-learning), and actually experiencing and practicing those new skills (which lends itself to classroom instruction, peer learning, and one-to-one coaching).

When deciding upon which medium to use here, consider the distinction between the theory (what they need to know) versus the practice (of demonstrating the skill).

As your company begins to evaluate e-learning options, it's important to beware of "techno-lust" – the desire to implement the latest and greatest technology to address your training needs. Too many call centers have failed with their e-learning initiatives by trying to force too much content into a self-paced medium. A safer approach involves taking small steps into e-learning conversion and realizing that not all aspects of your current training are appropriate for the virtual classroom.

31. How do you know if the training is working?

It's important to constantly assess the effectiveness of your call center training program. You'll want to measure immediate reaction, successful transfer of learning to the job, ongoing behaviors, and long-term results in order to evaluate the success or failure of the program.

Measure immediate reaction and test scores, transfer of skills to the job, and long-term results.

At a minimum, make sure you utilize an evaluation form for each training program and pre-class and post-class assessments to measure before and after learning. In addition, you should keep a formal or informal log of each new employee's performance where you track observations of actual performance once the training program has been completed.

There are five points at which the training program should be evaluated using formal assessments tools:

- ***Before training.*** Assessments used in advance of, or at the start of, a learning experience are sometimes called diagnostic assessments, pre-assessments, or placement exams. These assessments may include a self-assessment of knowledge, skills, learning style, and attitudes, or be used to place students within a suitable learning program.
- ***During training.*** Assessments used during the training process provide valuable feedback to students, training managers, and call center supervisors and help to confirm the student is progressing as expected through the program. These assessments may include practice tests and exams, or may be used to collect data that may contribute to an overall certification score.
- ***After training.*** Post-assessments are the best tools to be used for after the training program. The post-assessment scores should be compared to the pre-assessment scores to evaluate knowledge levels before and after the training.
- ***In the workplace.*** Observation by the supervisor is the best way to determine the utilization of new knowledge and skills on the job. Other ways to gather information related to the student's performance in the workplace after attending training include peer observations, checklists, interviews, and analysis of before and after performance data.
- ***Leaving the workplace.*** An exit interview can contain valuable information about the employee's opinion of training programs in the call center including the initial, ongoing, and development programs.

The call center management team must make a commitment to evaluate the end results of any training program to define the success or failure of each program. All training solutions should be analyzed to determine if the original goals of the program have been achieved and to create a process improvement strategy to correct any gaps.

32. How can you create a learning environment?

In a "balanced scorecard" business model, there are four areas that are evaluated for success. The first three are customer satisfaction, business processes (productivity measures), and financial measures. In general, these three categories of success factors are covered by the performance measures of the business and of the call center. The call center has customer-related performance measures (speed of answer, quality scores, satisfaction scores), business process measures (occupancy, handle time, resolution rate), and financial measures (cost per call, sales per call, sales conversion rate).

The fourth category that successful businesses utilize is a category related to learning and innovation. It is a category that addresses not how the business is doing today, but how well it is preparing itself for the future.

Successful companies evaluate not just how the business is doing today, but how well its employees are prepared for the future.

To successfully prepare for future business opportunities and challenges, it is important to provide not just "how-to" training for current job responsibilities, but also to provide an environment in which all employees are encouraged to continually learn and grow. Training should not be viewed as a one-time event, but as a never-ending activity.

No matter what you know today, it could be outdated next week or next month.

To create and sustain a learning environment, the management team must budget both the time and the dollars for ongoing training. Some training experts recommend a training budget of five percent of an employee's time – the equivalent of about one day a month. Studies done on Malcolm Baldridge Quality Award winners indicate that these companies regularly spend 3-5% of employee time and roughly 2-5% of annual payroll on training resources and activities.

Futurist Alvin Toffler writes of a need for people in the modern workplace to "learn, unlearn, and relearn." No matter what you and your team members know today, it could be outdated next week or next month.

Be a role model by learning new things yourself.

As a supervisor, you can facilitate team learning by doing the following:

- Encourage people to take risks and try new ideas.
- Model, coach, and reinforce behaviors that support learning as a strategy for facilitating change.
- Generate enthusiasm by sharing your learning experiences and portraying learning as a way to become more valuable to the organization.
- Help team members anticipate opportunities to enhance learning.
- Be a model by learning new things yourself.

Learning Activities

1. Work with other supervisors in your call center to develop a Pre-Orientation checklist. Include in this checklist what to gather for the new employee's first day on the job, what other departments or individuals that need to be contacted, what tasks need to be performed by you or others on the team, and specific plans for making the employee feel welcome and a part of the team.

2. Assemble an Orientation Welcome Kit for new employees. Gather appropriate information from human resources, telecommunications, IT, and other areas to provide to the employee. Include an overall training schedule and expectation checklists for 30, 60, and 90 days of employment.

3. Work with your call center manager and other supervisors in your call center to define the competencies needed to be successful as a supervisor in your call center. What are the knowledge and skills needed? Perform a self assessment and identify the areas where you are fully competent and where you have gaps. Map out a plan for self-study or group study to address your knowledge and skill gaps.

4. Outline all the components of your current frontline training program.Identify which content might be appropriate as an e-learning solution,which is best delivered as traditional, classroom training, and which could be either way. For the classroom training components, identify how the needs of visual, auditory, and kinesthetic learners are met or not met by the current classroom program.

Chapter 5 – Building and Managing Teams

Most call center organizations are built around a team concept. Some call centers have teams that are nothing more than a group of individuals that happen to report to the same person, or perhaps do the same kind of work, but there is no real interaction and work as a team. Other call centers have empowered teams that work together as a cohesive group and take responsibility for the productivity and success of the unit.

There has been much research to show that self-directed work teams foster continuous improvement and result in better quality, productivity, and customer service. People who work on functional teams are happier with their jobs than people who don't belong to a team. Team members feel better about their work because they are involved more in their jobs and see a link between their own accomplishments and those of the team and the organization.

As a supervisor, there is much you can do to make your team a success. Clearly defining the roles and responsibilities of the team will help ensure your team members know what is expected now and into the future. A team framework, with ever-increasing responsibilities, can provide career definition and help map out a training and development for the team as a whole as well as individuals.

This chapter outlines some of the basics of building and managing a successful team, including how to define roles and responsibilities, as well as how to develop the team over the long-term.

33. What are the benefits of teams in the call center?
34. What roles should your team perform?
35. What skills will your team members need?
36. How should your team grow and mature?

33. What are the benefits of teams in the call center?

Teams in the workplace are nothing new. Anthropologists believe that a major advancement in evolution occurred when early cavemen formed teams to hunt and farm more successfully. Early on, our ancestors learned they could accomplish more together than they could individually. Not only were teams more efficient, but more enjoyable too.

Teams throughout the years have allowed people to take on different roles, depending on their interests and skills. They have enabled human beings to help each other out, both personally and professionally. The pooled ideas of a group have proven to be superior to the ideas of an individual.

> Teams allow people to take on different roles depending upon interest and skills.

The growth of teams has been particularly evident in the past twenty years in the workplace. There has been much research to show that self-directed work teams foster continuous improvement and great strides in quality, productivity, and customer service. People who work on functional teams are happier with their jobs than people who don't belong to a team. Team members feel better about their work because they are involved more in their jobs and see a link between their own accomplishments and those of the team and the organization.

There can be two definitions of a team in the call center. A team can simply be a group of people that handle the same type of call or report to the same supervisor. A true team environment, however, will take the definition past just job function or supervisory structure. In an integrated team environment, team members will share job responsibilities and work toward a team vision and goals. Depending upon how self-directed the team is, the members may be responsible for anything from scheduling and assigning their own work to monitoring their performance as individuals and a team unit. Truly self-contained teams may even be responsible for peer performance reviews and coaching, as well as reward and discipline issues.

> Self-directed work teams foster continuous improvement in the workplace, resulting in better quality and productivity.

Cohesive teams have a great track record. There are many examples of improvements resulting from team implementations. According to the book *Succeeding with Teams*, teams at DDI's customer service center were able to handle 86% more work with only a 12% increase in labor through team innovations. At the Kodak Customer Assistance Center, the number of calls handled per hour doubled, as did first-call resolution rates, when a team structure was implemented.

34. What roles should your team perform?

As you develop your team, it will be useful to "charter" your team. A team charter will define the team's purpose and objectives. The more precisely you can define the purpose and objectives of the team, the faster your team members will understand where they're headed and how their roles fit into the bigger, overall plan for the call center.

Develop a team charter to define your team's purpose and objectives.

The team charter should answer three important questions:

- How much leadership will team members assume?
- What outside groups will the team need to coordinate?
- How will the team measure its effectiveness?

A key element in preliminary set-up and ongoing team development is identifying the roles that team members and the leader will play. As a supervisor you should define what responsibilities you will assume and which ones will be delegated to your team. Some of these roles and responsibilities can shift from you to the team as the team matures and develops.

A matrix of team roles and responsibilities should be shared with everyone on the team so all members know what the mission and goals of the team are, as well as who is doing what now and into the future. You may want to define responsibilities for the current time, six months from now, twelve months from now, and so on. It should show not just current responsibilities, but what the team is preparing to do for the future. A sample team responsibilities matrix is shown below.

The supervisor should define what responsibilities will be assumed by the team now and into the future.

Responsibility	Supervisor/ Team Mgr	Team Now	Team 6 Months	Team 12 Months
Customer liaison	X		X	
Administer timesheets		X		
Vacation scheduling	X			
Order supplies		X		
Lead team meetings		X		
Organize team training	X			
Monitor and score calls	X		X	
Monitor productivity	X	X		
Maintain team bulletin board/journal		X		
Interview new job candidates	X			X

A team responsibilities matrix serves as a roadmap to see where your team has been, where it is now, and where it is going. In addition to the matrix shown above, you will need to develop a matrix by individual that shows each team member's responsibilities. Clarifying roles helps your team members avoid misunderstandings and identify new opportunities for development. It shows who is currently fully occupied and who may have room for additional responsibilities. It can also help you identify training and development opportunities as your team members assume more and more responsibilities. Finally, it can also help people outside the team determine the best contact points for their needs.

A team responsibilities matrix can help you identify training and development opportunities as team members assume more responsibilities.

It is common for a team to get "off track" and to be going in too many directions at once. When that happens, it's difficult for the team to focus on its primary goals and objectives, which can frustrate both you and your team members. If your team members get off track, it's your role as their leader to work with them to reexamine their focus areas.

To help the team stay focused, you may need to help team members prioritize. Have each member make a list of responsibilities and work together as a team to prioritize their efforts. You may still keep all the tasks on the list, but items may need to move up or down the list so the team can readjust its focus to its top priority – meeting customer needs and expectations.

You will also want to ensure that team members are pacing themselves appropriately. In an effort to foster development, you may have shifted responsibilities to team members too soon in the learning and development cycle. Assess the tasks of each role and make sure team members have the appropriate skills and knowledge or they may be trying to do too much too soon.

To help the team stay focused, help team members prioritize their multiple tasks so the team can stay focused on its primary objective - serving the customer.

Always keep a focus on the team process and how the team can do the work better and more efficiently. This may involve rethinking processes and procedures. Be flexible and learn to adapt to inevitable surprises and conflict that are part of every team effort.

35. What skills will your team members need?

In addition to the skills and knowledge needed to perform their roles as service providers on the telephone, your team members may need to acquire some additional skills to support them in their roles as participative team members. Teamwork means sharing responsibility for the success of the team as a whole, and there are essential skills required to make this happen.

There are essential skills needed to help your employees be participative team members.

These skills involve learning to work with others to solve problems and improve team effectiveness. According to the book by Richard Wellins, *Succeeding with Teams,* some of these skills include:

Participating in or leading meetings

Everyone needs to understand his role as a team participant and meeting participant to maximize individual contribution, avoid conflict, and help the group stay on track. As a supervisor, you will want to relinquish control of a team meeting to your team members at least part, if not all, of the time. Team members should know how to plan and prepare for a meeting, how to conduct a meeting that focuses the group's efforts, and how to follow up to ensure that decisions will be followed through. The meeting leader will also need to know how to handle conflicts during a meeting and facilitate for effective sharing of ideas.

Interacting and influencing others

You will want to equip your employees with the tools they need to work better with others whose work styles may be very different from their own. As working relationships improve, job satisfaction for everyone on the job will increase. Some team members could benefit by increasing their communications skills so they have confidence in making suggestions and interacting with all other members of the team.

Supporting team members

As the team grows and develops, there will be opportunities for team members to coach, guide, and influence one another. They should be equipped with knowledge on the quality monitoring process and how to deliver both positive and negative feedback, in the same way you might do as the supervisor.

Handling conflict

As multiple people from diverse backgrounds with different personalities work together, there is bound to be conflict. The better your employees are equipped to work out these issues on their own, the less you will need to be involved. Find ways for them to develop their listening, negotiation, problem-solving, and cooperation skills.

36. How should your team grow and mature?

It's tempting to hope for an overnight solution and to have your team fully functional right away. However, you need to be careful about growing your team too fast, as the best way to develop the team is to let it grow over time. Planning appropriate tasks and incorporating new levels of decision-making one step at a time will ensure the success of the team and prevent the kind of frustration that occurs when people expect too much too soon.

Incorporating new responsibilities one step at a time will ensure the success of the team over time.

Team members will be able to handle different responsibilities at various stages of their development. For example, you might expect team members to handle simple administrative tasks like timekeeping early on, but they may not be ready to take on more complex responsibilities like performance monitoring and review until much later in their development. Be realistic in your expectations and match the tasks and levels of decision making when the team and individual team members are fully ready to handle them.

It's important to know when to "stretch" the team and provide them with new challenges and opportunities. However, you don't want to stretch them to the point of breaking. While some failures are inevitable and help the team learn and grow, too many failures will damage individual and team morale.

There are also occasions where your team will hit a "plateau" where their improvement and development is stalled. Recognize that early efforts on team activities may yield significant results, and it's natural to assume that these productivity increases will continue. It is natural to reach a steady level of performance, and the team should not be discouraged when improvements fail to skyrocket. When this happens, it is simply time to celebrate the successes that have been achieved, and perhaps look for new and different ways to do things, or define new areas to be attacked.

Celebrate successes and then be ready to take on the next workplace challenge.

Top-performing teams constantly challenge everything. The work environment in today's call center is changing constantly, and teams that don't change to adapt to the new environment will fail. It is important to celebrate team successes, but also to be ready to move ahead with the next new challenge. As a supervisor, you should help the team identify those new challenges, and provide feedback and advice about their steps to improvement.

Learning Activities

1. Working with members of your team, develop a team charter if you don't already have one. Make sure this team charter aligns with corporate and call center goals. Outline the objectives of the team and your vision for the short-term and long-term.

2. Make a list of all of your tasks and responsibilities and those of your team members outside of answering calls. In creating this list, note the amountof time spent per week or month on each task and the priority of the task. Are there tasks that could be assigned to various team members to foster their growth and development? Are there activities that would be better performed by the team instead of you to encourage ownership and empowerment of the team?

3. Note the skills and knowledge needed to perform each of the tasks listed in Item #2 above. Do an inventory of current skills and knowledge of your various team members to identify knowledge gaps that would prevent your staff from taking on more of these responsibilities. Develop a training anddevelopment plan that would enable team members to take over more responsibilities in the next six months.

4. Meet with your manager and other supervisors and perhaps individuals outside the call center to discuss the coming year's strategic plan for your company. Identify any specific challenges that the call center is likely to face and communicate those with your team. Working with your team, design at least one new process that will help your team help the call center meet the challenge.

Chapter 6 – Key Performance Indicators

There are many different performance measurements that are used to gauge the efficiency and effectiveness of the call center operation. Some of these measures are for overall call center performance, while others focus on the individual employee. The main purpose of these performance measures is to ensure the call center is meeting its goals and objectives and that all personnel are living up to their work potential.

The performance measurement process begins with defining performance goals and expectations. These performance objectives for the call center and the employees working in the call center should link to enterprise goals and objectives.

For the call center, there are external measures of performance and internal measures of performance. The key internal indicators of performance that you probably use in your call center are typically categorized into service, quality, efficiency, and profitability measures. These same categories can be used to define team and individual measures of performance.

This chapter provides an overview of the performance definition and measurement process, including a look at external (customer) measures of performance as well as internal measures. These measures will ascertain how efficiently the call center is using its resources and meeting enterprise and departmental goals, as well as how individuals and teams are performing.

37. How do you begin to define performance objectives?
38. How do you measure success from the customer's point of view?
39. How do you measure success from an agent's point of view?
40. What are the most important measures of service?
41. What are the most important measures of quality?
42. What are the most important measures of efficiency?
43. What are the most important measures of profitability?
44. What are the most critical performance measures for agents?

37. How do you begin to define performance objectives?

It is critical for every call center operation to have a performance measurement and management strategy in place. The old adage "if you can't measure it, you can't manage it" is certainly true when it comes to the call center. A significant amount of information is needed to gauge how the call center, as well as every individual, is performing from an internal operational and external customer perspective.

An effective system of performance measures allows you to do the following:

- Review the call center as a whole.
- Review performance of each employee.
- Analyze performance trends.
- Investigate root cause of problems.
- Optimize use of call center resources.
- Support the call center and company's strategic plan and objectives.

When setting call center, team, and individual performance goals, it is important to link them to the organization's mission, vision, and goals.

When setting call center, team, and individual performance goals, it is important to link them to the organization's mission, vision, and goals. A company's mission statement describes the purpose of the organization. It defines why the firm exists, and therefore how it operates and makes decisions. The vision statement for an organization is a bit different in that it describes where the organization wants to be at some point in the future. This vision drives the strategy of the organization as a whole, and certainly should define the strategy and performance goals of the call center, as well as the performance goals and standards for each individual within the organization.

Sample strategic objectives for an organization might include some of the following:

- Increase customer satisfaction and retention.
- Increase productivity and efficiency.
- Introduce new products or services.
- Increase profitability.
- Gain market share.
- Expand into new markets.

The performance goals of the call center should be defined based on corporate goals and strategies.

In order to meet one or more of these corporate objectives, the goals must be communicated throughout the company, and then supporting goals must be developed in the call center. The performance measures for the center, for teams, and for individuals can then be defined.

The management team in the call center should fully understand the corporate mission and goals, and strive to create call center objectives to support the business purpose. Some examples of linking call center goals to corporate goals are illustrated in the table below.

Enterprise Goal	Call Center Goal
Maintain position as low-cost provider of services in the product sector.	Maximize technologies and offerings for self-service options to minimize cost of support.
Provide unique and valuable products and services that meet the unique needs of each customer.	Identify unique product requirements through customer interactions, and record them for use in product development and customization efforts.
Provide superior service that maximizes customer delight.	Implement customer contact strategy that maximizes accessibility and quality of customer interactions.

If the organization's goal is to provide superior service to maximize customer satisfaction and retention, then the call center's goal might be to maximize customer accessibility and quality. If these are the primary goals of the call center, then the top performance measures of the center should be ones that determine if these accessibility and quality goals are indeed being met.

To support the call center's goal to expand accessibility and increase customer satisfaction and retention, each team will need to identify specific steps they can take. Goals may be set for "one and done" completion by access channel, or each team may set goals related to "customer saves," customer satisfaction ratings, or quality scores. Likewise, performance metrics would be defined to gauge how well each team supports the mission and goals.

Finally, to determine how each individual's performance supports the corporate goal of improving customer satisfaction and retention, an approach similar to the one used with setting team goals should be used. Again, each agent will either directly or indirectly support the goal of increasing customer satisfaction, and this goal may be measured in a number of different ways. As standards are set for each agent, these individual and team goals will drive the performance expectations and performance measurements.

Another way to think about defining performance measures is to think about what is required to keep the various call center stakeholder groups happy. There can be many different call center stakeholders, but the primary three are customers, senior management, and frontline employees. You might think about developing performance measures that gauge how well your team is keeping these three groups satisfied.

The call center's performance goals and measures should be balanced among each of the three major stakeholders – the customers, the agents, and senior management. The basic concerns of these groups will be used later in this chapter as a structure for defining the key performance indicators (KPIs) in the call center.

38. How do you measure success from the customer's point of view?

The key to success for your team and your center involves listening to customers to learn how effectively you are meeting their needs. There are many different ways you can listen and get customer feedback. The three primary ways include:

- Customer surveys
- Customer praise and complaints
- Observation of customer interactions

> It is important for the call center to perform its own regular surveys to understand the perceptions of customers related specifically to call center transactions.

Customer Surveys

First, it is important for your call center to perform its own surveys in order to understand the perceptions of customers related specifically to call center transactions. Your company may perform regular customer satisfaction surveys, but these surveys probably focus on products, pricing, and a variety of other concerns with the call center experience sometimes buried in the overall questions and scope of the survey. To truly evaluate how effectively the call center is serving customers and representing the organization, it is crucial to do customer surveys solely focused on the call center experience.

As a supervisor, you may get involved from time to time in planning a survey or developing the survey questions. Your team may even be involved in actually administering the survey if you're doing a telephone or email survey.

If you're interested in learning more about developing and administering customer surveys, we recommend two books: *Customer Surveying* by Dr. Fred Van Bennekom and *The Survey Research Handbook* by Pamela Alreck and Robert Settle.

Customer Praise and Complaints

The second way to get customer feedback is to encourage open feedback from your customers and then pay careful attention to what they say. Complaint letters should be viewed not as a negative, but as an opportunity to build the customer relationship.

According to the book, *A Complaint is a Gift,* by Janelle Barlow, when customers feel dissatisfied with a product or service, they have two options – they can say something or just go away. If they go away, they give you no opportunity to fix their dissatisfaction. On the other hand, complaining customers are still talking to you, giving you a chance to fix the problem and salvage the relationship so they might buy from you again. So as much as you may not like to receive negative feedback or criticism, customers who complain can actually be viewed as giving you a gift.

Any complaint should be viewed as a way to grow the business. Complaints are one of the most valuable, yet most underutilized forms of market research information. They provide an opportunity for your company to satisfy a customer just by solving a problem or fixing an error. In both of these ways, the complaint is a gift to the company. You'll benefit by opening it and handling it carefully, just like you would a treasured gift package.

View a complaint as a way to grow the business through providing valuable market research information.

This view of a complaint as a gift starts from the top. Your outlook as a supervisor will be mirrored by your staff. Instead of dreading these types of interactions, adjust your own attitude – and eventually your employees' attitudes – not to dread these types of interactions, but to welcome them with open arms and ears.

Of course, not all customer comments are negative. It's just as important to note and celebrate the instances where a customer is delighted. Recognize why the customer was happy with the interaction so you can continue those practices over and over again. Communicate these successes throughout the call center so the good performers get the recognition they deserve and others can learn from the positive experiences, too.

Communicate and celebrate letters of customer praise so those good practices will spread.

Observation of Customer Interactions

Sometimes customers don't take the time to participate in a survey or send us a letter of praise or complaint. To keep our finger on the pulse of customer interactions every single day, it's critical to monitor and observe calls on a random basis. What's important here is to look for things that define a quality transaction in the eyes of the customer and not just by your own internal definitions of good service.

That's why surveys are so important – they tell us not only how customers feel about certain aspects of the interaction, but also what things are most important to them. Use this information as you observe calls to ensure what the customer cares about most is reflected in your monitoring and review process. We'll talk more about this monitoring process in upcoming chapters.

As you monitor calls, make sure you're observing the things that are most important to your customers.

39. How do you measure success from an agent's point of view?

Frontline employees are the key to customer satisfaction, so survey them regularly to make sure they're happy with the job and work environment.

Your business can't be successful if your employees are chronically unhappy. Just as it's important to measure how well your call center is doing in the eyes of your customers, it is likewise important to gauge each employee's level of satisfaction with the job and work environment.

Completion of a regular employee satisfaction survey can provide valuable insight into the current perceptions of your staff. Surveying should be a regular process that allows and encourages each employee to assess you as a supervisor, the management team, work environment, training, job resources, career opportunities, and so on. If there is dissatisfaction with some recent change or process, it is important to find that out as quickly as possible, since dissatisfaction plays a role in how the agents perform.

While the most effective way to gauge satisfaction of your staff is simply to talk to them regularly, you may also want to employ some more formal survey processes. Surveys are typically done in writing, with employees providing feedback on an anonymous basis. This "blind" survey ensures an honest feedback opportunity, without fear that the employee will be identified as the one who gave negative input. There are usually ten to fifteen questions, with a scale of choices and a few free-form comment areas too.

While the most effective way to gauge satisfaction of your staff is simply to talk to them regularly, you may also want to use a formal employee satisfaction survey.

A sample Employee Satisfaction Survey is provided on the following page. This survey assesses the satisfaction of the employee, and asks the worker to grade the effectiveness of the call center in serving its customers. The latter part of the survey provides an interesting comparison to a typical customer satisfaction survey that might ask many of the same questions.

This type of survey for employee satisfaction should be done on a regular basis with trend analysis to ensure that the performance and satisfaction is moving in the right direction. If your scores are below expectations, doing a survey every quarter may be needed, while you might survey less frequently if the work environment is stable and scores indicate overall satisfaction.

It's important to share the results with your employees so that they know that their input is being heard. Specific suggestions by employees should be addressed, and management's response shared with all employees. Just like with call monitoring, asking for the information and then doing nothing with it is worse than never checking it in the first place.

Sample Employee Satisfaction Survey

Your feedback is important to us. Please rate your satisfaction on the following items on a scale of 1 to 5, with 5 for very satisfied, 3 for neither satisfied nor unsatisfied, and 1 for very unsatisfied.

Scale Definition: 1—Very Unsatisfied, 2—Unsatisfied, 3—Neutral, 4—Satisfied, 5—Very Satisfied

1. Tools available to do job ○ ○ ○ ○ ○
2. Reference materials available ○ ○ ○ ○ ○
3. Training provided by company ○ ○ ○ ○ ○
4. Industry certification requirements for the job ○ ○ ○ ○ ○
5. Escalation process within group ○ ○ ○ ○ ○
6. Escalation process to other groups ○ ○ ○ ○ ○
7. Schedule you are assigned to work ○ ○ ○ ○ ○
8. Process/procedure documentation ○ ○ ○ ○ ○
9. Fairness of treatment by management ○ ○ ○ ○ ○
10. Career development opportunities ○ ○ ○ ○ ○
11. Coaching by management personnel ○ ○ ○ ○ ○
12. Peer support/coaching ○ ○ ○ ○ ○
13. Team spirit within group staff ○ ○ ○ ○ ○
14. Fairness of workload distribution in group ○ ○ ○ ○ ○
15. Willingness of management to assist with questions ○ ○ ○ ○ ○
16. Overall job satisfaction ○ ○ ○ ○ ○
17. Likelihood of staying with company > 1 more year ○ ○ ○ ○ ○

What could be done to improve your satisfaction with your job?____________________________

____

____

Below, please grade your view of the overall performance of the call center.

Scale Definition: 1—Very Unsatisfied, 2—Unsatisfied, 3—Neutral, 4—Satisfied, 5—Very Satisfied

1. Speed of resolution of problems ○ ○ ○ ○ ○
2. Quality of resolution of problems ○ ○ ○ ○ ○
3. Technical skills ○ ○ ○ ○ ○
4. Helpfulness to customers ○ ○ ○ ○ ○
5. Consistency of service provided ○ ○ ○ ○ ○
6. Handoff of problems to/from other groups ○ ○ ○ ○ ○
7. Overall performance ○ ○ ○ ○ ○

What could be done to improve service to our customers? ____________________________

____

____

40. What are the most important measures of service?

There are many different measures associated with service delivery in the call center. Some are associated with overall accessibility, while others are related to the speed of the service provided. Most of the service measures are those that gauge how the overall call center is performing. However, some of the measures can also be indirect measures of team or individual performance.

Service Measures	Call Center	Team	Agent
Accessibility			
Blockage	X		
Hours of operation	X		
Abandons	X		
Self-service availability	X		
Speed of Answer			
Service level	X	x	x
ASA	X	x	x
Longest delay in queue	X	x	x

X = primary measures; x = secondary measures

Blockage

Blockage is an accessibility measure that indicates what percentage of callers will not be able to access your call center at a given time due to an insufficient number of telephone lines. Your center may have plenty of telephone lines into the call center so that blockage is not a concern. However, in some cases, the number of facilities is adjusted to achieve a consistent level of access or blockage, such as no more than two percent of callers reaching a busy signal and being forced to retry the call.

Call Center. Measures indicating percentage of blockage by time of day or occurrences of "all trunks busy" are utilized by most centers. Failure to include a blockage goal allows a center to always meet its speed of answer goal by simply blocking the excess calls. This can have a negative effect on customer accessibility and satisfaction while the call center looks like it is doing a great job.

Team and Agent. The individuals in the call center can have an impact on trunk blockage. If understaffing exists due to lack of schedule adherence, then delays in queue will increase, driving up the workload on the incoming trunks, and perhaps causing a higher incidence of blockage experienced by callers. However, blockage is typically not a measure of individual performance.

Hours of Access

Call centers evaluate the hours of current operations to determine if these hours should be extended or shortened. A common measure is the number of calls that arrive outside the normal operating hours of the center.

Call Center. Call volumes and percentage of calls arriving outside normal operating hours are measured to evaluate completeness of coverage.

Team and Agent. Accessibility is typically not a measure of individual performance.

Call Abandons

Call centers measure the number of abandons as well as the percentage of calls that abandon, called the abandon rate. This abandon rate can translate into lost customers, so it's important you track it to identify patterns of abandon behaviors.

Call Center. Abandon rate is a typical measure of call center performance. It should be noted, however, that abandon rate is not entirely under the call center's control. While abandons are affected by the average wait time in queue (which can be controlled by the call center), there are a multitude of other factors that influence this number, such as caller tolerance, time of day, and availability of service alternatives.

Abandon rate is often measured, but is something not directly under the call center's control. It can be affected by what the center does, but is ultimately up to the customer to control.

Team and Agent. Abandon rate is not a measure of individual performance.

Self-Service Availability

Many contacts today are being offloaded from call center agents to self-service alternatives such as IVR and Web interactions. It is important to measure the percentage of customers that utilize these self-service alternatives, as this contributes directly to both service perception and the bottom line.

Call Center. Self-service utilization is an important gauge of accessibility for the call center, and is typically measured as an overall number, by self-service methodology, and by time of day or by demographic group.

Team and Agent. Self-service utilization is not a measure of individual performance. For those companies that wish to increase self-service usage, agents may be encouraged to tell customers about these services and encourage their use. In these instances, a performance objective may be the percentage of calls during which agents tell the customer about these alternatives, or even show how to use them.

One of the top key performance indicators in a call center is the speed of service at which calls are answered. There are several ways to define speed of service in the call center: service level, average speed of answer (ASA), and longest delay in queue.

Service Level

Service level is the most common speed of answer measure in the call center. It denotes the percentage of calls that are answered in a defined wait threshold. It is most commonly stated as x percent of calls handled in y seconds or less. Service level is generally measured by half-hour, and can be reported as a cumulative simple average over the day, a weighted average over the day based on the actual calls per half-hour, or can be gauged by the percentage of half-hours of the day in which the half-hour service goal is met.

Call Center. Service level is one of the most common measures of performance for the overall call center, and is measured by half-hour and typically reported by day.

Team and Agent. Service level is an overall call center measure and not an individual one. However, service level is directly impacted by staff being in their seats available when scheduled, so schedule adherence is the measure of individual performance that is typically in place to ensure that the call center's speed of answer goal is met..

Service level and ASA are overall call center or group measures of performance. Schedule adherence measures agent contribution to ensuring the speed of answer goal is met.

Average Speed of Answer

Average speed of answer, or ASA, is the average delay of all calls for the period averaged together. For example, if half the calls go into queue and wait there for an average of sixty seconds, and the other calls go immediately to an agent, the ASA is thirty seconds.

Call Center. ASA is a common key performance indicator and is used by many call centers instead of, or in addition to, service level.

Team and Agent. ASA is an overall call center measure, not an individual one. However, ASA is directly impacted by staff being in their seats and available to take calls when scheduled, so schedule adherence is the measure of individual performance that is typically in place to ensure that the call center's ASA goal is met.

Longest Delay in Queue

A real-time measure of performance that is used by many call centers is the age of the call that has been in queue the longest, or the longest delay in queue (LDQ). This is both a historical gauge of performance and a real-time measure.

Call Center. Many call centers use real-time LDQ as a measure to indicate when immediate staffing reactions may be required. Historical LDQ indicates the "worst case" experience of a customer over a period of time such as a day.

Team and Agent. The delay situation is a call center measure, not an individual gauge of performance. But like the other speed of service measures, this statistic is affected by schedule adherence.

41. What are the most important measures of quality?

There are many different measures associated with quality in the call center. Some are associated with resolution of the contact, while others are related to the actual process of the call.

Quality Measures	Call Center	Team	Agent
Resolution			
First call resolution rate	X	X	X
Transfer rate	X	X	X
Process			
Telephone etiquette	x	X	X
Competency/knowledge	x	X	X
Error/rework rate	x	X	X
Process adherence	x	X	X

X = primary measures; x = secondary measures

There are two main measures associated with the resolution of the call. One is associated with the call being completed to satisfaction within one contact, and the other is related to transfer rate.

First Call Resolution Rate

The percentage of calls completed within a single contact, often called the "one and done" or first call resolution rate, is a crucial measure of quality within the call center. It gauges the ability of the center, as well as of an individual, to accomplish the call in a single contact without requiring a transfer to another person or area, or without needing another call at a future time to resolve the customer problem or question.

First call resolution rate indicates the ability to complete a call in a single contact and is highly correlated with customer satisfaction.

Call Center. The one-call completion rate is tracked and measured by many call centers since it is a crucial factor in many customers' perception of quality. The satisfactory resolution of a call is tracked overall in the center, as well as by type of call, and perhaps by time of day or by group.

Team and Agent. The one-call resolution rate is also an individual gauge of performance, as it measures an individual's capability to handle the call to completion without requiring assistance via a transferred call or a subsequent call, meaning higher efficiency and better service.

Transfer Rate

The transfer percentage is an indication of what portion of calls has to be transferred to another person to be handled. There are many different reasons why a call is transferred, and tracking these can help fine-tune the routing strategies as well as identify performance gaps of the staff.

Call Center. Tracking transfers and measuring the percentage of transfers and the destination of the calls will indicate problems due to incorrect routing and sorting on the front-end processing of a call.

Team and Agent. Other calls are transferred due to lack of knowledge or lack of skills of the agent. These transfers should be tracked by individual in order to identify performance gaps that need to be addressed.

There are many reasons calls are transferred and tracking these can fine-tune routing strategies as well as identify individual performance gaps.

There are several measures of performance related to the actual process of handling the call or contact. All of these are important in the customer's perception of how well the contact is handled from a quality perspective. Some of these measures include telephone etiquette, knowledge and competency, error and rework rate, and adherence to established procedures on the call.

Telephone Etiquette

One of the critical factors that impacts the caller's perception of how well the call was handled is simple courtesy and telephone etiquette. The degree to which general telephone communications skills and etiquette are displayed is generally measured via observation or some form of quality monitoring.

Call Center. General telephone etiquette is typically not an overall call center measure, but rather, an individual gauge of performance.

Team and Agent. Following the call center's guidelines of telephone etiquette and overall communications, best practices are typically monitored and scored by most call centers on an agent-by-agent, call-by-call basis.

Knowledge and Competency

One of the components that lead customers to remark that a call was handled with quality is the ability of the agent to provide correct and thorough product and service information, and to be competent at handling customer questions and problems.

Call Center. The measure of knowledge and competency is closely tied to the "one and done" resolution rate mentioned above. However, observation of knowledge and skills is typically measured on an individual basis, not on an overall call center basis.

Team and Agent. Call centers typically monitor agents' calls to determine the extent to which the agents can satisfactorily handle a customer's request or problem. The level to which an agent can provide product information and solve problems is a critical measure of individual performance related to the quality of the call.

Error and Rework Rate

One measure of quality in the call center is the error rate – the degree to which errors have to be corrected or work redone due to poor quality the first time.

Call Center. Although not one of the most common measures of quality call processing, many call centers track the errors made on calls and the rework associated with those errors, since it costs the company in terms of productivity and service.

Team and Agent. In addition to tracking the error and rework rate overall, many call centers also track these elements by individual agent to identify performance issues and perhaps training and development gaps.

Error rate should be measured on a call center and individual basis since it costs the company both in terms of service and cost.

Adherence to Procedures

Adherence to procedures such as workflow processes or call scripts is another essential element of quality in the call center. This is particularly important to the perceived quality in terms of the caller receiving a consistent call-handling experience regardless of the contact channel or the individual agent involved in the contact.

Call Center. Adherence to processes and procedures is typically measured through simple observation and through the quality monitoring process. Overall adherence is observed, but is typically not a measure of overall call center performance.

Team and Agent. Adherence to processes and procedures is a crucial element of individual agent performance in the call center. Adherence to telephone procedures, call scripts, and so on is typically monitored through both general observation and a more formal quality monitoring process.

Adherence to procedures and scripts contribute to a consistent call-handling experience for the caller.

42. What are the most important measures of efficiency?

There are many different metrics used to measure efficiency in the call center. Some are associated with resource efficiency, while others are related to contact handling activity.

Efficiency Measures	Call Center	Team	Agent
Resource Utilization			
Agent occupancy	X		
Shrinkage	X	x	x
Schedule efficiency	X		
Schedule adherence	X	X	X
Availability	X	X	X
Contact Handling			
Average handle time	X	X	X
After call work	X	X	X
On-hold time	X	X	X

X = primary measures; x = secondary measures

Agent Occupancy

Agent occupancy is the measure of actual time busy on a call or doing after-call work compared to available time. It is the percentage of logged-in and available time that an agent is actually busy on a call. It is calculated by dividing workload hours by staff hours.

Agent occupancy is the primary measure of how efficiently personnel resources are being utilized. It is a call center, not an individual, measure of performance.

Call Center. Agent occupancy is an important measure of how well the call center has scheduled its staff. If occupancy is too low, agents are sitting around idle with not enough to do. If occupancy is too high, the staff is overworked. Occupancy should be tracked to evaluate how well the call center is using its resources.

Team and Agent. Agent occupancy is an overall call center measure, not an individual gauge of performance. Agents have no control over occupancy, since it is a function of how many calls arrive and how many people are in place to handle the work.

Staff Shrinkage

Staff shrinkage is defined as the percentage of paid time that agents are not available to the call center to handle calls. It is classified as nonproductive time, and is made up of meeting and training time, breaks, paid time off, off-phone work, and general unexplained time off the phones.

Call Center. Staff shrinkage is an important number to track, since it plays an important role in how many people will need to be scheduled each half-hour. Most of the shrinkage categories are "fixed," such as paid vacation time and breaks, as well as training and meeting time. Others are more controllable, and should be tracked closely to ensure productivity is maximized.

Team and Agent. Shrinkage is an overall gauge of productivity, not one used as an individual measure of performance. Time available to be on the phones is a component of shrinkage, and as such, availability and adherence to schedule are the associated individual performance measures associated with shrinkage.

Shrinkage is an important to track since it plays an important role in how many people will need to be scheduled each half-hour.

Schedule Efficiency

Workforce management is all about getting the "just right" number of people in place each period of the day to handle customer contacts – not too many and not too few. Schedule efficiency measures the degree of overstaffing and understaffing that exist as a result of scheduling design. It is also referred to as the net staffing measure – in other words, how many staff "over" or "under" for each half-hour of the day.

Call Center. Call centers gauge schedule efficiency in a number of ways. Net staffing may be measured by half-hour as an indication of how well the resources in the center are being utilized.

Team and Agent. Schedule efficiency is not an individual agent performance measure.

Schedule Adherence

Schedule adherence measures the degree to which the specific hours scheduled are actually worked by the agents. There are two forms of adherence – total hours worked and specific hours worked. The first looks at the total hours scheduled for the day and simply compares that number to the total hours worked. True schedule adherence matches the exact hours scheduled versus the exact hours available.

Schedule adherence is one of the most important measures of team and individual performance in the call center, as it affects so many other call center performance measures.

Call Center. Schedule adherence is an overall call center measure, both in terms of hours worked as well as specific schedules worked.

Team and Agent. Schedule adherence is one of the most important measures of team and individual performance in the call center, as it affects so many other measures. Each agent should be evaluated on total hours worked versus scheduled, as well as adherence to the defined work schedule of start and stop times and scheduled breaks and other activities.

Availability

Availability is the percent of time that staff are logged in and available to take calls. It is typically viewed as an overall availability, and may or may not be linked to schedule adherence. Availability can be affected by the amount of time that is needed off the phones to do research, projects, and other activities.

Call Center. The call center may measure total hours of availability and may break down availability by team or by individual agent. Another measure of availability is the percentage of time the overall staff were available in contrast to their paid time.

Team and Agent. Availability is another important gauge of team and individual performance. It can be measured as hours of time available or by a percentage of time available. However, if the agents are adhering to the schedule they are given, and if available time is low, the problem can only be solved at the team and call center level by changing the scheduled activities.

Several performance metrics exist that provide an indication of how efficiently the actual customer contact is being handled. These measures include average handle time, after-call work time, on-hold time, and transfer rate.

Average handle time (AHT) is a combination of talk time with the caller plus any after-call work.

Average Handle Time

The most common measure of contact handling is the average handle time (AHT). AHT is made up of talk time plus after-call work (ACW), and is a factor used in determining overall workload and staffing requirements.

Call Center. Average handle time is one of the most common performance indicators in the call center. To accommodate differences in calling patterns, it should be measured and identified by time of day as well as by day of week.

Team and Agent. Average handle time is also a measure associated with team and individual agent performance. While handle times will vary based on call content, the agent should typically deliver a consistent handle time within acceptable boundaries. However, a word of caution is appropriate. Putting too much pressure on shortening AHT can have undesirable effects on quality and sales results.

Measure AHT, but be careful about putting too much emphasis on this measure or quality of the call may suffer to meet efficiency goals.

After-Call Work Time

One of the components of AHT that is considered to be the most variable and the most controllable is the after-call work (ACW) portion of the contact. This is the time spent after the conversation is over, when the agent fills out associated paperwork, updates files, and so on. ACW is work that needs to be done in conjunction with the call before the agent is ready to handle the next contact.

Call Center. ACW should be measured and evaluated over time to determine what the appropriate amount of time should be to accomplish the needed tasks. This overall call center ACW number will then typically serve as the benchmark against which to measure an individual agent's ACW time.

Team and Agent. ACW is a component of agent performance that is typically measured with each agent compared to the average ACW time of the team or the center as a whole. It is important to ensure that the comparison is made for similar call types as the requirements can vary significantly among different kinds of call-handling situations.

When comparing individual ACW time, ensure you're comparing the same types of calls as the requirements may vary significantly by call type.

On-Hold Time

On-hold time is the amount of time a caller is placed on hold during the course of the conversation. Obviously, the goal is to minimize the number of occurrences of placing the caller on hold, as well as to minimize the length of the actual on-hold time.

Call Center. Most call centers measure on-hold time, but it is not necessarily one of the top performance indicators. It is more typically used as a gauge for individual agents. However, an overall high percentage of hold time may be an indicator that system performance is slow or that access to multiple systems is delaying the agents in processing the callers' requests.

Team and Agent. On-hold time is a measure of agent performance, as it can serve as an indicator of insufficient product knowledge or other learning or performance gaps. You'll want to review the percentage of calls an agent has to put on hold, as well as the length of the hold time.

Transfer Rate

The transfer percentage is an indication of what portion of calls has to be transferred to another person to be handled. There are many different reasons why a call is transferred, and tracking these can help fine-tune the routing strategies as well as identify performance gaps of the staff. Customers generally regard transfers negatively, so minimizing the requirement to transfer will increase not only efficiency but customer satisfaction as well.

Call Center. Tracking transfers and measuring the percentage of transfers and the destination of the calls will indicate problems due to incorrect routing and sorting on the front end of a call.

Team and Agent. Other calls are transferred due to lack of knowledge or lack of skills of the agent. These transfers should be tracked by individual in order to identify performance gaps that need to be addressed.

43. What are the most important measures of profitability?

There are many different financial measures in the call center operation. Some are associated with resource efficiency, while others are related to contact handling activity.

Profitability Measures	Call Center	Team	Agent
Sales or Revenue			
Conversion Rate	X	X	X
Up-Sell/Cross-Sell Rate	X	X	X
Gross Sales / Sales per Hour	X	X	X
Use of Financial Resources			
Cost per Call	X		
Return on Investment	X		

Several gauges of performance exist that are related to the revenues generated by the call center as well as by individual staff. Some of these performance measures include conversion rate, up-sell/cross-sell rate, gross sales, and sales per sign-on hour.

Conversion Rate

The conversion rate refers to the percentage of calls in which a sales opportunity is translated into an actual sale. It can be measured as an absolute number of sales or as a percentage of calls that result in a sale.

Call Center. Conversion rate is tracked and measured by most call centers as an overall number as well as by type of call or by group.

Conversion rate is a common measure of individual performance, especially if compensation is tied to sales performance.

Team and Agent. Conversion rate is also used as an individual measure of performance as an indication of an individual's ability to effectively sell the company's products and services. This is typically one of the key performance indicators for an individual agent in a revenue-generating call center, particularly if there is compensation tied to sales performance.

Up-Sell/Cross-Sell Rate

The up-sell rate or cross-sell rate is measured by many call centers as a success rate at generating revenue over and above the original order or intention of the call. It is becoming an increasingly common practice, not just for pure revenue-generating call centers but for customer service centers as well.

Call Center. The overall up-sell/cross-sell rate is measured by many call centers as a gauge of effectiveness at generating additional revenues for the company.

Team and Agent. The up-sell/cross-sell rate is also measured by individual agent to determine an individual's willingness and ability to make the sale.

Gross Sales / Sales per Hour

Overall sales are also measured and tracked, both by overall call center as well as by team and individual. These numbers may be tracked as sales per hour or more-defined sales per sign-on hour, or by time of day or day of week.

Call Center. Sales are typically closely tracked, and may be measured by overall call center, by type of call, or by group. Sales may also be tracked and measured by campaign to gauge the effectiveness of various marketing campaigns and strategies.

Team and Agent. Sales and sales per hour are common measures of performance in a revenue-generating call center. To distinguish between full-time and part-time staff, sales per sign-on hour is a frequently used measure of performance.

Cost per Call

A common measure of call center operational efficiency is cost per call or cost per minute to handle the contact workload. This cost per call can be simply a labor cost per call, or it can be a fully loaded rate that includes wage rates in addition to telecommunications, facilities, and other services costs.

In setting cost per call, it is critical to define the components being used, and to use them consistently in evaluating how well the call center is making use of financial resources over time. While commonly used to compare one company or site to another in benchmarking, this is not a good practice as the components included may vary and the types of contacts will also often vary.

Call Center. Cost per call is one of the key performance indicators of most call center operations. Regardless of whether it is tracked as only a labor cost or as a fully-loaded cost, it is used to evaluate the efficiency of the operation in terms of the use of the company's financial resources, and it must show a positive return on investment.

Team and Agent. While occasionally applied as a team performance measure, cost per call is generally applied only to the call center as a whole. It is not used as an individual measure of performance.

Return on Investment

There are many different financial measures associated with the use of capital budget dollars and the cost justification of the acquisition of products and services. Financial measures associated with return on investment dollars include payback period and calculation of net present value. These are gauges that are associated with organizational and call center financial performance, and are not individual measures of performance.

44. What are the most critical performance measures for agents?

The measurements that apply to an individual agent have been discussed in each of the four previous topics, but we'll summarize them here. A balanced set of measures should include both quantitative metrics, as well as some measures that are qualitative in nature.

Performance Category	Performance Measures	Quantitative Measure	Qualitative Measure
Service	Schedule adherence	X	
Quality	First call resolution rate	X	X
	Transfer rate	X	X
	Telephone etiquette		X
	Competency/knowledge		X
	Error/rework rate	X	X
	Adherence to procedures		X
Efficiency	Schedule adherence	X	
	Availability	X	
	AHT	X	
	ACW	X	
	On-hold time	X	
Profitability	Conversion rate	X	
	Up-sell/Cross-sell rate	X	
	Gross sales or sales per hour	X	

The most common quantitative measures of performance are attendance and schedule adherence, availability, AHT, ACW, on-hold and transfer rates, and one-call completion rate. If your call center is a revenue-generating center, they may also be measured on conversion rate, up-sell/cross-sell rate, and overall sales or sales per hour.

Individual agents will also be evaluated on qualitative gauges. These measures do not lend themselves as easily to being defined and scored. They include general telephone etiquette and communications skills, product and service knowledge, completeness of the call handling, and adherence to defined procedures and processes.

These qualitative measures of what an agent says or how the agent interacts with the customer are typically observed and evaluated by using a quality monitoring process. Some call centers want to know if the agent said the company's name in the greeting; used the customer's name appropriately; utilized the correct tone, pitch, and volume; and closed the call appropriately. Each of these items can be observed by using a manual or automated process with a quality monitoring form. Monitoring can include side-by-side monitoring, silent monitoring, and recorded monitoring.

Learning Activities

1. Write down your company's mission statement and review it with your team. How do the performance goals of your call center support the com pany's overall mission and goals? Should some of the performance goals for individuals or teams be changed or updated to reflect changes and new strategies of your business?

2. Research your call center's customer satisfaction surveying process. How often is it done and what percentage of customers participate and respond? Determine if the full scope of services you provide is actually addressed in the survey questions. Are there additional questions that should be added or old ones that are no longer relevant?

3. Discuss with your call center management team the best ways to assess employee satisfaction. Do you regularly perform employee satisfaction surveys, and if so, how are results acted upon and communicated to staff? Using the sample form in this chapter as a starting point, gather a task force of frontline employees to create an employee satisfaction survey that addresses the major areas of concern for the staff.

4. Make a list of all the service, quality, efficiency, and productivity performance measures for your center, your team, and individuals on your team. Are all the metrics in this chapter being addressed by your current measurement plan? Are there new ones you should add? Prioritize the list of performance measures to a "top ten" list and indicate which results senior management will want to see first and which ones are of more interest to the frontline staff.

Chapter 7 – Defining and Measuring Performance

Performance management is an ongoing, two-way communication process between you and each member of your team. It is a means of preventing poor performance, recognizing stellar performance, and working together to improve existing performance. Performance management involves talking, listening, learning, and improving. It isn't about filling out a performance review form once a year – rather it's about daily interaction and shaping of your employees' performance.

By investing the time to carefully define performance expectations and provide feedback about performance on an ongoing basis, you'll be making a worthwhile investment in your employees' growth and development, and saving yourself much stress and conflict in the long run.

Performance management begins with defining performance goals and expectations. There are many quantitative performance expectations (defined in the previous chapter) such as schedule adherence percentage, average handle time, call transfer rate, sales per hour, and so on. Other expectations will be defined around qualitative goals such as portrayal of positive company image, display of active listening skills, or use of proper pacing and voice quality. Many of these need to be defined down to a behavioral level in order for employees to fully understand what is expected, and in order for you to measure their performance fairly and objectively.

Once these goals and expectations have been set, the next step is to gather information about actual performance versus desired performance to identify performance gaps and problems. There are many sources of quantitative information from which to draw, while qualitative information will likely come from observation and monitoring to ensure adherence to the proper behaviors and actions.

This chapter will discuss the overall performance management process and focus on how performance expectations are defined and how actual performance is measured at an individual level, with attention given to the various aspects of the quality monitoring process.

45. What are the overall steps of performance management?
46. Should performance standards be unique to your team?
47. How do you create detailed performance standards?
48. What are the critical components of call monitoring?
49. What should be included in a quality monitoring policy?
50. How do you design an effective quality monitoring form?
51. What are the steps of call calibration?
52. How should calls be evaluated and scored?

45. What are the overall steps of performance management?

By definition, performance management is the application of scientific behavior analysis to the workplace. It is not a one-time management solution to a single problem with one of your employees. Done correctly, performance management provides a precise way of defining the work to be done, analyzing results, and implementing solutions that will not only deal with inadequate performance, but will provide practical ways to maximize performance of every individual on your team.

Performance management is the application of scientific behavior analysis to the workplace. Applying it properly will help you maximize performance of every individual on your team.

Health Care Metaphor

The best way to explain how the performance management process works is to use a metaphor to present the concept. The metaphor for this concept is a visit to the doctor and an attempt to diagnose a medical problem. There are many similarities between the performance management process and the medical diagnostic process, including:

- Symptoms alert someone to the possibility of a problem.
- A process is used to analyze symptoms and determine cause of the problem.
- The diagnostic procedure begins with small tests and builds to more complex (and expensive) ones depending upon severity of the problem.
- A plan or method of treatment is established.
- Intervention is planned and executed once the cause is determined.
- Progress is monitored and corrections or adjustments in treatment are made when necessary.

Performance standards should be defined by a management team to reflect call center strategy and goals and not be opinions of single individuals.

Step 1: Defining Healthy Performance

The first step in the diagnostic procedure is to define what is "healthy." The "norms" are determined by scientific research and in the medical world might include normal ranges for body temperature, blood pressure, heart rate, cholesterol levels, and so on. Individual doctors have the same basic definitions about what constitutes "good health" versus a medical variation or abnormality.

The link to the call center is similar. Within the call center, "healthy" is determined by management strategy and goals and not opinions of individual supervisors or team leaders. Your management team has likely determined performance standards and your job as a supervisor is to translate the information from management into workable behavioral standards for your agents.

Knowing what the "healthy" or ideal performance looks like enables you to identify when an agent's performance is "unhealthy" and in need of some type of intervention to facilitate improvement. Defining these specific standards and behaviors will be discussed in more detail later in this chapter.

Step 2: Measuring Current Performance

Doctors don't treat symptoms without diagnosing their cause. They know the presenting problem is not always the cause of the ailment. Doctors first analyze the symptoms and conduct tests to make sure of an accurate diagnosis or to establish a baseline. And in some cases, symptoms may not be present. For example, before beginning a new exercise program, a patient would want to check with the doctor to determine the "health" of his heart. In other words, not all diagnoses are driven by presenting problems; some are precautionary and preventative.

In the call center, you should analyze performance information to see if symptoms of performance problems exist. In some cases, you will review performance based on a certain incident or a concern, but in other situations the "check-up" is merely a routine one that assesses performance on a regularly scheduled basis.

A performance gap analysis compares what you have versus what you want in terms of agent performance.

The process of comparing what is "healthy" or "what you want" versus "what you have" is sometimes referred to as a performance gap analysis. Here you will compare an existing performance situation against a set of performance, standards. Performance will either be in the acceptable range, or out of range either as exceptional or below expectations. Performance below expectations is then evaluated and analyzed to determine a root cause for the problem.

Often supervisors make mistakes in diagnosing a performance, problem. Misdiagnosing a problem can waste money, lower performance, and create mistrust or lack of respect. Money may be spent on additional training when the real cause may have been an issue of feedback or conflicting goals. As a result, the agent's behavior doesn't change, even though time and money were spent on additional training or some other corrective intervention. Sometimes a misdiagnosis results in lowered morale and lessening of respect.

Step 3: Diagnosing the Problem

Doctors use a systematic diagnostic process to correctly determine the cause of symptoms or to assess general health. When a presenting problem arises, there is a diagnostic system in place that employs various types of tests (examination, blood tests, x-rays, etc.) to obtain information needed to correctly identify the cause of the problem. The severity of the symptoms will dictate the complexity of the test administered.

The link to the call center is similar. Instead of relying on your "gut" feeling, a systematic process to guide diagnosis and decision-making should be used. Some presenting problems are simple and don't require sophisticated analysis to identify or correct. Others are more complicated. Having a performance management model allows you to get to the real root cause of a problem.

Step 4: Applying a Treatment

Doctors plan interventions once the cause has been determined. Once the cause has been established, they can plan a specific intervention, requiring the least invasive process necessary to deal with the problem. A doctor's credibility would surely be affected should the patient learn the doctor performed unnecessary surgery or prescribed incorrect medication, not to mention the risk to the patient's health.

In applying a treatment to a call center performance problem, you will want to recommend the least invasive intervention to improve performance. This intervention must focus on the root cause. Focusing on the root cause helps establish the most effective long-term solution rather than a "quick fix" remedy.

Focusing on the root cause helps establish the most effective long-term solution rather than a "quick fix" remedy.

In many cases, misdiagnosing and treating a symptom creates a more difficult problem that must be dealt with later. While your misdiagnosis of a problem may not impact the agent as drastically as a medical one does, there is still a negative impact. Improper interventions are costly in time and performance and sometimes make the situation so much worse it becomes impossible to repair the damage.

Step 5: Monitoring Behaviors

When medical treatment is prescribed, a process for monitoring the patient's progress is established to make sure the treatment is effective and there are no side effects. The more complicated the situation and intervention, the more formal or elaborate the monitoring process is. Monitoring could be as simple as "take two aspirins and call me if the pain continues," or as complex as a hospital stay and observation after major surgery. In either case, the process serves the same purpose – to ensure the intervention has been effective.

In some cases the intervention may not be effective. The doctor may change a medication if desired results are not achieved with the first one. Anytime a treatment is not effective, the doctor goes back to the drawing board and tries another method.

As a supervisor, you should follow the same process. When an intervention is planned, monitoring should be included as part of the follow-up to assess the effectiveness of the action. In some cases, the prescribed treatment doesn't work, and you will need to work closely with the agent to try another solution until the desired performance is achieved.

Step 6: Practicing Preventative Maintenance

Preventative maintenance plays a major role in today's emphasis on managed care. With the shift to managed care programs, medical personnel have discovered it is more cost effective to intervene in the health process before negative symptoms are presented. The emphasis is shifting from treatment to prevention, which includes proactive measures to change unhealthy behaviors and habits before they can create bigger medical problems.

The link to the call center is similar. It is always better to correct simple performance situations before they manifest into complex problems. By using processes to continuously monitor and diagnose performance issues, you can prevent simple errors or misunderstandings from becoming widespread problems.

46. Should performance standards be unique to your team?

The first step of performance management is defining performance standards and expectations. However, this is not typically a job you will undertake on your own. These performance standards will need to be consistent across the center and probably not unique to your team. You probably won't define these by yourself, but will work with other members of the management team to define standards for the entire center.

It's dangerous to define expectations and performance goals based on your own personal management style. It would be difficult for your call center or your company to survive if all the managers and supervisors had their own individual styles of management and performance expectations. The overall performance management process and defined standards in place must support the company's mission and goals. Different management policies and performance standards will only serve to confuse the staff and cause inefficiencies in the workplace.

It's dangerous to define expectations and performance goals based on your own personal management style.

As Aubrey Daniels points out in the book, *Bringing Out the Best in People*, imagine a doctor saying "I've developed my own operational style. I'm going to operate on your brain a little differently than other surgeons would. I've had a few real successes with this technique, so don't worry." Or suppose you're on a plane and pilot announces that he's going to land a little differently than FAA procedures require based on his flying preferences. Performing surgery or flying a plane requires precision and the use of established processes. Managing people's behaviors is just as important to your business and therefore should not be made up of a wide collection of subjective approaches based on each manager's or supervisor's own personal style.

Managing people's behaviors is important to your business and therefore should not be made up of subjective approaches based on each supervisor's personal style.

Performance standards should be defined that explain what is expected of every person in the call center. Agents on one team that take the same kinds of calls as another team should have their performance judged in the same way, even though they work for two different supervisors. The standards should define what is expected in terms of desired behaviors and each supervisor should measure actual performance against those same standards. Every supervisor should follow the same steps of diagnosis and treatment. Employees must see in practice, not just in theory, that the same performance is expected of everyone. They should know that their performance will be evaluated in the same way, and that rewards and consequences will be applied consistently.

Employees must see in practice that the same performance is expected of everyone and that their performance will be evaluated in the same way.

Performance management is a science that works well for management, as well as for the employees. It helps shape desired performance to achieve business results, and it guarantees fair and consistent treatment for all the staff. As it turns out, the best way to run the call center from a management perspective is also the best way to treat people.

47. How do you create detailed performance standards?

The performance management process involves establishing clear expectations about the essential job functions the employee is expected to perform and then breaking down those job functions into clearly defined behavioral expectations and standards.

Quantitative Standards

The easiest expectations to define are the quantitative standards of performance for your organization. It's fairly easy to define a range of numbers in which you expect a person to fall within various categories. A list of quantitative measures and a sample range for each is listed in the table below. *(Note: The numbers listed in the table are not meant to indicate "industry averages" or suggested standards. They only indicate a sample.)*

Expectations of performance should be outlined with clear definitions of what makes up unacceptable, satisfactory, and exceptional performance.

Performance Category	Quantitative Performance Measures	Sample Target
Service	Schedule adherence	>97%
Quality	First call resolution rate	>90%
	Transfer rate	<10%
	Error/rework rate	<5%
Efficiency	Availability	>80%
	AHT	220 sec
	ACW	25 sec
	On-hold time	<30sec
Profitability	Conversion rate	50%
	Up-sell/Cross-sell rate	25%
	Gross sales or sales per hour	$225

Most call center measures tend to focus on quantitative performance measures, simply because they're easy to obtain.

The categories listed in the table represent the common categories of performance upon which an agent might be measured. These expectations of performance should be defined for each unique position in the center, with careful thought given to what an unacceptable number would be, what constitutes satisfactory performance, and what level of performance would be considered exceptional performance.

Different numbers may be appropriate based on the type(s) of calls the team receives or the length of time on the job. For example, you may have an expectation of an average handle time of 220 seconds, but that expectation may be defined a little higher for brand new employees still in a learning mode. They should be aware that they will be expected to reach this number at a certain point in time, but their performance expectation as a trainee may be legitimately lower.

Most call center measures tend to focus on quantitative performance measures, not because they're more important, but simply because they're easy to obtain. It's also more of a black and white definition of whether an employee met an expectation or not. However, much of what defines success in the mind of the customer has to do with how well the call was handled, and that expectation points to qualitative measures of performance.

Qualitative Standards

It is a much more difficult task to define qualitative standards of performance since definitions of quality tend to be more subjective in nature. For example, everyone would agree that agents should exhibit good telephone etiquette on a call, but two different people may have two different definitions about what constitutes good telephone manners.

Below are a few samples of competencies associated with providing quality service over the telephone:

- Adapt the call to the customer's tone and pace.
- Project a positive and professional corporate image.
- Demonstrate a supportive approach when dealing with customers.
- Maintain control of the conversation to balance service with efficiency.

Everyone would agree that these are certainly reasonable and desirable expectations. However, each of the above expectations needs to be defined in more detail in order to be a clear performance standard.

For example, you probably need to define in more specific terms what is meant by adapting the call to the customer's tone and pace. A full definition of that expectation should be provided, along with sample behaviors of what to do and what not to do, as illustrated below:

<table>
<tr><th colspan="2">Goal: Adapt call to the customer's tone and pace</th></tr>
<tr><td colspan="2">Definition:
Adjust to the mood and pace of the caller.
Refrain from imposing your own style or rate of speech on the customer.
Relate to callers as individuals and adapt presentation style and content to fit their needs.</td></tr>
<tr><th>Positive Behaviors</th><th>Negative Behaviors</th></tr>
<tr><td>Slow pace down for inexperienced caller.</td><td>Raise your voice to a caller who is yelling.</td></tr>
<tr><td>Adapt to slower pace for different language or accent.</td><td>Offer all the specials when caller has indicated he is in a hurry.</td></tr>
</table>

Another example might be the expectation of displaying a positive, professional corporate image. That phrase alone leaves much room for interpretation about what is meant by "professional" or what contributes to corporate image. Defining this expectation with a full definition and examples of positive and negative behaviors will make the expectation clearer, and therefore more likely to happen.

Defining the standards down to this behavioral level will accomplish two things. First, it will make it much clearer to your employees what to do and what not to do on a call. One of the reasons that employees don't live up to performance expectations is that sometimes they really don't understand what the expectations are. Too much is left up to the employee to figure out what would be appropriate or not. The more ambiguity you can remove, the clearer they will be on what to do, and be more likely to meet the performance expectation. Be as precise as possible with your definition and give both positive and negative examples.

Goal: Project a positive, professional corporate image	
Definition: Speak clearly and keep conversation focused on customer needs. Use the company name in the greeting and/or closing. Avoid slang and technical terms unfamiliar to the caller. Use "we" when referring to company to project cohesive unit.	
Positive Behaviors	**Negative Behaviors**
Offer assistance – "I'll be happy to help you with that question."	Use can't, don't, or won't – "I can't find that in your record."
Offer positive statements about company – "We're proud of our on-time delivery record."	Disclose undesirable things about company - "Delays have been really long all day."
Use "we" when referring to company – "We have a new discount policy now."	Use "they" when referring to company - "They don't give out that number to customers."

Defining standards down to a behavioral level will make it much clearer to your employees what to do and what not to do.

The other benefit of having performance standards defined all the way down to the behavioral level is that it will make performance evaluation much easier for you and other supervisors. Scoring a call becomes a matter of checking yes or no for the display of the behaviors you want to see, with little room for interpretation about whether an employee met the expectation or not. It's a much easier process for you and a much fairer process for the employees.

Scoring a call becomes a matter of checking yes or no for the display of the behaviors you want to see.

Defining performance expectations to this level takes time, but it is well worth the effort. It helps each employee better understand what to do, and ensures fairness and consistency in the evaluation process. Having these definitions in place reduces the possibility that you can judge two employees differently based on personal feelings about those individuals. The evaluation process becomes a matter of judging a set of behaviors and not an individual.

48. What are the critical components of call monitoring?

Measuring how well frontline staff are meeting qualitative standards is typically done through quality monitoring of calls. You may be doing this monitoring with simple one-to-one observation or you may be using sophisticated remote monitoring of both telephone calls and screen activities.

Side-by-side monitoring involves simply sitting next to your employee and listening to how the call is handled. The best procedure to accomplish this task, with minimal disruption to other agents, is to "double-jack" into the agent's telephone set. A double-jack refers to the agent's telephone set having dual headset connections that enables the agent and you to connect directly into the same telephone set using two separate headsets. Your headset will be placed in a "mute" position to enable you to hear both sides of the conversation, without the customer hearing any additional noise from your side.

The best approach for side-by-side observation and on-the-spot coaching is to double-jack with agents at their workstations.

The advantage to this approach is being there at the agent's side to provide "on the spot" coaching and guidance. The biggest disadvantage of using side-by-side monitoring is the potential for the agent to be more nervous since you'll be observing the call in very close proximity. Some agents are more comfortable without someone "watching over their shoulder," so the side-by-side monitoring procedure should be combined with one or more different monitoring procedures.

Silent monitoring allows you to access a call currently in progress, listening to both sides of the conversation between the caller and agent without either of them knowing that you are observing. There are two major drawbacks to silent monitoring. One is the requirement to do it when calls are happening in real-time. It may be difficult for you to fit monitoring into your busy daily schedule, so it is common for goals to accomplish a set number of observations to be missed.

In addition, when you do have time, it can be difficult to catch calls from the beginning unless you listen to a partial call and then wait for the next one to begin, wasting time and effort. Another drawback is that there is no record of the call except in your mind and your written notes. When you sit down with the agent to discuss the call, it is easy for the agent to deny having said something, or just not to understand what you mean by an "unenthusiastic manner." This lack of record can be particularly problematic in a situation where the agent is being considered for a disciplinary measure.

Disadvantages of silent monitoring include finding time to do it real-time within the day and the lack of a permanent record of the call.

A final category of monitoring involves remote monitoring and recording of the calls. This monitoring and recording function is typically accomplished through the use of a quality monitoring system. While some organizations record every call for business purposes, most do not. The quality monitoring system is usually programmed to record randomly, sampling each agent at different times of day and week to ensure a fair sampling. Generally, the programming calls for a specific number of calls or number of minutes to be recorded per agent.

Optionally, the system may also record the data screens and entries the agent performs during the calls so you can see exactly what the agents saw on the screen and what keystrokes they entered as they processed the call. This information will be displayed on your screen as the call is reviewed so you can determine if the agent is navigating through the system in the most efficient way, making appropriate notes in the customer files, and accessing the right information to solve the customer's problem.

Some quality monitoring systems may also record the data screens that accompany the voice portion of the call so supervisors can review navigation skills and proper note-taking.

The call recordings generated by the system can be stored for future use, or deleted immediately upon review. The random selection process supports a fair and unbiased review process, which can be important when disciplinary issues are involved or should accusations of bias ever be leveled against call center management. If the system instructions are to gather the same number of calls or minutes for each person during sometime in the shift, there can be little risk of the process being found to unfairly target one individual or group of agents.

It is possible in most of these systems to selectively record a specific agent or calls to a particular group, but this is more the exception than the rule in actual practice in most centers. Some centers choose to record all calls handled by trainees, for example, or those that come from a high-value customer group. However, in most cases the calls are recorded randomly.

The random selection process supports a fair and unbiased quality review process.

Another real benefit of having a call recording system in place is the ability for you to review calls along with the employee. Many call centers have a practice where the supervisor and agent listen to a call together and score it independently. This allows the agents to observe their own calls for self-feedback purposes in addition to the feedback that the supervisor provides. With this tool in hand, there possibility for denying certain behaviors is eliminated since the evidence is right in front of the agent.

Another capability of quality monitoring systems is the ability for an agent to actively select to record a call in progress. This feature was originally intended to allow the recording of abusive or threatening calls, but it is being used in many centers as a voluntary self-assessment tool for those agents that want to gauge how they're doing.

Another benefit of quality recording systems is the opportunity they provide for a supervisor and employee to jointly review and score a call.

One call center uses this feature to have a "Worst Call of the Week" contest in which agents can record a particularly difficult call to demonstrate how they've used proper call-handling techniques to handle it. The center rewards the agents that enter a call with a grand prize for the best technique.

49. What should be included in a quality monitoring policy?

If your call center monitors customer calls, you should have a formal quality monitoring policy in place.

You should first research the laws about one-party and two-party notification in your state to ensure you comply with legal guidelines. Much of the policy will outline the process by which employees will be notified of the call monitoring guidelines, both during the hiring process, as well as on an ongoing basis.

The policy will also describe the tools and instruments to be used and how scores of calls will be communicated to the staff.

The top ten items to include in a quality monitoring policy are summarized below:

Top Ten Considerations for a Quality Monitoring Policy
1. Research specific state regulations with respect to monitoring calls to define who must be notified that monitoring will occur.
2. Inform potential employees about monitoring policy during interview/hiring process.
3. Inform agents on a regular basis *when* they are to be monitored in accordance with legal guidelines.
4. Inform agents *why* they are being monitored – the purpose of the monitoring and how it will be used.
5. Obtain agent signatures on monitoring consent forms and post written monitoring policies
6. Use a standardized evaluation form that follows flow of call and gathers most critical performance information.
7. Monitor all agents periodically and set objective standards for varying the number of calls monitored based on performance.
8. Determine how monitoring scores will be communicated – how often, by whom, what communications channel, etc. Outline what information, if any, will be posted publicly and inform staff of posting procedures.
9. Permit only qualified personnel and those with a legitimate business reason to access monitoring capabilities.
10. Establish an objective calibration process that includes representation from all staff involved in the contact handling process.

50. How do you design an effective quality monitoring form?

Make sure your quality form is relevant, user-friendly, objective, and useful for coaching.

Every call center has its own version of a monitoring form. Much thought should go into creating a quality monitoring form to ensure it is relevant to your business, user-friendly, fair and objective, and most importantly, useful as a coaching tool.

Many call centers simply borrow forms from other centers, or use a form that was created back when the business was very different. The form should be carefully constructed and updated as needed to reflect the changing needs of the business. Some of the problems with existing forms from a management, supervisor, agent, and customer perspective are listed in the table below.

Agent Perspective	Supervisor Perspective
▪ Evaluation form is nit-picky and subjective. ▪ Quality form is negative and comments are all critical. ▪ Monitoring is not used to recognize performance, but rather to catch me doing something wrong. ▪ It doesn't matter how I score on quality because my performance is based on call statistics.	▪ It's difficult to locate the agent behavior on the form. ▪ I'm not sure what an evaluation item means, so I just give agent credit for it. ▪ There's no area to write notes and explain why agent received that particular score. ▪ I can't match quality form to related call for coaching purposes.
Management Perspective	**Customer Perspective**
▪ Evaluation scores do not match customer survey results. ▪ Scores are too high, so there is no room for agent growth. ▪ We're not able to recognize those with outstanding performance. ▪ We can't generate quality summary reports that correlate with call statistics.	▪ They say they're monitoring to improve quality, but nothing ever changes. ▪ I was clearly dissatisfied with that call, but nobody seems to care. ▪ They don't seem to get what's most important to me. ▪ They were nice and said the right things, but didn't solve my problem.

You'll want to review your quality form regularly and the first step will be assembling a review team. A sample of frontline agents, supervisors, and quality assurance specialists should participate in the review. The ideal size is probably eight to ten people with someone assigned to be the facilitator.

As you begin the review, keep in mind the call center's main performance objectives (which have been set to match corporate objectives). Note which corporate goals are most important and then which call center goals support that. Your main purpose for monitoring calls should be to ensure that those call center objectives are being attained on each call. Samples of corporate goals might be:

- Create unified customer experience.
- Improve/maintain accuracy and efficiency.
- Handle contacts as "one and done."
- Up-sell, cross-sell, cross-service.

Decide what you're looking for on a call that demonstrates support of these objectives. These goals should make up a significant portion of the form. For example, what behaviors best demonstrate that contacts are being handled in just one call?

List observable behaviors on the form and not vague objectives. Behaviors should be observable and measurable.

Another content issue to keep in mind is the extent to which you list observable behaviors on your form and not vague objectives. Performance objectives should be defined as specific, measurable behaviors that someone can clearly observe or not. As an example, "portrayed positive corporate image" would be subjective measure, while "used company name in greeting" is a clear objective behavior that can be checked yes or no on the form.

In terms of designing the overall form, you will want organize the sections according to the order and flow of the call for ease of use and speed of completion. Common sections that follow a logical order, along with associated behaviors are listed in the table below:

Opening	Discovery
▪ Uses standard greeting ▪ Verifies customer account ▪ Updates customer information ▪ Offers assistance	▪ Clarifies purpose of call ▪ Asks fact-finding questions ▪ Identifies correct nature of call
Resolution	**Closing**
▪ Matches best option to need ▪ Explains delivery schedule ▪ Follows resolution procedure ▪ Promotes additional services	▪ Summarizes actions taken ▪ Offers additional assistance ▪ Thanks customer for business

In addition to these basic components of a call, you will likely want to monitor and evaluate various types of skills or competencies being demonstrated on a call. It is useful to group these kinds of items together in a "skills" section on your quality form. Some examples of these kinds of skills are noted in the following table.

Customer Interaction	Technical Skills
▪ Maintains control of call ▪ Uses courtesy words and phrases ▪ Avoids long periods of silence ▪ Uses hold technique properly ▪ Uses customer name to build rapport	▪ Accurately updates customer profile ▪ Navigates through screen efficiently ▪ Uses reference system correctly ▪ Completes next action screen at the end of call

Quality Standards Document

You should have a quality standards document that is a comprehensive reference for all the components of your quality form. All the definitions of objectives will be noted here, along with samples of positive and negative behaviors that someone should watch for in the call monitoring process. This document should be updated regularly to add new examples and remove outdated ones.

Both supervisors and agents should be involved in updating this document. It is useful to review small pieces of it on a regular basis, to remind agents what the definitions are of desirable and undesirable performance, as well as to refresh and update the document as examples and types of calls change.

Include for each behavior the specific steps for performing the behavior. You may also want to include notes about when it should be performed during the call. It is also useful to include what call center goal or corporate goal the behavior supports to demonstrate its relevance.

A sample entry from a quality standards document is shown below:

	Quality Monitoring Behavior: **Verify customer address and phone number.**
How?	Ask customer for address and check information against Customer Account Screen. If different, update system before proceeding with call.
When?	During the opening of the call, following the greeting
Related Goal?	To ensure company has correct customer contacts for future billing and marketing contact.

51. What are the steps of call calibration?

An important step in the quality monitoring process is the regular calibration of calls. As a supervisor, you will likely be involved regularly in this process.

Call calibration is the process of standardizing the call evaluation and scoring process. The ultimate goal of the process is to make sure that when any two people listen to and evaluate a call, they arrive at exactly the same score. The process ensures fairness and objectivity in the evaluation and scoring process and is an absolute requirement for improvement through the call monitoring process.

Call calibration is the process of standardizing the call evaluation and scoring process.

There are benefits of call calibration for everyone in the call center, as outlined in the table below.

Agent Perspective	Supervisor Perspective
▪ Promotes consistency ▪ Ensures same scoring, regardless of who monitors or scores ▪ Shifts focus away from fairness and towards achievements and areas of improvement	▪ Defines call standards ▪ Clarifies procedures and processes ▪ Expands skill and/or knowledge base
Management Perspective	**Customer Perspective**
▪ Provides consistent service to customers ▪ Maintains integrity of quality program (fewer agent complaints) ▪ Supports center performance standards	▪ Improves service ▪ Promotes more reliable service ▪ Promotes more consistent service

There are three items needed for a call calibration session – the quality standard document with all the definitions of objectives and desired behaviors, the quality monitoring form, and some sample calls. It also requires participation by individuals that have been trained in the call monitoring process and are familiar with definitions in the quality standards document.

For a calibration session, you'll need the quality standards reference, the quality monitoring form, and some sample calls.

The following outlines the steps in the call calibration process:

1. Gather a representative group. This group should typically include supervisors, frontline agents, and quality assurance staff. Depending upon the type of call, you may wish to include folks from other areas of the company whose interests are represented in the center. The optimal size of the group is eight to ten people. If more than twelve people are going to participate, you should probably split into two teams.

2. Randomly select a sample of calls. Sample calls from various agents at various times of day. You may wish to ask for volunteers to be monitored so that nobody feels like they're being "picked on" during the review process.

3. Listen and score the calls. Everyone should listen to the calls with a complete "poker face." There should be no visual reaction from anyone, including laughing, rolling of eyes, etc. that might influence other people's reaction to the call. Verbal comments should not be allowed at this point either. Remember that the goal is a completely unbiased score from each person with no influence from others in the scoring process.

4. Treat each call independently. Even if you know the person who took the sample call, try not to think about what the agent "usually does" on a call, or the fact that the call may not be a typical one from a customer perspective. Don't let that person's status in the call center or overall performance influence the way you score that particular call.

5. Start calibration with a definition of excellence. Discuss several calls without using the monitoring form. Rather, discuss what was "excellent" about each call and perhaps add those items to the definitions in the quality standards document. If the calls had some problems, discuss what an "expert agent" might have done differently on the call. Note any negative behaviors exhibited and add those to your "not to do" list in the quality document.

6. Once definitions are set and everyone is clear on the attributes of an excellent call, score the next call using the monitoring form. Ensure that the definitions created in the step above are represented on the form.

7. List each judge's score on the board without any rationale of how the scores were determined.

8. Select the person who rated the call the lowest to explain the rationale. Determine what proficiencies need coaching and seek agreement from group. The majority of the group should agree that coaching opportunities are valid.

9. Have someone take notes regarding recommendations or changes in proficiency definitions.

10. Ensure that all the changes agreed to in the session are incorporated into the quality standards document and are added to the monitoring form.

52. How should calls be evaluated and scored?

There are many different ways to evaluate and score various components of a call. Some call centers prefer the "Yes/No" or "Pass/Fail" checklist, where the form indicates whether the agent displayed the desired behavior or not. Assuming that the behaviors are adequately defined, this is a completely objective scoring process.

This "Yes/No" scoring is illustrated in the scorecard below. This first example shows just the Customer Service skills from a more comprehensive quality monitoring form that also includes sections for Sales, Technical, and Specialized skills. In this scorecard, an agent's performance was observed over four calls. For some of the traits, the agent had the opportunity to demonstrate mastery of that skill or procedure on every call (such as prompt answer, positive corporate image, attentive listening, and using the customer name). On some calls, the agent did not have the opportunity to demonstrate a skill. For example, only two of the four calls required the caller to be put on hold during the call, and only one call provided the opportunity to demonstrate use of problem-solving steps and techniques.

Customer Service Skills	Opportunity	Compliance
Delivered prompt answer and salutation	IIII	II
Used company name in greeting and closing	IIII	IIII
Used attentive listening skills and responses	IIII	III
Adapted call to customer tone and pace	IIII	II
Demonstrated proper hold technique	II	I
Used customer name during call	IIII	II
Used problem-solving steps to diagnose problem	I	I
Displayed empathy and support	II	II
Maintained control of conversation	IIII	IIII

In this "Yes/No" scorecard, the agent had the opportunity to demonstrate proper behaviors 29 times, as shown by the marks in the Opportunity column. The marks in the Compliance column show the number of times the agent displayed the proper behaviors or processes. In this example, the agent did the right thing 21 times. Therefore, the agents score would be 21 out of 29, or a 72% score.

In this scoring process, there is no judgment about how well the agent displayed any of the skills. In this type of scoring, the agent is credited with a score as long as the behavior was displayed according to the definition of the proper behavior in the quality standards document.

For this particular organization, the same type of scoring might be done for sales skills, technical skills, and any other specialized skills that supported call center and organizational goals. The table below shows sample scores for sales, technical, and specialized skills that have been calculated the same way as the 72% score in the Customer Interaction category.

Skill Area	Actual Scores	Customer Service Emphasis	Sales/Revenue Emphasis
Customer Service	72%	60% factor	10% factor
Sales	97%	20% factor	70% factor
Technical	92%	10% factor	10% factor
Specialized	87%	10% factor	10% factor
Overall Score	**87% (B-)**	**81% (C)**	**93% (A)**

The four scores that the agent has earned in each of the skill areas can simply be averaged together for an overall score of 87% or a B- grade, as shown in the second column of the table. This grade assumes that all four of the skill areas and behaviors are equally important on a call.

As some skills become more important than others in supporting call center goals, this can be reflected by a different weighting in the overall scoring process.

Different scoring might be applied however, if corporate goals dictated more of an emphasis in one area versus another. If the current corporate focus is on customer service, for example, the call center might assign a 60% weighting factor to the customer service skills, a 20% factor to sales skills, and only 10% each to the two other types of skills. With customer service as a focus, the agent gets a lower overall score since the lower customer service skill score has gotten more weight than the others. In this case, the agent's overall score is 81% or a C grade.

On the other hand, if increasing revenue is the primary objective of the company, then sales skills may be deemed more important than the other three. The last column of the table shows an example of this kind of weighting, with sales getting a 70% weight factor and the other three categories only weighing in at 10% each. The overall score here is much higher since the 97% score in sales skills gets more emphasis. In this scenario, the agent scores 93% or an A grade.

"Yes/No" forms are the easiest to use, but may not indicate an agent's strengths and weaknesses in a specific skill area like a rating scale can do.

In addition to this type of "Yes/No" monitoring form and scorecard, other forms can be developed that allow calls to be scored in a variety of categories, with a rating scale for each element (i.e., 5 for excellent, 4 for good, 3 for fair, 2 for poor, and 1 for unacceptable performance). This type of scoring has the advantage of showing a range of performance on each behavior or skill, so agents can better see their strengths and weaknesses. However, it also adds some subjectivity to the scoring process, unless each rating has a specific definition and example showing what would earn a 5 score versus 2 score for each skill. There's more work involved in this approach, but it's worthwhile in terms of communicating more specifics about agent performance.

Learning Activities

1. Outline three competencies required of a frontline representative after the first few weeks on the job. Define each competency, giving at least three positive behaviors that indicate compliance and three negative behaviors that should not be demonstrated within each competency or new skill.

2. Write a description of the performance management process in your center. Explain how standards are set, how they are measured, and how performance issues are diagnosed and treated. Include at least one recommendation on how the process might be improved in your center, based on what you have learned in this chapter.

3. Review your company's call monitoring policy. Does it contain all the recommended components, including a statement of how and when calls will be monitored, how results will be communicated, and who will do the monitoring? Are there components that should be added to your current policy or elements that could be deleted?

4. Review your call center's current call monitoring form. Is it organized logically to follow the flow of a call? Do all items on the form have a complete definition and examples listed in a quality standards document? Do all items link back to corporate goals and objectives? What are the current strengths of the form and what could be done to improve it?

Chapter 8 – Diagnosing Performance Problems

Once you have defined performance expectations, it's time to observe and measure actual performance to identify performance gaps. This performance gap analysis involves comparing what you want against what you actually have in terms of behaviors and performance. Hopefully the two will match, but unfortunately there will usually be employees with performance gaps.

Your next step as a supervisor is to diagnose why these gaps are happening. A root cause analysis is important so that you can prescribe the proper treatment or intervention.

This chapter discusses the three basic reasons why employees don't perform and suggests strategies to deal with each of these types of problems. It also discusses the importance of recognizing desirable behaviors and what to do so that good performance will continue.

53. What are the main reasons that employees don't perform?
54. What are the signs of employees that "don't know"?
55. What are alternatives for staff who "can't" perform?
56. What can be done with staff who "won't" perform?
57. How should you recognize good performance?

53. What are the main reasons that employees don't perform?

The first steps of performance management involve defining performance expectations and communicating them to your employees. Once these standards are in place, you can observe actual performance to see how it measures up against your expectations. Hopefully you'll have a match between the two, but in many cases there is a performance gap. Identifying the gap and the reason(s) behind it is the next step of performance management.

Just as a doctor would use a systematic diagnostic process to correctly determine the cause of medical symptoms, you must use a diagnostic process to guide your analysis of an employee's performance problem. A doctor would order various tests to obtain the necessary information to make a diagnosis, and you must likewise observe and analyze all the information at hand to determine what's behind your employee's lack of performance. Just like in the medical field, the severity of the symptoms will dictate the complexity of the analysis that will be required.

Use a systematic process to guide your diagnosis and arrive at an accurate root cause of the performance problem.

Instead of relying on your "gut" feeling, you'll want to use a systematic process to guide your diagnosis. Some presenting problems are simple and don't require sophisticated analysis to identify the cause, but others are more complicated. Having a performance management model allows you to get to the real root cause of a problem. This root cause analysis is important so that you can prescribe the proper treatment or intervention.

There are three basic reasons behind all performance problems in the call center or in any other work situation. Each performance problem can be attributed to one of these reasons:

Don't Know

The first reason for undesirable performance is that an employee is unaware of performance. He may be not performing up to speed in a certain area because he doesn't know what the performance expectation is, or perhaps he's aware of the expectation or goal, but is unaware that his own performance is not meeting that goal.

Can't

Once the possibility of the "don't know" aspect of the performance problem has been eliminated, it may be that performance is due to the fact that the employees "can't" perform. The employees may lack the training required to do the task, or there may be barriers that are preventing them from completing the task as expected.

There are three basic reasons for non-performance: don't know, can't, or won't.

Won't

The last reason for performance problems is where an employee knows the expectations, knows her performance level, knows how to do the job, and all barriers have been removed. In this case the employee "won't" perform. She may have decided not to perform due to a lack of consequences for performance or non-performance, or she may simply not be motivated to perform.

54. What are the signs of employees that "don't know"?

The first reason that one of your employees is not performing in a certain area may be that he doesn't know he's not performing. In other words, he's unaware that there is anything wrong. There are two types of "unawareness" that may exist. Either the employee is unaware of what the performance expectations are in the first place, or alternatively, is aware of what's expected, but just unaware that he is not meeting them.

One reason that an employee doesn't perform is that he is unaware of expectations or how he is meeting those expectations.

As an example, suppose you have just listened to five of an agent's calls and he has failed to use the customer's name in closing on all five calls. The reasons why he failed to use the customer's name might include:

- He doesn't know he's supposed to do it.
- He doesn't do it because it helps shorten handle time when he leaves it out.
- He doesn't like doing it and so far nobody seems to have noticed.

The reason the agent didn't use the customer's name could be any of the above reasons. It's important for you to determine exactly which one of these is causing the lack of performance so you can address the situation in the appropriate way.

What if he was a new employee and it's only his second week on the phones? He may be fresh out of training and with so many different things to remember, he may not have retained the part about using the customer name in the closing. Or he may remember it being discussed, but thought it was optional – a "nice to do" rather than a specific performance expectation. So he may simply be unaware that there's a real performance expectation he's not meeting.

For new-hire agents, especially for the first several weeks on the phones, there will be many instances of performance gaps. Many of the gaps will be simply because the new agents are unaware of expectations. Either they learned it in training and have forgotten it, or perhaps it was never mentioned at all. When they aren't performing because they're unaware of expectations, your role is to simply tell or remind them of what is expected. In some cases, it's as easy as that.

For new employees, many of their performance gaps will be a simple "don't know" where they are unaware of a performance expectation.

In other cases, lack of performance isn't because a person has forgotten about the standards, but may be due in part to the expectations not being clearly defined in the first place. For example, adherence to scheduled start time is a problem common to many call centers. If an agent's shift starts at 7:30, there might be some ambiguity in what is meant by that start time. While your definition of start time probably means logged into the system ready to take a call, perhaps the agent thinks that as long as he's in the building getting a cup of coffee at 7:30, he's on time. Since there are many ways to interpret start times, it is important for you to clearly define what is meant by adherence to scheduled start time. That means explaining to the agents that they are expected to be logged into the ACD and available for the first call of the day at 7:30, not just in the building.

The other "don't know" situation that can occur is when the employee is aware of the expectation, but just not aware or informed about the degree to which he's meeting those standards.

A "don't know" performance gap can be caused by an unclear definition of the performance expectation.

For example, one of your agents may be aware that there is a performance goal of completing after-call work for each call within 30-45 seconds. He is a speedy typist and feels like he's getting the forms completed in about 15 seconds, giving him a 30-second "breather" before having to go back into available mode to take another call. His supervisor is puzzled to see that his average statistics for wrap-up time show that he's way beyond the norm at an average of 65 seconds per call, even though all his other performance indicators are in the excellent range.

As his supervisor, you could:

- Assume that since he excels in every other area, there's a valid reason his wrap-up time is high and leave him alone.
- Provide a sample of his performance statistics to him, and ask if there's a reason he's having trouble with wrap-up activity.
- Write up the poor performance as part of his employee record.

The correct approach is for you to provide him with a representative sample of his performance statistics, pointing out the difference between what is happening (his actual wrap-up time of 65 seconds) and the performance standard (30-45 seconds). It may be that he's simply unaware of what the performance standard is (just like the first agent was unaware of the expectation of using the customer's name). Or, in this agent's case, he is aware of the goal, but is simply unaware that he's not meeting it.

Employees may be aware of the goal, but not getting enough regular feedback to know that they're not meeting the expectation.

A common reason for non-performance in the call center is that frontline agents simply don't have enough information about how they're performing against performance standards. Timely and consistent feedback about all areas of performance is the key.

There are mirrors in a dance studio so that dancers can see themselves and polish their moves. Likewise, you must find ways in the call center to "turn agents to the mirror" so they can "see" and "hear" their performance. To do this, you should:

Providing regular, timely feedback is the key to preventing the "don't know" performance problem.

- Provide daily performance statistics to individuals that want or need them.
- Provide weekly performance statistics showing team and center averages.
- Provide recordings of calls for agents' review.
- Review and coach using recorded calls and screen activity.

Providing consistent feedback is the key to shaping desired behaviors. In addition to providing feedback about undesirable behaviors and performance, it's just as important to provide feedback and reinforcement when performance is on target. Informing agents when they're on track and demonstrating the proper behaviors will reinforce those behaviors. This can be reinforced even more strongly by attaching a positive consequence or reward to the feedback (more in later chapters), but sometimes just the feedback alone is enough to support and reinforce the desired behaviors.

In addition to informing the agent that his after-call work time is too high, you may want to take that same opportunity to show him how well he did on talk time. If you only point out the lengthy wrap-up time, the agent may think he needs to pick up the pace a little during the conversation with the customer too, resulting in an unsatisfactory customer experience. So you might have to correct two areas when only one problem area needed to be addressed.

Feedback should be given that shows where performance is on target, as well as where it needs to be corrected.

Think about different ways you can provide feedback to the agents on your team. You should look at all the options available to you to provide daily statistics from the ACD to each agent so everyone is always aware of where they stand in terms of quantitative performance measures. Giving them the capability to listen to recordings of their own calls is also useful, particularly if you can note the positive and negative aspects of each call.

If you are too busy to do this on a regular basis, think about implementing some peer monitoring and feedback mechanisms. These types of programs can simply provide more feedback to each individual. It has an extra benefit in that the feedback is likely to be more immediate and linked closer to the behavior that needs to be corrected or reinforced.

Once communications is in place, and "don't know" can be ruled out as a diagnosis for a performance problem, then it's time to move on to the next possibility of why employees don't perform.

Peer monitoring and feedback can provide agents with more information about individual performance and on a more frequent, timely basis.

55. What are alternatives for staff that "can't" perform?

If the agent is aware of the expectation and aware that she is not meeting it, you can rule out the "don't know" reason. The next diagnostic step is to determine if your employee has the ability to perform. With employees who can't perform, you will need to establish if they don't know how to do a task, or if there are any barriers that are preventing them from doing the work.

When employees "can't" perform, it can be due to a lack of know-how or a barrier that's preventing the behavior from occurring.

If you have employees that "can't" perform because they don't know how, then you must provide them with the appropriate training resources to improve their knowledge and skill development.

The employee may have been trained, but still not be able to perform. Sometimes that is due to an ineffective training program. Chapter 4 discussed various training approaches and the need to incorporate different approaches and styles to meet the needs of different types of learners. If knowledge is not being absorbed from your standard training program, you may need to reexamine the content and delivery of the classes. Your training needs to address the needs of visual, auditory, and kinesthetic learners. It should also be based on adult learning principles that incorporate these steps:

- Tell them.
- Show them.
- Let them try.
- Provide feedback.
- Let them try again.
- Reinforce their efforts.

By implementing the adult learning format, you will increase retention in the first place and improve the chances of performance improvement when subsequent training is required.

Make sure your training program employs adult learning techniques and addresses the needs of visual, auditory, and kinesthetic learners.

One example of a "can't" situation where the agent doesn't know how is someone who is having difficulty closing sales. The agent may have been through a classroom course on selling techniques, but may not have fully understood the closing techniques and how they work. It may be appropriate to send that agent back through that portion of the class again. On the other hand, perhaps the agent would learn better by reading about the techniques on her own or sitting with an experienced sales agent to see real-life examples of how to do the work. It is your job to determine what the best means will be to see that the knowledge and skills are gained to perform the needed tasks.

If training isn't the issue, then the other reason an agent "can't" perform may be a barrier or obstacle that is preventing the person from reaching her performance goals. When you take the time to fully investigate and review the issue, you may often discover barriers that impede the ability of the agents to succeed. A key element of the investigation involves getting input from the agent. These conversations save valuable time because the agent may very well pinpoint the barrier or problem for you immediately.

Sometimes the reason an agent "can't" perform is a barrier or obstacle in the way.

Some common barriers to agent performance include:

- Unrealistic productivity goals – You may have the same goals all the time without consideration of seasonal change in call volumes, capability of technology, call overflow, or skill coverage.
- Conflicting goals – It is impossible to meet one goal while trying to achieve another, such as better quality and shorter handle time.
- Resources – There may be a lack of reference materials and resource personnel readily available, or limited staffing in other departments to support the call.
- Technology – There are often system delays or complete shutdowns that impede a call. Poor user interfaces or system design can also restrict the flow of a call.
- Processes and Procedures – You may have cumbersome or outdated procedures that lengthen call with no value to customer.
- Time Shortage – There may not be enough time to learn procedures before an evaluation, or not enough time for you to review and coach properly.

Once you have identified a barrier to performance, the next action is to take the steps necessary to remove the obstacles. Sometimes the action is simple and one that you or your manager can correct immediately, such as adjusting the steps in a process or procedure, or changing a break schedule which has too many agents off at the same time. At times, the obstacle may be complex and involve one or more other departments. In these situations, you may not be able to remove the barrier without coordination with others.

Once you have identified performance obstacles, outline the process required to remove the internal or external barrier to performance.

Removing performance barriers that involve outside resources will involve an identification of all the parties involved and communicating the situation to them. In many cases, you may identify common barriers that can be solved jointly, such as lack of support staff, outdated reference information, insufficient inter-departmental communication, and so on.

56. What can be done with staff who "won't" perform?

The last reason for performance problems is where an employee knows the expectations, knows his performance level, knows how to do the job, and all barriers have been removed – but still won't perform. At this stage, you probably have an employee who "won't" perform. In other words, this employee has made the conscious decision not to demonstrate the desired behaviors.

The most likely reason that employees won't perform is that the wrong consequence is being applied to their actions.

The most likely reason that these employees won't perform is that there are improper consequences associated with their actions. They are either getting an inadvertent negative consequence for displaying the right behaviors, or they're getting a positive consequence for not performing. It is your job to be on the lookout for these mismatched consequences.

It is important to remember that rewarded behavior is repeated behavior. People continue to do those things for which they are rewarded and avoid behaviors that are unfulfilling. Reinforcement actually shapes behaviors. Positive consequences will encourage behaviors and negative consequences will discourage them.

Rewarded behavior will lead to repeated behavior.

It is not uncommon to have mismatched consequences in a call center. Since positive consequences are the most powerful, you will first want to determine if any of your employees are receiving positive consequences for non-performance or non-compliance.

As an example, one call center has a reward system that is based on the number of calls handled per hour. The center has established an environment to motivate productivity, but at the same time it may be counter-productive to quality. Agents may increase their call volume by rushing through calls so they will be available for the next call in queue. Many agents sacrifice service quality (exhibiting a negative behavior), yet they are rewarded.

Another example is one in which a supervisor accepts escalated calls from certain agents who have less than adequate problem-solving ability. This action is actually a form of reward. These agents are spared the difficulty and stress often involved in these situations. Plus, a negative message is being sent to the top performers who are expected to handle all types of calls.

There can also be situations in which good performance gets a negative consequence. For example, a call center may use skill-based routing to send difficult calls to high performers and easy calls to low performers. The outstanding performers are given all the really difficult calls because the lower performers are unable to handle them. The outstanding performers typically take fewer calls since the calls they handle are longer and more complex. The lower performers handle more calls since they are easier and take a shorter time to resolve. If rewards are based on productivity, the lower performers or new-hire agents may have an edge in this particular element of reward and recognition since they handle more calls and the better performers get treated negatively.

Most reinforcement mistakes are made because supervisors are unaware of what is being reinforced. You may get so caught up in meeting your own goals that you don't stop to think about how your actions might be creating an environment that de-motivates performance.

Awareness is the key in preventing the practice of reinforcing the wrong behaviors. You must be on the alert for inconsistent and inappropriate reinforcement and request agent feedback on an ongoing basis. You should also monitor agent reactions to determine what they respond to, how they react to recognition programs, and what their responses are when rewards are announced. The key to success is to reward what you want to see repeated.

Supervisors must be on the alert for inconsistent and inappropriate reinforcement and request agent feedback on an ongoing basis.

(Note: The role of consequences and rewards is discussed in more detail in the next chapter.)

Finally, if improper reinforcement is not the issue and appropriate consequences are matched to behaviors, and employees are still not performing, you may have reached a final diagnosis stage. This final stage is where the employees have simply made the conscious decision not to perform as expected. In many cases, motivation is a key factor in this type of performance management situation.

Motives are what drive behaviors and sometimes all the best-planned consequences can't overcome a simple lack of motivation. The best environment can't provide the motivation for employees who are not a fit for the job. They may have been a misfit for the job in the first place or may have simply grown to dislike it over time. In either case, even though they are capable of performing the right behaviors, their lack of motivational fit can render them less than effective. These employees often create dissension simply because of their unhappiness. They will work in spurts but even this requires "micro-management" on your part as their supervisor.

Sometimes consequences can't overcome a simple lack of motivation. The best environment can't provide the motivation for employees who are not a fit for the job.

The key in addressing motivational fit issues is to make sure you are hiring the right people for the job in the first place, as outlined by the steps in Chapter 3. Then you must constantly strive to create a motivating environment for your employees. Motivational tips and techniques are outlined in Chapter 10. However, it is important to recognize when there is nothing you can do as a supervisor to get the employee to perform satisfactorily and when it is time to move the employee to another position or terminate.

57. How should you recognize good performance?

Part of your role as a supervisor will be to do an ongoing review of all your team members' performance, not just the problem employees. You'll want to do this "preventive maintenance" type of review to catch small issues before they become big problems and to catch employees exhibiting desired behaviors so they can be rewarded.

A common supervisory mistake is to spend the majority of time with problem employees and to ignore the staff performing well.

One of the biggest mistakes that supervisors make in managing performance is to spend nearly all their time with the problem employees and to ignore those employees that are performing well. It's a common situation where "the squeaky wheel gets the grease" and the parts that are working well are virtually ignored.

For example, consider the two employees listed in the table below. The scores needed for an A, B, or C grade are listed in the second, third, and fourth columns. The actual scores of the two agents, Ann and Bob are listed in the last two columns. Bob has scored below a C in quality, a B in after-call work, a C in sales percentage, and a C in schedule adherence. Clearly, you would need to spend time with Bob, first determining why he is scoring so low in each of the categories. Some of the reasons might be a "don't know" or "can't" for some categories, while it may be a "won't" reason for others.

	A	B	C		Ann	Bob
Quality Monitoring Scores	100	90	85		95	82
After Call Work Percentage	20	25	30		24	25
Sales Percentage	25	15	10		24	12
Schedule Adherence	98	96	94		97	94

Now, the question is …what would you do about Ann? Would she get the same time and attention from you that Bob would receive? Ann has scored an A- in quality score, B in after-call work, A in sales, and A- in schedule adherence. She's obviously doing well, so if you're like most supervisors you might assume she's doing fine and not feel the need to spend much time with her.

Recognize good performance to ensure it will continue.

However, Ann deserves just as much of your attention as Bob does. You should be devoting as much time to your good performers like Ann, giving them feedback and recognition, as you spend in coaching time with your problem employees like Bob. It may seem as if she does not need as much of your attention, but she does. If she doesn't get the attention she deserves, she may stop performing well.

You must take time to recognize and reward good performers so they will continue to excel. Remember – rewarded behavior is repeated behavior. If employees are doing something right, you must spend the time to let them know you are aware of it and appreciate it or they may stop.

Learning Activities

1. Review the items on your performance appraisal form and all the items required to be eligible for contests, bonuses, etc in your center. Are there items that need to have clearer definitions of what behaviors are expected for a reward? Are employees getting enough feedback to be able to monitor and correct their own performance? Write a 2-3 page analysis of how your behavioral standards are documented and for each category explain how feedback is provided, along with recommendations on how to improve the feedback cycle.

2. Identify one area of performance in your center where performance might be improved by a change in the training program. Review the current training content and delivery methods and make recommendations on how training might be altered to be more effective in this area.

3. Work as a pair with a fellow supervisor. Identify for each employee on your team an example of what may be conscious or unconscious delivery of an improper consequence for performance. Are some employees getting no reinforcement or negative consequences when performing well? Are there situations where negative behaviors are inadvertently being rewarded? Review each other's lists and discuss appropriate actions you can take in each case.

4. Create a checklist for each of your team members of what behaviors each demonstrates each day that should be rewarded. Determine which of these are most critical to the team's and call center's success and reinforce at least two of these behaviors every single day for a week. Keep a log of the behaviors and the rewards and any noted change in performance.

Chapter 9 – Fundamentals of Coaching

Coaching is the process of instructing, directing, guiding, or prompting employees as they work toward desired outcomes. It is all about developing each employee's potential and encouraging the success of every individual.

There are several different forms of coaching. It can be as informal as stopping by your employee's desk to offer a suggestion or to correct a small call-handling procedure. It can be a session where you sit down with the employee to review some sample calls to identify what went well and/or what could be improved. There may be certain individuals who have performance problems where a more serious counseling session is required to correct a behavior. In addition to these types of interactions, you will likely be responsible for a formal performance review or appraisal session on a periodic basis.

One of the most critical components of any coaching session is the application of consequences or reinforcers. Both positive and negative consequences can be used to shape performance and there are situations where each is appropriate. The proper application of consequences is one of the most powerful tools a supervisor has in managing employee performance, but there are many common mistakes in how consequences are used, resulting in problems rather than successes.

This chapter outlines the various types of coaching sessions and provides some suggested approaches to coach and shape employee performance. The roles of feedback and consequences are discussed, along with the proven techniques and best practices in delivering feedback and consequences.

58. What are the benefits of effective coaching?
59. What should you do in a coaching session?
60. Should you use positive or negative consequences?
61. What are common mistakes in applying consequences?
62. What is the role of mentoring in the coaching process?
63. What are the recommended steps of performance counseling?
64. What are the components of a formal performance review?

58. What are the benefits of effective coaching?

Coaching takes many forms in the call center and there are benefits and drawbacks to each approach. As a supervisor, you will want to do coaching in many different ways – informal side-by-side coaching, formal quality review sessions, counseling sessions to correct performance problems, and formal performance appraisals.

Regardless of the type of coaching used, the benefits are many:

- Increased productivity
- Better quality of work
- Decreased stress levels
- Fewer performance surprises
- Increased team unity
- Increased job satisfaction – yours and theirs!

Coaching will increase job satisfaction for the supervisor and the frontline employee.

The primary benefit of unscheduled side-by-side coaching is that it brings you in direct personal contact with each of your employees to build the employee/supervisor relationship. You can regularly and frequently stop by the agent's desk and listen to a call side-by-side so you can see exactly what the agent is doing. Take the opportunity to point out what is going well as often or more often as you point out mistakes. Recognize desirable behaviors on the spot and do it frequently to ensure good performance continues. If you do this kind of coaching on a regular, frequent basis, you can catch the small errors before they become big performance problems.

The benefit of impromptu side-by-side coaching is that you can do it informally and often.

Some might argue that side-by-side monitoring and coaching isn't effective because the agent is aware he is being observed and as a result will perform better than he normally would. However, this shouldn't be a problem, as the ideal coaching situation is to find someone doing something well to recognize and reward the performance. If having you there in person is likely to generate better behavior, then absolutely do it!

The ideal coaching situation is to find someone doing something well so you can recognize and reward the performance immediately.

Another type of coaching involves monitoring and scoring calls and providing the agent feedback. In a smaller center, the monitoring and coaching are both done by the supervisor, while in larger centers, a quality specialist may do the monitoring and evaluation. These quality specialists may do the actual reviews of the calls and provide a standardized score sheet to the supervisor identifying the areas that the agent handled well and those that need improvement. In a few cases, the quality assurance or training specialists may also do the coaching, but in most cases, coaching is the direct supervisor's responsibility.

In a significant number of centers, monitoring is done on a regular basis, but coaching is not. The scores become merely report cards of performance with little emphasis put on the opportunities to identify gaps or reward excellence. Failure to coach after monitoring is really worse than not monitoring at all. The scores are used to provide input to the agents and to report elsewhere in the organization, but the agent has no real idea how the score was determined or what to do to affect the score. This kind of situation builds resentment at worst and confusion at the very least.

In many centers, monitoring is done on a regular basis, but coaching is not. Monitoring without coaching may be worse that not monitoring at all.

If coaching has so many benefits, then why isn't it done more often? There are many reasons or excuses that supervisors use not to coach. Some supervisors may say they don't have enough time, but not coaching leads to bigger, more time-consuming problems in the future. Supervisors may also have too many employees, and may genuinely have difficulty getting around to everyone on the team on a regular basis. If you have more than fifteen employees, then you may want to enlist the help of lead agents or incorporate peer monitoring and coaching programs to make sure everyone is observed and coached regularly.

Other supervisors, particularly new ones, may avoid coaching due to fear. They may have a fear of frightening the employee or feel awkward in delivering feedback or criticism, especially to team members that were recently peers. Others are in a denial mode, assuming employees will change on their own or ask for assistance if they need it. Regardless of the reason, avoiding coaching is dangerous. It is only through coaching and performance management that your team members' performance will improve.

If you have a large number of employees and don't have time to coach them all regularly, enlist other team members to help.

As a supervisor, you should regularly evaluate your own performance as a coach. There is a coaching characteristics scorecard on the following page. It contains twenty characteristics that employees use to describe supervisors who are good managers and leaders. Rate yourself in each of the categories and then add all the circled numbers to arrive at a final coaching effectiveness score.

Suggested scoring:
Above 50 points – Excellent
40-50 points – Good
Below 40 points – Needs improvement

Avoiding coaching is dangerous to you and your team. It is only through coaching that your team will improve and develop.

Coaching Characteristics Scorecard

As a coach, I:	Seldom	Sometimes	Always
1. Give assignments that capitalize on employees' strengths.	1	2	3
2. Give employees visibility with higher-level managers and customers.	1	2	3
3. Provide freedom and empowerment for employees to do their jobs.	1	2	3
4. Set standards of excellence for the team and for individual team members.	1	2	3
5. Orient the employee to company values and business strategies.	1	2	3
6. Hold the employee accountable for both successes and failures.	1	2	3
7. Protect the employee from undue stress in the work environment.	1	2	3
8. Encourage employees when they are discouraged or about to undertake difficult assignments.	1	2	3
9. Provide information about the company's vision, products, and goals.	1	2	3
10. Define performance expectations and priorities and communicate them clearly.	1	2	3
11. Take time to build relationship and trust with each team member.	1	2	3
12. Provide appropriate training and support when needed.	1	2	3
13. Solicit and listen to the employee's ideas even when I disagree.	1	2	3
14. View the employees as partners and critical to the success of the company.	1	2	3
15. Serve as a good role model in all aspects of job performance.	1	2	3
16. Encourage employees to try and never give up in a difficult situation.	1	2	3
17. Keep confidential information secure and don't divulge confidences.	1	2	3
18. Explain reasons for decisions and procedures and give advance notice of changes if possible.	1	2	3
19. Provide employees with feedback about team and individual performance.	1	2	3
20. Give employees recognition when they deserve it and discipline when they need it.	1	2	3

59. What should you do in a coaching session?

What happens in a coaching session depends upon the development stage of the employee. Some of your newer employees will be in learning phase and the coaching time you spend with them will mostly addressing "don't know" or "can't" issues, where they need to be informed about expectations or perhaps receive some training on how to perform a certain task. Your role as a coach with these employees is mostly to enlighten and to train.

A supervisor's main role as coach with new employees will be training.

Intermediate level employees will have passed through the initial learning curve and know how to do most things. They will also most likely be aware of what is expected of them. These team members may still fall into a "can't" category, but are more often classified in the "won't" category. Your job as a supervisor will be to fine-tune their performance and reward them for the things they're doing well.

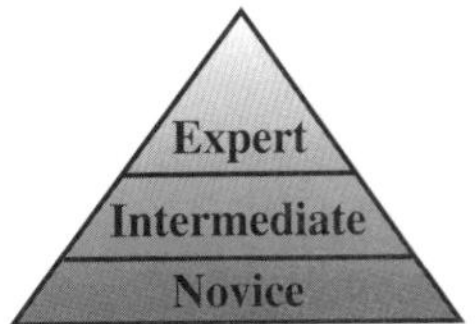

Once an employee has reached the expert level, it is rare that performance issues fall into the "don't know" or the "can't" category. When performance problems exist at this stage, they generally belong to the "won't" category. It is your job to apply proper consequences in the form of rewards and disciplinary consequences to shape desired performance. Just like a sports coach with a star athlete, your role with the expert employee is probably no longer a teaching role, but one of advanced development, team strategy, and motivation.

Your role as a coach will vary depending upon the developmental level of the employee.

A common mistake that supervisors make in a coaching session is to talk the whole time. A coaching session should be a two-way interaction between you and the employee, not a lecture. Spend at least half the time listening to what your employee has to say. Listen to what he is saying, both with words and actions. Read the meaning behind his words and pay attention to body language and non-verbal messages. Put more of the responsibility of current situation description and possible solutions on the employee's shoulders and they will feel more ownership of the end result.

A coaching session is a two-way discussion, not a lecture. Listen to what the employee is saying with words and non-verbal actions.

In general, there are six steps in a routine coaching interaction:

1. Ask a question.
2. Listen to the answer.
3. Ask a follow-up or probing question.
4. Listen to the answer.
5. Reward if behaviors are what you want.
6. If not, make suggestions for improvement.

Review the dialogue of a brief coaching session below and see if you can identify the positive and negative aspects of the discussion.

Coach: *How do you think that last call went?*
Agent: Not very well.
Coach: *Why do you think it didn't go well?*
Agent: I had to put her on hold and I forgot to do the "hold thing" right.
Coach: *Well, putting her on hold was unavoidable. What could have improved that experience for the customer? What would you do differently next time?*
Agent: I'll ask permission first?
Coach: *That's right. Anything else?*
Agent: Umm, I'm not sure.
Coach: *Well, if the delay is long, we want to check back in and tell them we're still checking so they don't feel like we've disconnected or forgotten about them.*
Agent: OK, I'll do that next time.
Coach: *Great, I know you'll get it right in the next call or two. And keep up the good work on the up-sell technique. You did a good job on offering the extended warranty. Even if she didn't accept, you did all the right things, so keep at it!*

There were several positive aspects of this discussion. The coach started with a question, listened for the answer, and then fed back another couple of questions to clarify the agent's knowledge on the hold technique. The coach provided the agent an opportunity to identify the strengths and weaknesses of the call before jumping in to provide corrections and assumptions.

Every coaching session should support the employee's self-esteem, even if negative feedback is being given. In this example, the coach has provided constructive criticism, but without damaging the agent's self-esteem. The statement where the coach expresses confidence in the agent's ability to get it right the next time is an excellent example of supporting self-esteem while delivering negative feedback.

One poor aspect about this dialogue is the closing statement made by the coach. The main point of the call was to correct the hold technique, and by jumping to a different topic with positive feedback, the impact of both is lessened. The coach should have saved recognition of the up-sell technique for a different time so the agent can focus on just one aspect at a time. The fact that the agent is doing the sales step well should not be ignored, but rather recognized separately. Mixing positive and negative messages in a single session diminishes the effectiveness of both. This concept will be discussed in detail later in this chapter.

60. Should you use positive or negative consequences?

The main thing that influences someone to do something is what happens to him when he does it. There are things that can cause an event to occur in the first place called antecedents. The things that happen after an event are called consequences. Both of these can shape behavior. Antecedents like an order or a request can set the stage for behaviors to happen in the first place. However, whether or not the behaviors will continue to occur depend upon the consequences of that behavior.

> The chances of a behavior occurring over and over depend upon the consequences that happen when that behavior is displayed.

Applying consequences is critical to shaping behavior. While some consequences occur naturally, others will need to be consciously applied. For example, agents may demonstrate some desirable behaviors such as telephone etiquette because they get an immediate consequence for doing so – a friendly, thankful reaction from a customer. Other behaviors that you would like for them to display, such as schedule adherence, don't come with natural built-in positive consequences, so you will have to apply consequences to shape the behavior you want to see.

Both positive and negative consequences can be used to influence behavior. If you can catch someone demonstrating desirable behaviors, then you will want to immediately apply a positive consequence. Positive consequences work more effectively than negative consequences. People like positive reinforcement better, it produces a less stressful environment, and it also maximizes performance.

Negative consequences can also be used, but they are not as effective as positive consequences. Negative reinforcement will shape performance, but it generally produces behaviors that are just enough to get by. Discipline and punishment will generally stop a negative behavior, but in some cases only for a little while, and it will never encourage employees to give maximum effort like positive consequences can do.

> Negative reinforcement will shape performance, but it generally produces behaviors that are just enough to get by.

The key to successful performance management is to define desired results, isolate the behaviors that drive them, and then provide appropriate consequences and rewards when those behaviors are observed. It is better to catch employees doing something right and reward them than to have to deliver negative consequences. Rewarded behavior is repeated behavior, so look for behaviors to reward and do it consistently.

Sometimes situations occur where even though positive consequences are given for desired behaviors and negative consequences are attached to the wrong behaviors, employees still do the wrong things. This is because there are other characteristics of consequences in addition to just the positive and negative aspects. In addition to the positive/negative aspects associated with a consequence there are also the aspects of how personal a consequence is, how immediate it is, and how certain it is. These other aspects of a consequence can sometimes outweigh the positive/negative aspects.

Let's look at an example where positive aspects for the right behavior and negative aspects for the wrong behavior are in place, but still don't yield the desired result.

In this example, the employee issue is failure to adhere to the assigned work schedule. Let's examine both the positive and negative effects associated with this lack of schedule adherence, along with the personal, immediacy, and certainty aspects of the consequences.

Lack of Schedule Adherence Consequences	Positive/ Negative	Personal/ General	Immediate/ Future	Certain/ Uncertain
Impact on service level	N	G	I	C
Impact on peer occupancy	N	G	I	C
Bad appraisal	N	P	F	U
Loss of bonus	N	P	F	U
10-minutes extra sleep	P	P	I	C
More time to socialize	P	P	I	C
Fewer calls to take	P	P	I	C

Even though there are many negative consequences associated with a lack of schedule adherence, the employee may continue to do it. Two of the negative consequences are of benefit to the overall call center and customers, but not felt as a personal effect. The bad appraisal and loss of bonus are also negative, but they are not immediate. Those things will likely happen sometime out in the future, and may be viewed as uncertain by the employee.

These negative consequences may be outweighed by the positive consequences. The benefits may include an extra ten minutes of "snooze" time in the morning, or an extra few minutes to socialize in the break room, not to mention fewer calls to take. All these consequences are personally felt by the employee, and they're all immediate and certain. Even though they're not as significant as the negative ones, the fact that they're personal, immediate, and certain may sway the employee to continue his errant schedule behavior.

The best consequences to shape employee behavior are positive, personal, immediate, and certain.

You can liken this dilemma with the difficulty of sticking with a diet. The positive consequences of eating healthy foods and exercising are clear – weight loss, better health, more attractive physique, better-looking clothes, and so on. However, there are millions of overweight individuals that aren't being influenced strongly enough by these consequences, mainly because they're not immediate enough. The personal, immediate, and certain consequences of the taste and enjoyment of high-calorie foods is enough to keep some people from sticking to a healthy eating plan.

The key when developing a plan of consequences is to apply consequences that are positive to shape desired behavior. However, it's not enough that the consequence is positive. It also has to be personal (something that means something to the employee), immediate, and certain for it to work as an influence on behavior.

61. What are common mistakes in applying consequences?

There are several common mistakes in defining and applying consequences to shape employee performance. Some of these common mistakes are described below.

Delay error

The first and most common mistake is the delay error. This is the case where the consequence may be appropriate, but it is not delivered close enough to the observation of the behavior. As discussed on the previous page, a reward must happen immediately if it is to be effective. The longer you wait to deliver it, the less effective it will be and the less mental link there will be to the desired behavior.

According to Aubrey Daniels in *Bringing Out the Best in People*, effective leaders do not necessarily reinforce more often than ineffective ones. They simply reinforce while the people are performing or immediately thereafter. That means spending more time in direct contact with the staff so you can reinforce good behaviors on the spot.

A reward will be more effective if delivered during or immediately following the desired behavior.

Frequency error

One positive reinforcer will not change behavior. To be effective, there need to be consistent, frequent consequences for positive actions. Occasional reinforcers will not sustain desirable behaviors. That's why you must coach and reinforce often. The recognition you supply once a quarter in a performance review is not enough to sustain good performance. It needs to happen on a daily basis.

Motivational speaker and writer Zig Zigler once said "People say that motivation doesn't last. Well, neither does bathing. That's why you should do it often." If you don't have time to do it often enough, think about having peer recognition programs in place so that everyone can get feedback and recognition on a more frequent basis, even if all of it doesn't come from you.

Contingency error

This error relates to the relationship between a behavior and a consequence. If an employee can get recognition without engaging in the prerequisite behavior, then that consequence is said to be noncontingent. This error happens often in a team environment. A team may be rewarded for reaching a certain goal, yet some of the employees on the team may not have contributed to the end result that earned the reward. If these people share in the team reward, this is an example of a mismatched or noncontingent consequence.

Watch out for instances where a non-performing member of a team unfairly shares in a team performance reward.

As a supervisor, you need to be watch out for these instances where you may be inadvertently rewarding non-performance. Make rewards contingent upon displaying the expected behaviors and you will see performance begin to improve to meet at least minimum acceptable standards.

Perception error

This error is related to the degree in which an employee perceives a reward or consequence to be desirable. It's important that your reward system takes into consideration what would be viewed as a negative and positive consequence by each person. It's common to think that people should want to receive the rewards you want to give them. But what is viewed as a reward by one person may be viewed as having no value or even as negative by someone else.

What is viewed as a reward by one person may be viewed as having no value or even as a negative by someone else..

When in doubt about how a reward or consequence is perceived, all you have to do is ask. Ask each employee what would be viewed as a positive or negative consequence. It may be that some people love public recognition and would put that at the top of their positive list, while others would consider the attention to be embarrassing and negative. Don't assume that what you would like to receive is what another person would enjoy.

Sandwich error

Consider the case of delivering positive feedback and recognition to an employee. You begin with the words "You did a great job" or "I really appreciate what you did." However, in your role as coach, you feel compelled to offer some advice with the statement, so you don't stop there. You might follow that positive statement with another phrase that begins with "but you could have done…"

As an example, consider the coaching statement, "You did a great job on the hold technique, but you forgot to use the proper closing on the call." From your perspective, you may think you've reinforced the hold technique behavior and just added a little hint on how to fine-tune the call a bit for next time. Although well intended, your statement may be more punishing than reinforcing. Whenever you use the word "but" in a statement of praise, you are using a verbal eraser. It essentially erases whatever words came before it and all that remains is the criticism.

Do not use an occasion for praise as an opportunity to instruct or criticize.

Likewise, if negative information or consequences need to be applied, many supervisors have the tendency to "sandwich" a negative response in between two positives. While it's important to maintain the self-esteem of an employee when supplying feedback and negative consequences, it's important not to mix the positives and negatives together. This "love sandwich" may help you feel better, particularly if you're new at providing negative feedback, but in general, mixing the two is not a good practice.

Criticism should be short and to the point and make clear what negative consequence will happen if behavior does not change. The positives should be saved until there is improvement in performance and then be rewarded without a mention of a negative. You can maintain the self-esteem of the individual even in a negative feedback situation. Use statements that show you have trust in their ability to succeed. Attack the behaviors they've exhibited and not them personally and their self-esteem will remain intact.

Do not pair positive reinforcement with punishment.

62. What is the role of mentoring in the coaching process?

Mentoring may be viewed as another form of coaching. One organization may have a different definition of mentoring than another. In some companies, a mentor may be simply a senior agent assigned as a "buddy" to show a new employee the ropes. In others, a supervisor may take a selected individual or two under her wing for extra instruction and guidance. In other organizations, senior level managers serve as mentors to "rising stars" to nurture their growth and speedy progression up the career path.

In any of these cases, a mentor's role is to guide. While you might think of a coach as walking behind an employee pushing, and a counselor walking ahead pulling the employee along, a mentor would be the person walking alongside. This person would be gently guiding and giving advice. Most of the time, coaches and supervisors tend to be "change-oriented" or "goal-oriented," focused on shaping the performance of an individual on certain tasks. A mentor is more "growth-oriented" and focuses on career and long-term development of the individual.

According to the book, *Coaching, Mentoring, and Managing* by Micki Holliday, the following guidelines should be followed by anyone that is selected to serve as a mentor for another employee:

1 ***Know your work.*** Review the work you've done, the problems you have faced, and how you have dealt with them. Be prepared to answer questions about all phases of the work ahead.

2. ***Know the organization.*** One of the mentor's most important roles is to teach organizational realities. Help your employee understand and overcome office politics, and both written and unwritten company policies.

3. ***Get to know your employee.*** Take the time to learn about the employee's background, education, skills, and interests. Use this information to help guide this person to the best fit in the organization.

4. ***Learn to teach.*** You'll be instructing and guiding, so figure out how people learn. Research adult learning theory and the various learning/communications styles and determine how to apply them to the individual you will support.

5. ***Learn to learn.*** You will need to continually acquire and assimilate new information. You'll want to have a solid company background and knowledge as well as knowledge of the industry.

6. ***Be patient.*** Understand human nature and develop compassion for the different levels and ways in which people learn. Be especially patient if your employee is from another generation or a different culture than yours.

7. ***Take risks.*** Give your associate assignments that are challenging. Give support but also enough room to succeed or fail. Recognize that some small failures along the way will contribute to learning and development.

8. ***Celebrate successes.*** Let your employee know how proud you are of his/her accomplishments and progress. Celebrate significant milestones and make this a fun and exciting collaboration.

63. What are the recommended steps of performance counseling?

Unfortunately, you will have some employees with performance issues that have grown more serious than what can be addressed in an informal coaching session. In these cases, you will need to schedule and conduct a performance counseling session.

If you're in doubt about whether a performance counseling session is warranted, ask the following questions:

- Have employee duties been clearly communicated?
- Has feedback been given on performance?
- Is employee adequately skilled to do the job?
- Is the employee's behavior willfully inadequate toward these duties?
- Is the behavior ongoing?

A counseling session is called for if behavior is willfully inadequate on an ongoing basis.

If you answer yes to these questions, then it's time for a counseling session.

There are several things to consider in scheduling a performance counseling session. The first is where the session will take place. There should be a private area in which you can talk with your employee without being overheard by others and where you both feel free to express thoughts and feelings. This should certainly not be done in an agent's cubicle. If you have an office with doors, or an out-of-the-way private cubicle, you may conduct this in your office. Conference rooms are another possibility but are often in short supply. Sometimes the coaching may place in the break room or cafeteria during low traffic periods. This lack of an easily accessible private area is often an impediment to scheduling counseling sessions as frequently as they should be done.

The time of day that the counseling session is scheduled can be important too. If it is likely that the agent will be upset by the discussion, it might be best if it is held at the end of the day or before the agent's lunch period to allow time to regain composure outside of the call center. However, if the coaching session will be largely praise, then it is reasonable to schedule it during the working day.

Schedule a counseling session for an appropriate time of day.

When you schedule the session, decide on a set amount of time and then stick to it. It is common for these sessions to go on and on, and setting a time limit up front will help keep it on track and to the point. You can always schedule another session should more discussion be needed.

During the session it is important to keep distractions to a minimum. Don't answer your phone and politely turn away people that come to your door during the session. Avoid looking at the emails or instant messages coming across your computer screen. Your employee deserves your complete, undivided attention during the session.

Respect your employee's needs and avoid all distractions during the counseling session.

The main steps of a counseling session are:

1. State the purpose of the session.
2. Describe actual behaviors versus performance expectations.
3. Define recommended steps to improvement.
4. Communicate consequences.
5. Gain commitment.

Stating the Purpose

As the counseling session begins, you'll want to state the purpose of the meeting so that the employee knows why the session is being held. You may want to give your employee the opportunity first to describe why he thinks the session has been called.

Give the employee the opportunity to define the performance issue and why it is occurring.

The employee should understand that the goal of the coaching session is to identify areas of excellence and areas for improvement. Even if the employee is performing so poorly as to require some disciplinary action, the coaching process should remain as positive as possible. The focus of the session must be specific so that the agent knows exactly what is being praised and what areas need adjustment.

Describing Behaviors and Expectations

Once the stage has been set for the counseling session, the next step is to discuss the actual performance and compare it to the defined performance expectations. This process must be done with as many facts and as few personal impressions as possible. Describe the specifics, play back call recordings, show samples of productivity reports, or do whatever else is needed to illustrate the deficient behavior. Provide as much detail as possible so there is no doubt in the mind of the agent what the issues are. Discuss the potential or actual impact of the agent's performance so he clearly understands why you are bringing up this performance for review.

As part of this current situation discussion, you may discuss why the gap in performance is occurring. You may have already determined the root cause of the problem through the "don't know/can't/won't" model, but it is useful here to get the employee's viewpoint and reason(s) for the performance gap. If you have been coaching regularly, this discussion should not contain any surprises for the employee.

Defining Steps to Improvement

Once you have discussed the performance gap and the reason it is occurring, the next step is to define one or more solutions to address the problem. You will want to come to the session with at least one solution to suggest to the employee. However, it's best to ask the employee to suggest a solution to the problem before you make any suggestions. If the employee suggests the solution, there is greater buy-in and commitment to the solution than if you suggest it. Working together with the employee to arrive at acceptable solutions shows your willingness and effort to help the employee improve behavior and get performance on track.

Communicating Consequences

Whether the failure to perform is due to a lack of knowledge or a willful decision not to perform, the counseling session should clearly communicate the consequences of future behavior. This can be the promise of positive consequences should the performance improve, or negative ones if the undesirable behaviors continue.

Consequences must be aligned with the severity of the performance gap and the impact it has on the center and company. Consequences for failure to perform should be the same for all individuals performing at the same level in similar circumstances so you are not accused of personal bias.

Gaining Commitment

As you discuss the performance gap with the agent, the goal for improvement must be clearly defined, including the specific improvement expected and the timeframe for its achievement. It may not be realistic to expect the employee to reach the full goal in one step if performance is considerably below expectations. If the goal is set for a reasonable increment in a realistic period of time, the employee can see that it is possible and work toward it more effectively. Unrealistic expectations generally result in the agent giving up so that little or no improvement is made and disciplinary action is required.

If the performance gap is large, set small incremental goals that the employee has a better chance of achieving along the way.

It is important to document all interactions in these sessions whether they are positive or negative. It is common to see deep files of documentation on poor performers and virtually nothing on the best agents. This can be troublesome when the poor performer requires disciplinary action. Having documentation on only the poor performers may suggest evidence of personal bias and is one of the situations that can prevent you from being able to terminate a poor performer.

Once the counseling session has concluded and both parties have agreed to the performance improvement plan, the steps that were defined and documented must be carried out as agreed. If the agent is to have two weeks to develop the missing skill or demonstrate the appropriate behavior, then you must allow this time to pass before new measurements are taken. However, when the agreed date arrives, the new measurements should be done on a timely basis. Agents can suffer from considerable stress if they are under pressure to meet a target and then receive no feedback as to whether the goal has been achieved or not. In addition, failure to follow up sends a signal to the staff that you don't take performance plans seriously.

Failure to follow up after a counseling session sends a message that you don't take performance improvement plans seriously.

When the time is up, another meeting must be scheduled to discuss the results – positive or negative. If the results are acceptable, then the agent needs to be rewarded for success. If the achievement was one step in a multi-step improvement program, then reward the agent for achieving the first step and outline the next step in the process and the timeframe for achievement. If the agent failed to achieve the required results, the promised negative consequences must be applied.

64. What are the components of a formal performance review?

In addition to informal side-by-side coaching and as-needed counseling sessions, you will likely also be responsible for doing periodic formal performance appraisals or reviews. In most companies, these are scheduled every six months, but may occur more or less often depending upon your company and HR policies.

The formal performance review should be used to recognize good performance, provide coaching and feedback, and identify development opportunities.

This performance appraisal process is an ongoing exchange between you and your employee throughout the year. During each of these exchanges, you have the opportunity to recognize good performance and provide coaching and feedback when performance is not meeting the expectations. In addition, these reviews should be used to identify development opportunities for your staff.

The performance review period should begin with you and your employee meeting to set goals for performance in the coming period. These goals should be related to the overall goals of the call center as well as to the specific assignment of the agent and his stage of professional growth. You should both agree to the goals, and you should provide feedback throughout the performance period to let the agent know how he is doing, so that there are no surprises once you sit down for the formal review meeting.

Quarterly or annual reviews should be routine meetings and few surprises should arise. If feedback is constant (even daily, in some cases), these more formal reviews are typically used for adjusting the goals up or down, and for the sole purpose of simply reviewing performance.

You will want to maintain a performance file on every member of your team. Each employee file should contain notable and specific examples illustrating an employee's job performance or results and should also include instances when you provided feedback to that person. These files serve as a source of information from which to track performance throughout the year. Over time you will accumulate a file filled with detailed examples of an employee's work contribution. These examples can be drawn upon to support and give credibility to performance ratings on the performance appraisal form. This file can also assist when the employee is transferred to a different supervisor, especially near the time that performance reviews are due.

Keep a file of notable and specific examples of each employee's performance throughout the year.

Performance appraisal forms are an integral part of the performance appraisal process. These tools are used to evaluate how well employees perform their jobs compared to a defined set of standards. When appraisals are completed correctly and consistently, these appraisal forms should provide employees with a written record of what they are expected to do, identify if they are meeting their goals, identify their strengths and weaknesses, and provide suggestions for improvement.

One sample of a performance appraisal form is provided on the following two pages.

EMPLOYEE PERFORMANCE APPRAISAL FORM		
Date of Appraisal:		
Employee Name:		
Manager Name:		
INSTRUCTIONS: Enter the appropriate description of performance and include comments to support. The employee should be rated on every skill listed. Use specific examples and write your evaluation so as to help the employee understand what is needed to get to the next higher level of performance. **Guidelines:** **P** = Professional development needed **M** = Meets and may exceed some expectations **E** = Consistently exceeds expectations. A "+" (**plus**) or a "-" (**minus**) may be used in addition to these guidelines to better describe the employee's performance.		
KNOWLEDGE: Demonstrates a thorough understanding of job duties and has sufficient knowledge and skills to successfully perform job responsibilities.		
Experience level requires considerable assistance.	Experience level requires appropriate assistance.	Knowledgeable in all phases of job responsibilities.
P	M	E
Comments:		
RELIABILITY: Completes tasks within agreed upon schedules, reports on progress accurately; works independently without frequent supervision; considers and deals with all aspects of a task. Adheres to applicable guidelines with respect to care of equipment, safe working practices, attendance, and punctuality. Meets assigned work schedules.		
Requires supervision and reminders of schedule.	Requires normal supervision and generally completes tasks on time with consistent performance.	Always completes tasks on time. A self-starter who can always be relied upon.
P	M	E
Comments:		
QUALITY: Does the right thing the first time, every time, on time. Exhibits specific examples of being personally involved in generating and implementing quality improvements that benefit customers and fellow employees and lead to increased productivity.		
Workmanship and service need improvement.	Workmanship and service are professional.	Workmanship and service are consistently outstanding and highly professional.
P	M	E
Comments:		

PROBLEM SOLVING: Develops new approaches to problems and considers a variety of solutions, rather than just orthodox approaches; open to new ideas. Assists in additional work areas, enlarges abilities, and provides solutions to problems when able. Develops effective solutions and identifies and involves appropriate people and resources.		
Demonstrates minimal initiative for problem-solving or contributing ideas.	Demonstrates initiative and reasoning for sound problem-solving skills and contributing ideas.	Highly resourceful; often develops time or money saving ideas. Easily grasps issues and enthusiastically contributes practical solutions.
P	M	E
Comments:		
COMMUNICATION: Demonstrates ability to present ideas orally and in writing to provide others with a clear and exact understanding of an issue or situation. Adjusts communication style to accommodate different audiences. Practices active listening. Is persuasive and skilled at influencing others.		
Quality of communication needs improvement.	Communication, listening, and interpersonal skills meet professional expectations.	Demonstrates highly professional interpersonal, communication, and listening skills.
P	M	E
Comments:		
CUSTOMER SERVICE: Demonstrates dedication to meeting and exceeding customer expectations by providing superior services and products in a timely, accurate, and courteous fashion for external and internal customers.		
Needs better understanding of role in customer satisfaction and enjoyment.	Generally provides professional level of customer satisfaction.	Consistently provides excellent customer satisfaction. Delights the customer.
P	M	E
Comments:		
ANNUAL PERFORMANCE SUMMARY		
P	M	E
Comments:		

Employee Signature and Date:	
Manager Signature and Date:	

On this sample form, you can select a rating for a several different evaluation factors. You should select the rating that best reflects the employee's performance, based on achievement of defined objectives, behavior patterns, impact of behaviors, and patterns of work.

The description for an employee who achieves the highest rating includes individuals who focus on innovation, new ideas, process improvement, and who have achieved tangible results in the areas being rated. These employees consistently exceed expectations. The description for an employee who receives the lowest rating representing poor or unsatisfactory performance includes individuals whose work results are less than acceptable or adequate. Your employee whose performance is at this level should be on a written performance improvement plan so that if work results do not improve, the employee is aware of potential disciplinary action, up to or including termination.

Additional areas of performance that might be utilized as part of a performance appraisal form for call center employees include:

- ***Customer Focus*** – Supports corporate strategy for a high level of service delivery for internal and external customers. Seeks opportunities to offer assistance. Accepts ownership of issues. Anticipates customer needs. Seeks understanding by asking the right questions. Prioritizes services needs. Goes beyond what is required to resolve issues/restore service failures.
- ***Decision Making/Judgment*** – Demonstrates the ability to analyze the components of a problem and develop logical solutions. Chooses best option after reviewing all available and relevant information. Takes ownership, accountability and responsibility for actions.
- ***Professionalism*** – Approaches daily work responsibilities as well as new assignments with a positive attitude. Avoids negative conversations and gossip. Supports and acknowledges needs of co-workers. Supports corporate strategy. Takes a proactive approach to new and weighty projects or assignments. Accepts and welcomes change. Maintains composure in difficult situations.
- ***Quality of Work*** – Displays results in the caliber of work produced. Demonstrates ability to complete work assignments accurately, completely, and in a timely manner to meet set schedules.
- ***Teamwork*** – Actively contributes and/or supports team efforts and establishes positive working relationships with co-workers and supervisors. Seeks and accepts constructive feedback. Shares due credit with co-workers; displays enthusiasm and promotes cooperation and trust within the group environment. Works closely with other departments as necessary. Supports group decisions and solicits opinions from co-workers.

As part of the performance appraisal process, you and the employee should complete an employee development plan for the next review period. The key to any successful performance management process is the continuous development of the employee, and this review can be used to help employees to achieve their full potential, to increase job satisfaction, maximize job contribution, and to plan for career growth.

Learning Activities

1. Identify a common performance problem and non-desirable behaviors from an individual on your team. Think about the positive and negative consequences associated with these behaviors and make a table like the one listed in Question #60 where you list all the aspects of the consequences (positive/negative, personal/general, immediate/future, certain/uncertain). How could you change either the positive or negative consequences to make them more effective in shaping the desired behavior?

2. With a partner, set up role-play examples of common coaching scenarios from your call center. Demonstrate common mistakes made in coaching a frontline agent and then demonstrate the proper techniques to be used. Audio tape or video tape the "dos and don'ts" demonstration to serve as models for new supervisors to review.

3. Review the Coaching Characteristics Scorecard provided in this chapter. Fill out this scorecard, rating yourself in each area and determining a total score. Circle the three characteristics that need the most improvement and create an individual plan of action to work on these areas. (As an option, ask several of your employees to anonymously provide feedback in each of these areas and compare to your self-scoring.)

4. Select some of your better performers and form a peer mentoring group. Assign each one of these employees to a new employee and set aside time each week in their schedule to spend with their new protégés. Track the performance of these new employees with the ones that were not assigned a specific mentor. Note the performance of both groups after 3 weeks and 6 weeks, and discuss with your team what was positive and negative about the mentoring program.

Chapter 10 – Motivating for Performance

Creating a motivating environment is one of your most important jobs as a supervisor. You need to motivate each employee to perform to the best of his ability for the sake of customer service and the bottom line. Employees that are happy in their jobs will have higher levels of performance, both in terms of quality and efficiency, resulting in higher levels of customer satisfaction and retention.

Motivating employees is vitally important, but not necessarily very easy to do. Everyone is motivated by something different and it's your job as an immediate supervisor of an employee to find out what those motivating factors are for every single team member.

Motivating employees does not have to involve a huge budget for monetary rewards and prizes. Much of what the supervisor can do to motivate staff involves simply building relationships with employees, recognizing their work and accomplishments, and providing ongoing guidance and support.

Given the difficult nature of the work and the need to keep satisfaction levels high, most call centers use various promotional programs, competitions, and games to keep employees motivated to perform to their maximum potential.

This chapter will outline the various ways to motivate call center employees, providing examples of many programs that have been used successfully by call centers.

65. ***What are the different types of motivational techniques?***
66. ***What are ways you can provide guidance and support?***
67. ***What are ways to effectively recognize good performance?***
68. ***What are the most effective rewards for good performance?***
69. ***Should you use monetary rewards?***
70. ***How should rewards be matched to employee values?***
71. ***How can you develop teamwork and unity?***
72. ***What role do fun and games play in motivating staff?***

65. What are the different types of motivational techniques?

Selecting the right motivational technique requires a basic understanding of motivational theory. Psychologist Abraham Maslow described a hierarchy of motivational needs that is the basis of most motivational theory in the workplace. In this hierarchy, Maslow outlines five levels of human needs, as illustrated below:

Maslow's Hierarchy

Each level of the hierarchy represents a different human need. Starting from the bottom, each level of need must be satisfied before the next level up matters to the person. Level 1 needs are the most basic ones – food, water, and shelter. People won't care about much else if these needs are not met. Level 2 needs relate to safety and security. In the workplace, this need can refer to financial security. If basic compensation needs are not met, addressing higher level needs is irrelevant. The basic financial security and personal security needs must be met before any of the higher needs matter.

Levels 3 and 4 of the hierarchy are the levels that most workplace motivational programs address. The social needs of an individual are addressed through team activities, games, and competitions that provide a way for employees to interact with one another. Self-esteem needs are met through recognition and reward programs, both at a team and individual level. The top level need is individual self-actualization which addresses intellectual and spiritual needs.

Some of the ways to create a motivating environment in order to foster these social and self-esteem needs are:

- Guidance and support
- Recognition
- Rewards
- Team-Building

66. What are ways you can provide guidance and support?

One of the most important ways of creating a motivating environment is to simply offer continual guidance and support to your employees. No special skills or tools are actually required to do this. Listening to your employees and providing coaching and feedback on a regular, consistent basis is an important factor contributing to motivation.

> Listening and providing feedback are important steps in motivation.

As a supervisor, you need to show you care about your team members and their personal and professional growth. While you may think that being results-oriented or customer-focused is your most important attribute, you may need to re-focus in your role as a supervisor, since having an employee-focus is your main objective. Your employees are the ones that must concentrate on customer excellence, and your role is to support and guide them in that role since they're the ones dealing directly with the customer, not you.

Communication is critical in shaping your employees' performance and building a relationship with them. If your team members feel heard, understood, and valued by you, they will work harder and produce better results. The key ingredient to this communication is effective listening. This may sound easy enough, but most supervisors do more talking than listening, and could use some "brushing up" on their listening skills.

> If your team members feel heard, understood, and valued, they will work harder and produce better results.

You may have good listening skills, but you may be selective in how and when you use them. If you're like most supervisors and managers, you have a lot on your plate, and multi-tasking is a necessity. However, you should be careful that this multi-tasking doesn't happen during your one-on-one time with an employee. When you tune out, you miss out on having a respectful interaction and relationship with that person.

There are several common listening mistakes. Review the characteristics of each of the following types of bad listeners and see if any apply to you.

The Interrupter. This person finishes other people's sentences or breaks in to share thoughts before the other person is finished. If you constantly do this, your employees will lose patience with you and will quit coming to you with their ideas and problems.

The Defender. Defensive listeners also interrupt. You may be defending your opinion or your standing on a certain topic. Don't always feel the need to defend your way of thinking or it may prevent you from hearing the ideas and thoughts of others.

The Transmitter. These people spend much more time talking than listening. Do you know what percentage of the conversation you generally spend talking rather than listening? A wise person once said we were given two ears but only one mouth for a reason – that we should spend twice as much time listening as talking.

There are many different listening techniques you can use to more actively listen to your employees. One proven strategy is to use the "blinking word" technique. In this technique, you listen for key words in the sentences the other person is using and repeat that word back in your next statement or question, as shown in the example below:

To be an effective communicator, spend more time listening than talking.

Agent: We're getting lots of questions about the new assembly instructions.
Coach: ***What kinds are questions are you getting?***
Agent: One of the steps left out some information and we have to walk customers through it.
Coach: ***Tell me about the missing information. What steps do you need to explain?***

Use open-ended questions as you follow the blinking words from sentence to sentence. Use questions that begin with "how," "why," or "tell me about" to delve deeper into a situation and to show that you are fully tuned into what your employee is saying. You cannot tune out and still follow the blinking word so it forces you to actively listen.

Practice using various listening techniques with your staff. You'll want to listen for the following kinds of information:

New ideas. Your team members will have great ideas for improving service and efficiency, and they want to be heard and recognized.

Motivations. Talk to your team members regularly to find out how they're doing on the job and what they need from you to excel.

Challenges. You need to be communicating with your employees every single day to better understand the obstacles and challenges they face on the phones.

Think about the last time you sat and just listened with each of your employees. Make a list of several things you have learned from or about each of your employees in the past couple of weeks. If you can't name at least one item for each employee, you're either not spending enough time with them, or you are not listening attentively.

Your employees don't always expect a solution – just someone to listen.

Don't be afraid to listen for fear that you might not have an answer to some of their problems and concerns. Your employees don't expect you to have an answer or solution every time. Sometimes they just need to talk and have someone listen and provide some words of encouragement. A quote by William Arthur sums up this idea nicely:

Flatter me and I may not believe you.
Criticize me and I may not like you.
Ignore me and I may not forgive you.
Encourage me and I will never forget you.

67. What are ways to effectively recognize good performance?

Recognition is one of the most effective ways to motivate staff. One-on-one feedback from you serves to both build the relationship with the employee, as well as to reinforce behaviors that you want to see repeated, as discussed in Chapter 9. You'll want to take time each day to recognize your employees' efforts and successes. Provide recognition for improvements along the way, for initiatives, as well as achievement of the desired end results.

Recognition reinforces desirable behaviors and also helps build a personal relationship with an employee.

The following are some of the basic rules of recognition that you should follow:

1. Recognize desired behavior so it will be repeated. Chapter 9 discussed the important relationship between behaviors and consequences. Reinforced behavior is repeated behavior, so make sure you recognize the actions you want to see happen again.
2. Recognize improvements along the way. The ultimate desired goal some times seems out of reach for some employees. Be sure to recognize progress towards a goal, as well as the ultimate achievement of it.
3. Recognize initiative as well as results. This is related to the item above. Sometimes an employee is making every effort to display the right behaviors, but isn't succeeding in reaching the goal. Sometimes it's important to simply recognize the effort that's being made so they'll keep trying.

Recognize progress towards a goal as well as the achievement of it.

4. Recognize on the spot. Chapter 9 discussed the importance of a consequence not just being positive, but also being immediate. The closer the reward to the action, the stronger the reinforcer it will be.
5. Recognize verbally. Don't just send a memo or an email related to desired behavior. Make an effort to personally deliver the news and spend a few minutes talking with your employee. They'll cherish the recognition and the time spent.
6. Recognize in writing. Most people have a folder tucked away in their desks with memos or letters of praise from bosses or customers. Take time to write a note of appreciation that is a permanent record of their success.

Recognize both verbally and in writing.

7. Recognize privately. Another objective of recognition is that it builds the one-on-one relationship between you and the employee. Spend some time where just the two of you discuss recent actions and achievements.
8. Recognize publicly. The biggest reward for some people is to be the center of attention. Recognize good performance in front of others as well as privately, assuming that the employee is the kind of person that doesn't mind all the fuss.

Recognize both publicly and one-on-one.

Think about all the types of behaviors you'd like to see repeated from your team members. Some of these may be the quantitative performance expectations such as call handle time, sales results, or availability. Others may be quality scores or demonstration of new skills and knowledge. In addition, think of the other things that make the team more effective, such as volunteering for overtime, making a time-saving suggestion, or going beyond the call of duty for a customer or another team member. These may not be listed in a formal recognition policy, but are valuable actions that you want to see continue. Be on the lookout for all types of positive behaviors and reward them quickly and frequently.

Be on the lookout for all sorts of positive behaviors and reward them immediately and frequently.

Recognition and signs of appreciation are vitally important in motivation, yet many supervisors and managers don't take time to recognize the efforts of their employees on a regular basis. The table below lists some common excuses and the implication of those thoughts.

Supervisor Excuse	Implication
I don't have time.	If you don't take time to do it, you'll end up spending more time in dealing with problems.
Employees don't care about it much.	Employees crave praise and recognition more than anything else, even money.
It's enough to pay them to do the job.	Employees may only do enough to just get by unless they are recognized and rewarded.
It's meaningless if done too much.	It's impossible to recognize too much. There's almost never enough recognition.
People will become complacent.	Instead of slowing down, most people will work harder if they're recognized.
I'm limited in what I can do.	Recognition doesn't require a budget. It's time and attention that are the best reinforcers.
I don't get any...why should I give it?	Maybe your immediate boss needs to review these rules, too.
It's not my job.	It's the supervisor's job to recognize a job well done – nobody else's.

To determine whether or not you're doing recognition often enough, make a list of all the people who work with or for you. Note the last time you gave recognition for a job well done to each person on the list. If you can't remember the last time you recognized or praised someone on your list, you are probably not doing it enough.

Think about recognition this way, as a quote from management consultant Rosabeth Moss Kanter suggests: "Compensation is a right, but recognition is a gift." Give your employees a regular gift of recognition and appreciation and watch quality, performance, and satisfaction improve.

68. What are effective rewards for good performance?

It is important not just to recognize desirable performance, but to reward it in some way so that it will be repeated. Designing and administering an effective reward program is critical to your call center employees' ongoing performance improvement.

Rewards or reinforcers fall into two categories. The first category includes natural reinforcers. These are the consequences that happen naturally after a behavior occurs. Thanks from customers or the internal satisfaction of solving a problem may be enough of a reward to support certain behaviors with some staff. However, if you really want to see desirable performance continue, you probably need to go beyond the natural reinforcers.

Rewards are made up of social reinforcers and tangible reinforcers.

The other category of reward is "created" reinforcement and it is made up of social reinforcers and tangible reinforcers. Social reinforcement is the simple act of noticing and remarking on performance. Simple words of appreciation are samples of social reinforcers. The other reinforcers are tangible items that are given to the employee as a reward for desired behavior.

A tangible reward should be unique and relevant to each employee, so that it is viewed as a positive consequence, rather than neutral or negative. You will want to ask each employee what would be viewed as a positive, neutral, or negative consequence. Don't assume that just because you and most employees view an item as valuable that everyone will like it. An example might be tickets to a professional football game. While many people would work hard towards earning this as a reward and relish the experience of attending a game, others might not see the reward as valuable at all.

To be effective, a reward must be viewed as valuable by the person receiving it.

The table below lists some common items used as rewards for performance in a call center. Using these items as a starting point, create a list of possible rewards for your employees.

Movie passes	Catalog certificate	Restaurant certificate
Personal services	Theatre tickets	Sporting event tickets
Hotel stay	Weekend trip	Limo ride
CDs or DVDs	Catalog credits	Flowers or balloons
Lottery tickets	Mall gift certificate	Charity contribution

Create a list of desirable and non-desirable rewards for each employee.

Review the list with all your employees and have each person note which rewards would be most and least desirable.

It is common for call center managers and supervisors to use lack of budget as an excuse for having few rewards. However, there are many rewards that can be created that cost little to nothing at all. The table on the next page lists some of these possibilities.

Best parking space	Time off the phones	Featured newsletter "spot"
Pick of schedule	Participation on committee	Job trade for the day
Off-site project	A day off	Praise in front of the team
Working on exciting project	A thank you in writing	Posted praise letter

Some of these rewards that don't cost anything may actually be much better motivators than the prizes or gifts that you buy.

Some of the most effective rewards are those that cost little to nothing.

When defining the most effective reward, careful consideration should be given to the "trophy value" of the reward. The effect of the reward will have more lasting value if there is visible evidence of it in the workplace, either on the wall, on the employee's desk, or in writing somewhere.

Items with trophy value could be an actual trophy or plaque of some kind that either belongs to the employee forever, or it could be one that travels from place to place on a regular basis, as different employees earn the rights to it. The trophy could be earned and belong to an employee or to a team.

A few examples of rewards with trophy value are outlined below.

1. One call center uses the "Best Seat in the House" award to its performer of the week. The reward is a big soft leather chair. Not only is it more comfortable for the employee that gets to sit in it for the week, but it is has visible trophy value.

Consider the visible trophy value of a reward to maximize its long-term benefits.

2. An award that started small in one call center has taken on a life of its own. Teams compete for the "Quality Cup" in one center based on a combination of average quality and productivity scores. The actual trophy began as a 1950s bowling trophy confiscated from someone's attic, and it gets a new component added each month as the last winning team adds its own special mark to the trophy.
3. Agents in another center can earn snap-on beads that can be put on headset cords. It's a visible sign of excellences and fun for the agents to trade. Once an agent has accumulated a certain number of beads, they can be traded in for a gift certificate or day off with pay.

Many call center rewards center around earning "chances" in a drawing. This is an effective reward since it allows all to participate and have an opportunity to win, but gives better performers more chances in the drawing. The tickets earned can be redeemed at a casino party, a country fair with games, or for catalog shopping, just to name a few.

69. Should you use monetary rewards?

There are clear advantages and disadvantages of giving cash or some other kind of monetary reward to recognize performance.

On the one hand, cold hard cash has the advantage of being easy to administer and simple to handle. Cash is understood by everyone and each employee understands its value. Everyone likes it, and it can certainly provide an extra boost to a long-term program.

However, even if you have the budget for it, monetary rewards are not always the best idea. One of the main drawbacks to using cash is that there is no lasting value or trophy value of the award. It is often spent with nothing to show for it afterwards as a remembrance of the good performance.

It is also not really considered to be a very exciting award. Unlike a catalog of prizes or a weekend trip that the staff might work towards with pictures and images posted to remind them of the reward to be gained, cash doesn't lend itself to being advertised as well.

Cash can also be confused with regular compensation, and may not be recognized as the "extra" that it is for excellent performance. It may be more difficult for the employee to make the link between excellent performance and the award, if it's just extra cash that gets paid as part of a paycheck.

A non-monetary reward might be something that the employee might not otherwise have – a guilt-free pleasure. On the other hand, employees may feel guilty about splurging on a non-essential item and use it for a necessity, removing the excitement from the reward.

The other drawback to cash rewards is that they tend to become expected and not appreciated. If employees continually receive a cash reward, they become accustomed to it being part of their income and may become upset if it goes away since their spending may have adjusted to the extra amount over time.

These advantages and disadvantages are summarized in the table below.

Non-Cash Reward	Cash Reward
Tangible symbol of achievement	Intangible – disappears into wallet
Something physical to show off	Difficult to show off to friends and family
Socially acceptable to brag about	Not fashionable to brag about
Lasting reminder of achievement	Short recall what was purchased with cash
Reinforced association with the call center	Minimal association with call center
Appeal to recipient's need for psychic income (social acceptance, increased self- esteem, self-realization)	Used to satisfy basic needs (car payments, groceries, etc.)
Provide guilt-free enjoyment of reward	Guilty feeling for not spending award on necessities
Provide strong emotional appeal to participants' personal wants and interests	No "warm fuzzies" attached to cold currency
Higher perceived value than actual dollar value	A dollar is a dollar; participant attaches no greater emotional value to cash

70. How should rewards be matched to employee values?

As you define an appropriate reward or working environment that will best suit and motivate various individuals, think about the kind of personalities they have and what rewards and work situation would be the best match for that those personalities. In their book, *Love 'Em or Lose 'Em*, consultants Beverly Kaye and Sharon Jordan-Evans suggest using a values questionnaire to match a working environment with individual employee values. An excerpt of this questionnaire and its implications for defining rewards is shown below.

Employee Values Questionnaire

1. When you go to work, what do you look forward to the most? a. Having new challenges b. Enjoying being with co-workers c. Planning my own day d. A relaxed, routine day	2. You work best when: a. Your curiosity is high b. You're working with a team c. You're working primarily alone d. There are no deadlines
3. When you have a new project to work on, you're excited if: a. You will learn new things b. You will work with new people c. You will be in control d. It will be easy and low stress	4. If you won the lottery, what might keep you from quitting your job? a. The excitement of competition b. Missing friends at work c. Having challenging work goals d. Having too much extra time
5. In your ideal job, you would: a. Have opportunities to be creative b. Help society c. Start your own business d. Only work a few hours each day	6. Looking back, you felt most satisfied with work when: a. You had many exciting projects b. You were helping others c. You worked totally independently d. You never had to take work home

Have each employee answer these specific questions or design some of your own. Tabulate their responses to determine if there is a pattern to their answers.

People with mostly "A" answers are goal-oriented. You should find opportunities for them to work on stimulating projects with a sense of accomplishment. Employees with mostly "B" answers are people-oriented. For these employees, you should look for ways to increase their interpersonal contacts at work, perhaps through participation on task forces and project teams. People with mostly "C" answers are self-starters. Find situations that reward self-motivation with as much freedom and independence as possible and try not to micromanage these people. Finally, those employees with "D" answers are those that seek balance and an orderly work routine. Try not to vary their routine and give them plenty of attention and reassurance during change.

71. How can you develop teamwork and unity?

Another strategy for creating a motivating environment is to instill a sense of belonging in each employee. The more your employee feels a part of a team, a department, or an organization, the more motivated that person will feel to come to work every day and give the maximum effort.

The more employees feel a part of a team, the more motivated they are to attend and perform.

The best way to create a sense of belonging is to use teams. In addition to the many productivity benefits of a team structure that were discussed in Chapter 5, there are many motivational benefits of teams. Friendships develop more easily in a team environment and people are more likely to look forward to coming to work each day if they feel a part of a group.

There are many ways to foster teamwork in the call center. The work lends itself to a team structure where team members have the same type of skills and must all contribute to handling the workload. All the team members face the same types of challenges and difficult calls and sharing these experiences can help form a bond among team members.

People are more likely to want to come to work each day if they feel an important part of a group.

Many call centers choose to set up competitions between teams related to the call center work. Team members may work together to be the first to reach an aggregate productivity goal for example. If designed well, these competitions can be effective at building the team. Competition can bring team members together for a common goal, provide a sense of belonging, and create a spirit of cooperation. However, if the competition is not carefully designed, it can reinforce the "end justifies the means" thinking, limit learning and sharing between teams, and can shift the focus away from performance to "winning."

Competition can bring team members together for a common goal and create a sense of belonging and cooperation.

Another way to develop team cohesiveness simply involves organizing events or activities where team members can interact and get to know one another. Birthday celebrations, pot-luck meals, and activities outside the call center such as softball games, bowling parties, or movie outings are ways for employees to get to know one another in a relaxed atmosphere and build relationships beyond the workplace.

Activities that allow team members to work together toward a worthwhile goal are effective ways to build team unity. Preparing food baskets for the needy, supporting local school programs, or volunteering together for a local charity are all ways to bring people together in a positive way.

Look for ways for employees to get to know one another in a relaxed atmosphere outside of the workplace.

72. What role do fun and games play in motivating staff?

Let's face it – taking calls all day long can be a monotonous job. You'll want to look for ways to add a little fun to the work environment to keep everyone happy and motivated to stay on the phones. All work and no play can make the call center a very dull and unmotivating place. Research shows that a fun-filled workplace generates enthusiasm – and enthusiasm leads to increased productivity, better customer service, a positive attitude about the company, and much higher odds that your employees will stay with you over the long haul.

Can you remember the last time your team members had fun? If you can't, you may not be having enough fun. Unfortunately, there are many workplaces that are fun-free zones. In one study, employees graded their supervisors on the degree to which they supported or allowed fun at work. The average grade was a measly C-. Some of these supervisors were perhaps just not raised to have fun, with their previous (or current) bosses being serious taskmasters. Others think that having fun at work will cause a loss of control or failure to achieve results. Some may view moments of levity as bad precedents and fear the team can't get back to business.

People can have fun in the workplace and still maintain a professional work environment.

It's a fact that you can have fun in the workplace and still maintain a professional work environment. Most concerns have to do with inappropriate humor, loud behavior, or poor timing. But fun doesn't have to be laugh out loud funny, embarrassing, or disruptive. It also doesn't have to cost much money.

It's good to laugh in the workplace. Laughter has been referred to as "internal jogging" since it has the same positive benefits as an aerobic run. It releases endorphins, the healing element of the body. You can't laugh without a smile on your face, and it's a proven fact that you will sound much friendlier on the phone with a smile. Therefore, laughter isn't only just good for you – it's good for your customers too!

Laughter has been referred to as "internal jogging" since it has the same positive benefits as an aerobic run.

Research shows that fun-loving environments are actually more productive than their humorless counterparts. A fun break can reenergize your employees and get them ready for the next concentrated stretch of work. In one software company's support center, employees are encouraged to surf the Web or play games in between calls, with the thought that they will return to the next call fresher and sharper. You might think that your employees couldn't be trusted to that degree, but the key is to be crystal clear with your employees what the performance goals are, and let them have fun as long as the goals are met.

There are many ways you can foster a fun environment and you don't have to think up all the ideas on your own. Get your team members involved in defining ways to make your workplace more fun and a more inviting and motivational place to work.

Learning Activities

1. Make a list and note what you have specifically done in the last month to show that you care about your team members and the work that they do. This list should not include any reward and recognition systems that are done by the call center as a whole. Instead, focus on ways you have provided guidance and support to your individual team members. Create a plan for the coming month outlining specific dates, activities, and programs you will use to increase the support you provide.

2. Invite your team members to list the behaviors of their worst (unnamed)bosses. Have them describe what past supervisors and managers did (or didn't do) to demotivate them. Keep a written list of these behaviors and grade yourself each month, noting what you can do to minimize or eliminate these behaviors in the future. Encourage your team members to tactfully let you know when you're exhibiting "bad boss" behavior.

3. Assign frontline staff to a team and have each team develop a list of motivational programs for a coming month in your call center. Provide prizes for the team with the most ideas and a prize to the individual with the best implementable idea (as voted on by all the teams). Form a team to plan and implement the new idea in the center. Encourage them to structure the program to minimize cost and maximize the number of rewards.

4. Working with members of your team, develop a list of twenty no-cost items that would serve as recognition and reward items for good performance. Have each person on your team select the top five items they would most like to receive. Keep a file of these for each employee and make it a point to deliver at least one of these rewards each week, looking for opportunities for positive reinforcement.

Chapter 11 – Retention Strategies

One of the biggest problems that call centers face today is staff turnover. Finding and then retaining qualified staff has a huge impact on the bottom line as well as to quality of service.

It is important to quantify staff turnover, in terms of both the turnover rate and its cost. Turnover rate should be calculated for both voluntary and involuntary turnover. It should also be looked at to compare the numbers of staff leaving the company entirely versus going to another department in the company. You will also want to calculate the turnover rate by type of call, by skill, and by team so that the center can identify the main reasons that staff are leaving and address those issues promptly.

Quantifying turnover also means calculating what it is costing the call center and the organization in terms of dollars. The obvious hard costs of turnover include recruiting, hiring, and training costs. However, in addition to these costs, there are many other indirect costs that should be considered that can make the total cost of turnover unacceptably high.

Your call center management team will want to identify all the reasons that people are leaving the center. Some of these issues may be related to job fit or compensation issues, but many of the reasons are due to factors that are under your direct control as a supervisor.

This chapter will discuss the importance of the supervisor in staff retention and outline many of the strategies you can employ to retain your best people.

73. How is staff turnover rate calculated?
74. What does staff turnover cost the organization?
75. What are the main reasons that staff leave or stay?
76. What is your role in supporting staff retention?
77. What can you do to better understand staff needs?
78. How can you create passion for the job?
79. What can you do to enrich the job?
80. What growth and career opportunities can you provide?
81. What can you do to support a life/work balance?

73. How is staff turnover rate calculated?

Turnover is at an all-time high in today's workplace, and some of the overall turnover statistics have significant implications in the call center. According to the United States Bureau of Labor Statistics, workers aged 20-24 stay with an organization only 1.1 years on average (compared to 1.5 years just 15 years ago), and workers aged 25 to 34 stay 2.7 years (compared to over 3 years in the 1980s). Compared to these longevity numbers, call center workers who generally fall into this age group (ages 20-34) stay only about one year, according to callcenter-jobs.com.

Research studies by callcenterjobs.com indicate that the rate of turnover varies by area of the country, employment factors in a specific region or city, and by industry. There is a much higher turnover rate in routine, order-taking positions or in outbound telemarketing where burnout is high. Turnover is lower in more specialized, higher level jobs and also lower in union environments. Overall averages for the call center industry as a whole range between 30-45%, with some centers having almost no turnover, and other centers having turnover in the triple digits.

Turnover rate varies by regional employment factors, the type of industry, and the level of the position.

The turnover rate for a call center should be calculated and tracked on a regular basis for trending purposes and business case justification for programs to assist with retention. In calculating this turnover rate, most organizations use an annualized rate to describe the proportion of staff that leaves. The formula for turnover is the number of staff that leave divided by the average number of staff. For the numbers in the table below, the turnover rate would be 54 divided by the average number of staff positions (81.5) for an annual turnover rate of 66 percent.

Month	Departing Staff	Avg Number of Staff
1	4	75
2	2	78
3	3	80
4	6	80
5	5	82
6	5	84
7	4	85
8	5	85
9	6	85
10	4	82
11	5	82
12	5	80
Total	54	81.5

The turnover rate should be reviewed to analyze internal (employees leaving for other positions within the company) versus external (employees leaving the organization) turnover. Both are costly to the call center organization, but obviously some benefit exists to the organization if qualified people are leaving to fill other roles within the company.

Calculate the rate at which people leave the company entirely compared to moving to a different position within the company.

Turnover should also be analyzed to understand the proportion of agents who make the decision to leave the company compared to those that are being terminated. If your company has to terminate significant numbers of employees due to poor performance, there may be a problem at the recruiting and hiring phase. The company may be hiring too quickly in order just to fill seats and may not be screening carefully enough for necessary knowledge and skills or evaluating the personality match with the work environment.

Exit interviews should examine those reasons that are unavoidable, such as someone returning to school full-time or relocating for a spouse's job. These exit interviews can shed light on what reasons are unavoidable and what reasons could have been addressed by the call center.

This turnover rate should be calculated for the center, but should also be calculated for smaller defined groups. For example, turnover should be examined by call type, by location, and by team. In particular, calculating turnover rate by team may help pinpoint problems where employees are leaving due to supervisory issues and not because of compensation, job fit, or other factors.

Calculating turnover rate by team may help point out reasons that are supervisory issues and not overall call center problems.

You should also review the turnover statistics to see if there is any correlation with the skill or type of calls being handled. Calculation by call type in one organization revealed nearly double the turnover rate for one particular type of call versus any other one due to its difficulty and higher stress levels. When that center was able to allocate more resources to that call handling group and alter performance expectations slightly to make it a less stressful environment, retention improved significantly.

It should be noted that while turnover almost always has a negative effect on the call center, there are some positive aspects. If you are losing personnel that were not performing well, the opportunity to hire replacements can be a positive experience. Bringing in new personnel provides an opportunity to gain new ideas and to obtain some fresh perspectives.

If poor performers are the ones leaving, turnover can actually be a positive experience.

74. What does staff turnover cost your organization?

There are many costs associated with call center staff turnover. Some of these are direct, measurable costs to your organization, while others are indirect costs that may not be so obvious.

Some of the direct costs associated with turnover include the following:

Recruiting Costs. Track the cost of classified advertising, either in traditional newspaper listings, or in magazines and online postings. Your center may do radio or television advertising, or promotions at local events. You should also consider the costs of job fair participation or any other event used to attract candidates.

Hiring Costs. Consider the cost of screening and interviewing all the potential candidates. You should include time for your human resources department to process applications and screen employees, as well as the time for various call center staff to interview candidates.

Training Costs. Calculate the total cost of training, which should include the cost of the facilities, trainer time, and student training materials. These costs should be considered for orientation and initial training, as well as ongoing training.

Supervision Costs. Consider how much additional time each new employee takes in terms of additional supervisory time. This time may be spent to assist new staff in their early learning stages and is time the supervisor will be unavailable to do other things.

Unproductive Paid Time. Include the cost of the new employee's wages during the time they are in training and not yet available to process calls. This time may extend into their early time on the job when they are not fully productive in handling customer contacts.

Overtime Costs. Consider the cost of paying overtime to existing staff to cover call workload for missing staff. Either the work is simply not handled, or you must pay others to cover it, and this generally equates to overtime charges which can be very expensive.

When calculating the cost of turnover, consider the costs of recruiting, hiring, training, additional supervision, unproductive paid time, and overtime costs.

Another hard cost of turnover can be the revenues lost if not enough people are in place to handle the call workload. Let's assume that delay times are longer while you have a staff shortage and as a result of that, more callers are abandoning their calls. If you are a revenue-generating call center, such as a catalog or reservations center, then there is lost revenue associated with those lost calls.

If your center receives 3,000 calls a day and an additional 5% of those calls abandon due to the long delays caused by understaffing, that results in 150 lost calls.

If those calls are worth an average of $100 per call, that's $15,000 of lost revenue per day – a true "cost" to your company of not having enough staff on the phones.

Consider the following example of a customer service center with 100 employees whose turnover rate is 20%. The average wage rate in this center is $12 per hour. Each person handles an average of 12 calls per hour (x 6 available hours = 72 calls per day). It takes approximately 2 weeks to fill the position, 3 more weeks to train new staff. In order not to lose any revenue opportunities, this call center has asked existing staff to work overtime to fill in the staffing gaps, and that overtime rate is reflected below as 1.5 times the regular wage rate.

The costs of turnover for this organization to replace those 20 people are as follows:

Sample Turnover Costs	
Recruiting cost = Campaign to hire 20 employees = $5,000	$ 5,000
Hiring cost = (40 HR hours (2 per candidate) @ $20/hour)	$ 800
Hiring cost = (60 call center hours (3 per candidate) @ $20/hour	$ 1,200
Training cost = (5 sessions x 80 hrs @ $20 trainer cost)	$ 8,000
Training cost = (Materials/expenses @ $500 per person)	$10,000
Unproductive training time = (3 weeks salary x 20)	$28,800
Supervisory time = (10 add'l hours per person @ $15/hour) =	$ 3,000
Overtime costs = (25 days x 8 hours x 20 people @ $12 x 1.5 rate) =	$72,000
Total Cost of Turnover =	**$128,800**
Per Person Turnover Cost =	**$ 6,440**

This 20% turnover rate results in a cost to the organization of over $128,000 to replace these 20 people, or $6,440 per employee. These costs could go higher still if you were to consider the potential loss of revenue and damaged revenue due to poor service.

The hard costs of turnover are extremely high, and go much higher when you factor in the cost of dissatisfied customers, lost business, decreased productivity, and low morale.

In addition to the "hard costs" outlined above, you should also consider the harder to measure, but just as important costs of customer dissatisfaction, damaged reputation, lost skills and knowledge, and low morale. When these costs are factored in too, the costs simply skyrocket.

It is important that your call center be able to quantify all these hard-dollar and soft-dollar costs in order to accurately calculate the true total cost of turnover to the organization. The resulting numbers can be used to justify retention programs that will likely pay for themselves many times if they reduce turnover even a small amount.

75. What are the main reasons that staff leave or stay?

There are many reasons why turnover is so high in the call center industry. Some of these reasons are under your control and are "fixable," while some must be chalked up as simply costs of doing business. One of the responsibilities of the managers and supervisors in the call center is to consistently assess the reasons why people leave the center. Perhaps more importantly, it's also critical to talk to the happy staff and find out what is keeping them there.

Some of the reasons that employees leave fall into a category that may not be under your direct control as a supervisor. These reasons are compensation, job fit, and career path.

Identify all the reasons that people leave, as well as why they stay.

- ***Compensation.*** Inadequate compensation is a reason often cited in agents' exit interviews. This will be a common factor for call centers located in highly saturated call center labor markets such as Phoenix or Dallas where competition for qualified call center staff is high. Your call center should do periodic compensation benchmarking studies to ensure your wages are commensurate with the wages of nearby centers for the same type of work, particularly in highly competitive areas. It is also important to weigh the cost of turnover (as outlined in the last section) against the cost of increased wages. If raising wages would increase retention significantly, then the turnover costs that are saved can go a long way to pay the additional compensation.
- ***Job Fit.*** Many times the reason an individual leaves the center is simply due to a poor job fit. This type of turnover can be reduced significantly by better defining the job, widening the advertising process to attract a bigger field of candidates, and working harder at screening and hiring for a proper job fit. More effort during the selection phase will pay for itself many times over in improving retention. The key element for change here is taking time to assess motivational fit and ensure that the candidate will be happy with the unique working conditions found in most call centers: solo work, confined space, repetitive tasks, constant monitoring, and inflexible work schedules.
- ***Limited Job/Career Opportunities.*** Many individuals leave the call center due to limited possibilities for career growth or opportunities for advancement. While some organizations have multi-level job ladders with numerous levels of agent positions and multiple career paths to many areas, others are severely limited in growth potential and see turnover as a result. In a survey conducted by callcentercareers.com, 27% of people that had left one call center job and were looking for another cited lack of promotional opportunities as their primary reason to leave. Redefining job levels and looking for career advancement opportunities within the call center should be evaluated often.

All these factors contribute to turnover and should be examined by the call center management team and perhaps senior management to address needed changes and strategy. Some of the other reasons that employees leave may fall under your realm of control as an immediate supervisor.

Assuming that compensation meets local standards and that you have done a thorough job in your recruiting and hiring so that these two are not a factor, it's time to look elsewhere to fix the problem. Most of the other reasons that employees leave the call center are directly under the supervisor's control.

After compensation and job fit have been addressed, most of the other reasons for turnover are attributable to supervisory issues.

For the most part, the adage "people don't leave companies; they leave leaders" is certainly true in the call center environment. In the majority of cases, the supervisor can be either the greatest contributor to staff retention or the primary cause of turnover.

In a survey by callcentercareers.com, staff exiting call centers and looking for positions in other call centers cited the following reasons they had left their most recent job. These reasons included:

- 20% felt they were not recognized for their work.
- 18% felt bored and unchallenged by the job.
- 11% felt they did not receive enough training.

All of these items are ones that are directly under your control as a supervisor.

A supervisor is the biggest contributor to whether an employee leaves or stays with the organization.

There are many different factors that affect why staff will leave or stay with a job. According to a study on staff retention done by The Call Center School, the reasons that people give for staying with the job are a little different than leaving, as shown in the table below.

Reasons They Leave	Reasons They Stay
Job fit	Job fit
Compensation	Pride in work
Lack of career path	Training and development opportunities
Stressful work environment	Empowerment
Lack of recognition	Reward system

It's interesting to note that job fit is the top reason listed both in terms of why people leave as well as why they stay. Either they're a fit or they're not, and getting people matched to the right job in the first place is one of the top things you can do to improve long-term retention. While compensation is an issue for people that leave a place, it is generally not mentioned in the top reasons of why people stay. If people truly enjoy what they are doing and find other advantages in the job, compensation is less of a factor.

Job fit is the most critical factor for predicting whether an employee will leave or stay with the job.

Keep in mind there is much the supervisor can do to address many of the reasons that employees leave or stay. The next few topics in this chapter discuss some of these strategies.

76. What is your role in supporting staff retention?

When it comes to retaining staff, it's the supervisor that matters most. You have more power than anyone else in the company to keep your good employees. Many of the important factors that drive employee satisfaction and commitment are more in your control than you might think.

When it comes to retaining staff, it's the supervisor that matters most.

There are many different studies on employee retention that support the supervisor's role in retention. Here are just a few that show a supervisor's relationship with employees is key to satisfaction and retention:

- An emerging workplace study by the Saratoga Institute in the late 1990s was made up of over 20,000 interviews with workers who had just resigned from a job. The main reason cited for leaving their last employer from most of these workers was supervisor behavior.
- Another 25-year long poll by the Gallup Organization based on interviews with over 12 million workers at 7,000 different companies also found that the relationship with their manager was a major factor in most employees' length of stay with the company.
- Research by the Corporate Leadership Council found that a quality manager was of more importance than any other factor in attracting and retaining key talent.

Although senior management, organizational policies, and culture play a role in how an employee feels about the job, it is clear that most of an employee's work satisfaction is determined by the relationship an employee has with his or her immediate boss.

Talented employees should be viewed as valuable assets that you are responsible for keeping.

Think about a $50,000 company car you've been given to drive. You would take excellent care of this company asset, wouldn't you? You would probably be held accountable if something happened to the car or if it were damaged due to your neglect.

Likewise, you should be held accountable for taking good care of your employees. Talented people in your company should be viewed as valuable assets. It's your workforce that gives you and your organization a competitive advantage and you'll want to hold on to your best people. Supervisors in many organizations are being held increasingly accountable for retention of their good employees.

Good supervisors help employees find what they need and want from the workplace.

A good supervisor who cares about keeping good employees will simply help them find what they want from the workplace. For some people, that will mean guidance and support and a sympathetic ear. Some will be seeking new and exciting challenges each day, while others will yearn for recognition for achieving clearly defined performance goals. Therefore, a good retention strategy will be driven by an individual's direct supervisor, not the people in the human resources department.

77. What can you do to better understand staff needs?

If you're trying to reduce turnover, it's important to figure out why your employees are leaving. There are many ways this is done in the workplace – exit interviews, human resource consultants, focus groups, and benchmarking surveys. However, the best way to find out is often overlooked – simply asking them what would make them stay and what would drive them away.

> Simply ask employees what would make them stay and what would drive them away.

Supervisors may not have asked their employees what would make them leave for fear of putting ideas in people's heads (as if they'd never think of this on their own) or fear that the discussion would put false hope in the employees' minds that all they ask for will come true. Other managers may say they don't have the time for these one-on-one discussions with staff – but just like coaching, not finding time for these interactions can be dangerous in the long run.

If you don't ask, you may have the wrong idea of what would make an employee happy and what would be undesirable. Many supervisors think money is the biggest factor, and for some employees, it is. However, for many others, money ranks way down on the list and other factors like growth potential or work flexibility are much more important. You'll never know until you ask.

> You may have an incorrect perception about what makes each employee happy if you don't ask frequently.

Just the act of asking is a positive step. Employees will feel like you care about them and feel valued if you take the time to ask what is most important to them. That alone can lead to stronger loyalty and commitment. Sometimes just asking is a retention strategy in itself.

Asking these questions is better done one-on-one and not as a group activity. People are too easily led in a group and may be uncomfortable about voicing what is important to them in a group setting. Spend time with each employee and find out why he left his last job, what would make him leave this one, and what things will keep him happy.

> Retention interviews are best done individually, not as a group activity.

You should do these employee interviews often – perhaps as often as monthly or quarterly and not just once a year. Here are some of the questions you might use to uncover their reasons for staying with the job:

- If you were to win the lottery and resign, what would you miss about working here?
- What about the job makes you jump out of bed each morning? Hit the snooze button?
- If you had a magic wand, what is the one thing you would change about your job?

Use these ideas as catalysts to create your own questions. Make time to sit down with each employee and ask these questions. Listen carefully to their answers to develop an individualized retention plan for each employee.

78. How can you create passion for the job?

Think about ways you can help employees find the work they love to do. If all they're doing is answering phones all day, it may not be easy, and you will probably lose some of them. But if you can partner with your employees to find something they're passionate about in the work, you'll have a much better chance of keeping talented staff.

Confucius said, "Choose a job you love and you'll never have to work a day in your life.

Helping employees find passion in their work means finding something they like to do in their work role. The other option is to bring something they love to do to the workplace. When people are doing what they love to do, they are at their best. If you can create a link between people's passions and their jobs, you'll have happier employees that will perform better and stay with you longer.

Ask employees what they love to do at work and away from work. Use their answers to think creatively about how you might put their passions to work. Here are three examples of how an employee's passion was put to work in the call center:

Hobby

One employee had taken classes on desktop publishing. Her supervisor suggested she put those skills to use and create a team newsletter. The newsletter was a big success and became a regular monthly publication. Another agent that had an interest in photography offered to take pictures around the center and the newsletter added photos of team events and awards and served as a nice keepsake. Other teams joined in and the newsletter spread to be a call center wide project, with many different agents sharing their talents and skills at poetry, cartoons, and interviews.

Sport

One call center had a problem with scheduling for weekend coverage. The supervisor noted that several of the staff were avid skiers and worked with the workforce planning team to create some schedules that provided a four-day ski weekend if employees would work two Saturday/Sunday combinations in a row. The schedule variation addressed needed coverage, as well as supported a passion of several of the staff.

Career Calling

Look for ways for employees to bring their passion to the workplace.

One call center agent was going back to school to earn a teaching degree. The supervisor noted the interest in teaching and asked the agent to help out in teaching some components of the new staff orientation. The agent's talent was apparent and her training role expanded so that she spent about half her time taking calls and the other half training with new staff. When she finished her degree, she stayed with the call center and organized a training department as the company grew.

If passion is missing from the workplace, your best people may not bring their best efforts to work. Collaborate with them to uncover what they love to do and find a way to link it to their jobs. They'll be more enthusiastic and excited about coming back to work each day.

79. What can you do to enrich the job?

One of the most common reasons that an employee leaves a call center is the monotonous nature of the work. Workplace boredom is particularly common in call centers and can be a major cause of turnover. Your job as a supervisor is to identify when the job is becoming too routine for an employee and to find ways to enrich the job.

Workplace boredom is a common cause of turnover in call center jobs.

It may be that all the other aspects of the job are fine. The position may provide good wages and benefits, enjoyable co-workers, adequate job security, and a good company reputation. However, the job itself may simply not provide the stimulation and sense of achievement that many people need in order to justify them staying with the job.

Unfortunately, the employees that this boredom is more likely to affect are your good performers. They are likely the creative, energetic ones and will also be the ones that need personal challenge and growth to stay satisfied. The point at which they feel they have outgrown the job is the point at which they will likely consider leaving. Even if they don't physically leave, they may check out psychologically, as evidenced by absenteeism and declining performance scores.

Unfortunately, the employees most affected by boredom are likely to be some of your best employees.

Your role as a supervisor is to find ways to provide job enrichment. The key is to change some of the content in the agents' jobs or change some of the processes. Job enrichment generally involves allowing employees to take on different tasks and responsibilities or to accomplish them in ways that promote more personal autonomy and creativity.

There is no one recipe for enrichment. The right set of ingredients will be different for each person. Once again, the key to tailoring this job enrichment is to ask each employee questions like:

- What talents do you have that you currently don't use?
- Which of your talents are put to best use here?
- What about the job do you find rewarding and what is boring for you?
- In what areas would you like to have increased responsibility?
- What would you like to be doing a year from now? Three years? Five years?

The idea is to work with your employees and help them evaluate their jobs and ideas for enrichment. Many of their ideas will likely revolve around the following themes:

- Greater autonomy, need for empowerment, and more ownership of processes
- Participation in decisions related to work processes
- Opportunities to work with team members or other departments
- Increased variety in tasks
- Opportunities to learn new skills

80. What growth and career opportunities can you provide?

Another reason for turnover in the call center is that the position is viewed by many working in it that it is a dead-end job. If your employees keep doing one thing for too long with no change in sight, you will lose many of them. However, if you can keep your staff on a continual path of growing, developing, and adding new skills, you may be able to keep them around. Any organization that ignores the ambitions of good people cannot expect to keep them.

To retain good employees, keep them on a path of growing, developing, and adding new skills.

Providing career options and opportunities for growth involves developing a talent pipeline. This pipeline development is made up of four steps:

1. Know their talents.
2. Offer your perspective.
3. Discuss trends and options.
4. Co-design an action plan.

The first step involves having a career conversation with all your employees. Get to know each person professionally and personally. Talk about their talents, skills, values, and interests. Find out about past accomplishments and what they think makes them unique in the particular work environment. Find out what kind of roles and responsibilities they would like best.

The second step is to provide constant feedback to the employee about current performance and the impact of that performance on future aspirations. Help them see what they need to do now in order to move to the next stage of development.

Provide feedback on current performance and its impact on future development opportunities.

The third step is to help your employees to understand what potential positions and responsibilities are possible for them. Help them understand the broad call center and company perspective, as well as shifts and trends in the industry and how those might affect future positions. Work with them to understand all the potential next steps including lateral moves to other positions, enriching and expanding within the current position, and realigning job responsibilities.

Finally, you should work with each employee to identify a career path, the knowledge and skills needed to accomplish it, the steps for development, career obstacles and how to avoid or remove them.

Investigate and communicate all possibilities including lateral moves, enrichment opportunities, job realignment, and specialized roles.

According to the book, *Love 'Em or Lose "Em*, there are several do's and don'ts of career development planning. These are listed on the following page.

Career Discussion Do's and Don'ts

Step 1. Know their talents.	
Give plenty of encouragement and support.	Don't take employees for granted.
Ask open-ended probing questions.	Don't interrogate – investigate instead.
Engage individuals and find out what makes them "tick."	Don't tell them what to do – listen for what they want to do.
Step 2. Offer your perspective.	
Ask agents to assess themselves.	Don't agree just to avoid confrontation.
Clarify standards and expectations.	Don't just focus on weaknesses.
Give specific, concrete examples when delivering constructive feedback.	Don't give just performance feedback – give developmental feedback, too.
Step 3. Discuss trends and options.	
Provide information on organization and industry and trends.	Don't underestimate the impact of constant change.
Allow talented staff to access your network of peers.	Don't avoid talking about an unpredictable future.
Discuss your perspective on current challenges.	Don't side-step the importance of company culture and norms.
Encourage individuals to envision their future.	Don't make promises you may not be able to keep.
Help set goals that are aligned with business goals.	Don't forget to plan for several possible outcomes.
Step 4. Co-design an action plan.	
Suggest resources and on-the-job activities.	Don't depend on training alone for development.
Be direct to help strengthen their plans.	Don't be afraid to suggest resources outside of your department.

Some questions to ask in the career discussion might include:

- What skills do you think you would need to accomplish your goals?
- What abilities do you already have that would help you reach your goal?
- Can you identify someone to network with to help you reach your goal?
- What kind of training or support will you need from me?
- What kinds of on-the-job tasks would support your development?

Keep in mind that your role in this discussion is to assist your employee in identifying skills, knowledge, and development areas for each career alternative. Your job is not to build a plan for them, but to support them along the path.

A supervisor's role is not to build a career plan for each employee, but to assist each person in moving along a chosen path.

81. What can you do to support a life/work balance?

People leave jobs when rigid workplace rules prevent life balance or cause family stress. Businesses are realizing this today and many are implementing policies that are more "family friendly." Your company may be responding to a call from employees to make the workplace adapt to help them balance the demands of work with personal and family needs. Those businesses that don't become more family friendly will definitely have a harder time attracting good employees and getting them to stay.

Employees are demanding a friendlier workplace that helps them balance the demands of work with personal/family needs.

Some of the family-friendly policies that employees are looking for include childcare facilities or subsidies, job sharing, telecommuting, eldercare assistance, and flexible family leave programs. Some of these policies give talented employees an option for meeting personal responsibilities while still being productive at work. Talk to your management team about what policies your company has in place now or might be willing to try in order to keep valued personnel.

Keep in mind that there are different definitions of families in today's world. Some of your employees might have traditional, two-parent households, but there will be single-parent families as well. You may have a large percentage of young people who haven't had children yet and consider their family to be a roommate and a pet. Others may be caring for elderly parents. Your family-friendly strategy needs to accommodate the needs of all these types of families and living arrangements.

Family-friendly policies should be flexible enough to meet the demands of any definition of family.

You may really need to stretch to meet some of these demands, since you may not be able to provide one of the most common family-friendly policies – a flexible work schedule. Your company may have this policy in place for most employees, but it is likely not a benefit that can be granted to most call center employees. Because the center is at the mercy of the incoming calls, you have to have a certain number of staff there every period of the work day, and it matters greatly to service and productivity if the right number of staff aren't in place precisely as their schedule defines. Because you can't take advantage of this benefit in the call center, see if management is willing to make a concession in another area and grant more flexibility in some other area to make up for the stringent schedule demands of the call center.

Flexible scheduling is typically not one of the benefits the call center has the luxury of granting.

Brainstorm ideas with your staff about innovative ways you can help them balance family and work. Tailor your family-friendly policy to meet the needs of individual staff in order to improve job loyalty and retention.

Learning Activities

1. Review turnover reports for your call center and identify the loss rate for agents that leave the center, as well as for those that leave the area for other departments. Analyze the trend over the last twelve months for the reasons that employees leave the center. Identify at least one solution for preventing the most common reason that employees depart.

2. Select one or two of the retention strategies outlined in this chapter to apply in your call center. Write a plan for how the strategy will be implemented, what results are expected, and how results of the program will be measured in terms of improved morale and retention.

3. Create an invitation for frontline staff on your team to meet with you individually to discuss job satisfaction. Make a list of three things each employee has indicated that they like about the job and what would keep them motivated to perform well and stay in the position. Create an action plan/calendar of how you will provide reinforcement of these items over the next month.

4. If you don't already know about the hobbies and interests of each of your employees, make a concentrated effort to find out this information in the next few weeks. Identify two or three hobbies, interests, or talents for each individual and then create a plan that links these interests to the workplace.

Chapter 12 – Call Center Technology Overview

Your call center uses a variety of technologies to answer and handle customer contacts. As a supervisor, you should be aware of the technologies used to carry the contacts to and from the call center so that any problems experienced by a customer can be diagnosed and resolved quickly. With self-service options such as interactive voice response (IVR) and the company's web site, customers can do some transactions for themselves, but may need help in understanding the options and functions provided.

In addition to call delivery technologies, there are many tools available in today's call center to assist in managing performance. You can be a much more effective supervisor thanks to the availability of timely information about performance of your team and individuals.

Other technologies assist with other critical functions of the call center such as getting the right staffing resources in place, monitoring and recording calls, and assimilating knowledge about customers to better handle their requests.

This chapter will explore some of the more common technologies and their applications within the call center.

82. ***How does a call travel from the customer to the agent?***
83. ***What are the options for distributing calls to agents?***
84. ***What ACD reports are available to manage staff performance?***
85. ***What is IVR and what does it do?***
86. ***What does a workforce management system do?***
87. ***How are outbound calls placed to customers?***
88. ***What are the options for monitoring and recording calls?***
89. ***How can customer contacts be tracked and managed?***
90. ***How can employee knowledge be accumulated and accessed?***
91. ***How are email transactions tracked and managed?***
92. ***What technologies support customer relationships?***
93. ***What systems help manage the training curriculum?***
94. ***What are the steps of technology needs assessment and acquisition?***

82. How does a call travel from the customer to the agent?

Have you ever wondered how a call from one of your customers actually reaches you at your desk? When a customer dials your call center's phone number, it will travel through the Public Switched Telephone Network or PSTN. When the call reaches your call center site, it is generally answered by a private switching system. This switching system distributes the call, puts it in queue if there's no live body to answer it, and provides announcements for the caller and reports for management.

The telephone call generated by a caller to the call center can be handled in three primary ways. The call can be a:

- Local call when the caller and company are in the same town and the caller dials a 7-digit number
- Long-distance call in which the caller pays for the call and dials a 10-digit number of the company
- Toll-free long distance call in which the caller dials a special 10-digit number and your call center pays for the call

Local Service

Local telephone service is provided by your Local Exchange Carriers or LEC (commonly referred to as the telco – short for telephone company). The dialing plan for local calls is typically 7-digits, where the first three digits designate the telco central office that supports that group of numbers. The last 4 digits indicate the specific line of the subscriber.

Outbound Long-Distance Service

When a call needs to travel beyond the serving area of the LEC, the call is handed off to a long distance carrier, referred to as an Inter-Exchange Carrier (IXC or IEC). These companies (such as AT&T, MCI, and Sprint) do not generally provide local services, but take the call handed off to them by the LEC and transport it to the receiving town's LEC to connect to the called party location. Calls that are international are handled by an international carrier that may be the same as the IXC or a separate company.

Toll-Free Services

Toll-free is a bit of a misnomer because someone is paying for the call. Callers dial a special number that means they will not pay, but the receiving company will be charged. This is sometimes referred to as 800-Service because the area code for toll-free calls was 800 for many years. However, since all of the 800 number choices have been depleted, area codes have been designated for toll-free calling, including 888, 877, 866, and others. This special numbering plan makes it easy for callers to know when they are dialing a call they will pay for or not, and easy for the LECs to know that this is a call to be handed off based on receiver preference of carrier rather than caller preference.

Toll-free is a bit of a misnomer because someone is paying for the call. Callers dial a special number that means they will not pay, but the receiving company will be charged.

Your call center may have toll-free services in place so your customers can reach you more easily. These toll-free services also provide many features to assist with the routing and ongoing management of the calls. Within the network, callers can be identified based on the number they dialed (Dialed Number Identification Service or DNIS) or the number from which they are calling (Automatic Number Identification or ANI). Calls can be allocated among multiple company sites or be routed different places based on time of day or day of week. All of these features are selected and paid for by the receiving company.

Automatic Call Distribution (ACD)

Once a call arrives at your site, it is probably answered by a telephone switching system called an automatic call distributor (ACD). The role of the ACD is to receive the call, connect it to an agent in the center, provide queuing and announcements when agents are not available, and provide reports that assist in managing the operation.

The basic features of the ACD are designed to automatically answer calls and place them in the order defined by the programmed rules. Generally, that means the first call in is the first call handled. This ensures that your callers wait the shortest time possible and a fair workload is distributed to your agents. While the caller is in the queue, there is generally music or some kind of delay message.

A wide variety of features are also available to help the agent process the call. These include such things as a display that tell the agent what greeting is appropriate for a particular call, buttons that allow the agent to enter different work states, codes that can be dialed to indicate what the caller requested, and buttons to summon a supervisor for assistance on a difficult call.

The basic features of the ACD are designed to automatically answer calls and place them in the order defined by the programmed rules, distribute the calls to the staff, and provide reports to manage the operation.

Quality control features allow the supervisor to silently monitor both sides of a call so that neither party knows the call is being observed. This capability is used to monitor the quality of the work in the center and aid in identifying training needs.

83. What are the options for distributing calls to agents?

Once the call has reached the ACD, it will usually control the call until it is disconnected. In some cases, the ACD must determine which agent team would be the best match to the caller's needs, determine if an agent is available to handle the call, choose among a group of idle agents where needed, or queue the call if no agents are available. While the call is queued, the system will deliver delay announcements, and perhaps even estimate how long the caller will need to wait. The ACD monitors the status of all agents to ensure that as soon as one is available, the caller is connected. It then monitors the call in progress to be ready to transfer the call, record information the agent enters about the call, or disconnect the call when either party hangs up.

The ACD must determine what agent team would be the best match to the caller's needs, determine if an agent is available to handle the call, choose among a group of idle agents where needed, or queue the call if no agents are available.

Traditional Call Routing

Making the decision about which agent should receive the incoming call is one of the most important jobs the ACD performs. The most common form of call distribution matches the needs of callers to the skills of the agents. This is done by having the agents log into specific call handling groups and having the ACD direct the appropriate types of customer calls to those groups.

For example, some of your customers may want to place an order while others have questions on their bills. You can publish different telephone numbers for callers to use to help direct the calls to the right agent team. You might publish the Order phone number on catalogs and advertising, while putting the Billing phone number on invoices for your customers. Alternatively, you can publish one number for everything, and then have your callers go through an automated menu process to select the type of question they have (to place an order, dial 1; to check on your payment, press 2).

This is referred to as traditional call routing. It can meet the needs of fairly simple operations where customers can be effectively sorted and directed to the right teams. In this environment, each agent generally knows how to handle one kind of call.

While having universal agents who can handle all calls would minimize caller hassle; it's typically unrealistic from a cost and a training standpoint.

An ideal situation would have all agents trained to handle every type of question a customer might have. This scenario would only require one phone number and need no menu to direct the calls. However, training agents to handle every type of call can be expensive, and in some call centers may not be realistic. Therefore, sorting into some reasonable types of categories can ensure customers will reach someone who can help while keeping training costs down.

Skill-Based Routing

The addition of skill-based routing (SBR) has allowed some call centers to find a middle ground in terms of call sorting and training. Skill-based routing assumes that calls will be sorted into specific types based on the needs of the caller (defined through different phone numbers or menus) and then matched up to the staff in the center who can best handle them.

Skill-based routing assumes that calls will be sorted based on the needs of the caller and then routed to the individuals who can best handle them.

Various priorities can also be set. One priority setting ranks callers against other callers and is used to ensure priority callers receive special service. When agent skills are given different priorities, the result is that if several calls are in queue when the agent becomes idle, the next call handled by that agent will be the one with the highest ranking for that agent, generally the one that person handles best.

Skill-based routing can be very complex to manage. The mix of skills represented by the specific agents logged in at any point in time could be quite different from another time even on the same day. Therefore, the workforce management process is much more difficult in terms of determining staffing requirements and schedule options.

Your job as a supervisor is more complex in a center where SBR is employed. You will need to deal with the complexities of ensuring adequate coverage for all skills at all times, so decisions about when to allow someone time off the phones are more difficult. You should be aware that shifting skills and priorities for agents in the routing pattern of the ACD will throw off the planning process for staffing and should be done only in a crisis. It is a complex world that can work very well when carefully planned and executed, but it can create chaos when it is not well coordinated.

Your job as a supervisor is more complex in a center where SBR is used because of the complexities of ensuring adequate coverage for all skills at all times.

Multi-Site ACD Options

There are many companies who have call center operations in more than one site. They can serve these dispersed operations with separate ACDs that can be connected or not, or with dispersed hardware of a single ACD. If your centers take different kinds of calls, then separate ACDs is a reasonable option. Networking the ACDs together is a good alternative if workload is shared among sites.

84. What ACD reports are available to manage staff performance?

There are two primary types of reporting capabilities available from your ACD. One provides historical data and the other real-time snapshots of activity.

One type of ACD report provides historical data and the other real-time snapshots.

Historical data provides information on call handling, agent performance, volumes, and services levels over the last half-hour, day, week or longer. There are many standard reports offered by the ACD vendors and customized reports can be provided, generally with an export of the data to a software package designed for customizing reports. A table showing some of the typical kinds of historical reports is provided below.

Report Type	Report Information/Title
Application Reports	Application performance report
	Application delay before answer report
	Application delay before abandon report
	Application call treatment report
	Activity code by application report
	Application by activity code report
Skillset Reports	Skillset performance report
Agent Reports	Agent performance report
	Agent performance by supervisor report
	Agent directory number performance report
	Agent short calls report
	Agent average calls per hour report
	Agent log in/log out report
	Agents by skillset report
Resource Reports	Trunk performance reports
	Route performance reports
	IVR queue statistics report
	IVR port statistics report
	Call-by-call statistics report

Real-time data is generally provided on a color-coded computer screen to allow “corner of the eye” management. Parameters set by the center show all data in one color (such as green) to indicate that performance is within guidelines, while yellow might indicate slight variation and red more substantial variations. You can monitor how long an agent has been on a call or in a work status, what the service level is, how long callers are waiting in queue, and many other activities.

In addition to the standard reporting packages that come with the ACD from the manufacturer, there are also third-party reporting tools. These include wall-display boards and TV monitors that provide the current queue status, service level information, and other customized messages for all in the center to see. These displays can keep you and your staff informed and serve as a quick communications tool when updated information needs to be communicated quickly. Other tools can also provide the same kind of data on a line on the agent’s monitor.

85. What is IVR and what does it do?

An interactive voice response (IVR) system provides a menu of choices to your callers, routes the calls according to the caller's selection, and may interact with a database to look up information and allow the caller to interact with that data. The purpose of the IVR is to offer an automated, self-service option to complete transactions that would otherwise require an agent.

The purpose of the IVR is to offer an automated option to complete transactions that would otherwise require an agent.

Information Mailbox

The simplest form of IVR is a basic menu that lets callers access information stored in a voice mailbox or an announcement. The primary role of the information mailbox or announcement is to provide a recording that callers can listen to for frequently asked questions. For example, you may find that a significant percentage of callers who dial your main telephone number simply want driving directions to your site. Rather than have someone spend five minutes with each of these callers, a menu option can route the call to a recording that gives the driving directions and allows the callers to have them repeated until they get everything they need. Offloading these simple kinds of calls allows your staff to focus on the more complex calls that really need human interaction.

The primary role of the information mailbox or announcement is to provide a recording that callers can listen to for frequently asked questions.

Voice Response System (VRU)

The next step after menus and recordings is to allow your callers to interact with a computer system over the telephone. This capability is provided by the Voice Response Unit (VRU) that is also known as an Integrated Voice Response System (IVR). These systems use the touchtone dialing tones as input, pass that data to an attached computer for processing, and then "speak" information from the computer back to the caller.

IVR systems generally have a menu of choices and may include a menu tree structure that branches to take the caller to additional choices as a selection is made. If the caller does not make any selection, or selects a live operator option from the menu, the caller can be transferred to an agent queue for live handling in most cases.

IVRs use the touchtone dialing signals as input and then "speak" the computer information back to the caller.

Speech Recognition

In the last few years, the technology has been developed to allow a computer to understand spoken commands rather than requiring input from the telephone keypad. If your company has a large number of products, your speech recognition system can simply ask the caller to say the name of the product, rather than having multiple layers of menu choices to list them all.

This ability to handle spoken commands has greatly improved the willingness of most callers to use these automated systems, and reduces the amount of time the call takes to handle as well. Speech recognition technology is maturing rapidly and penetration in the market is expected to continue to grow substantially in the next few years.

A speech recognition system can simply ask callers to say the name of the service they need, rather than having multiple layers of menu choices to list them all.

As a supervisor, it is important for you and your agents to understand the functions of the IVR, the menu structure, and what applications customers can complete. Any caller who asks for an agent to do something that could be done in the IVR should be encouraged to use it, and the agent should offer to walk the customer through the process. Some people are intimidated by the machine at first and need some hand-holding, while others may simply not know that the option is there. It is particularly useful when the IVR can provide services to callers when the agents queues are closed such as overnight, holidays, and so on. Customers who have been led through the process by a helpful agent are likely to try it again in the future, resulting in higher customer satisfaction and lower cost to the company.

Any caller who asks for an agent to do something that could be done in the IVR should be encouraged to use it.

86. What does a workforce management system do?

The workforce management process was discussed in Chapter 2. The process of workforce management ensures that the right number of staff is in place to answer the calls within the time set by the service goal. This process requires that a reasonably accurate forecast be developed as to how many contacts are expected by half-hour and how long it takes to handle each one. With the forecast of workload done, the next task is to determine the number of staff required to meet the service goal. Workforce schedules are then developed that match the staff to the workload. Tracking the actual performance each day against the plan helps management determine if adjustments are necessary and what they should be. All these forecasting and scheduling steps are automated in a workforce management (WFM) system.

A workforce management system automates the process of forecasting workload, calculating staffing requirements, creating schedules, and tracking daily staffing and service.

Forecasting is based on historical data. This data is typically fed into the workforce management system over a data link from the ACD. When the workload has been forecast, the system generates a staffing forecast. This is the number of agents needed for each period in order to meet the service goal, but it does not take into account the scheduling rules or preferences of the staff.

The next step of the workforce planning process is to generate the actual work schedules for the staff. This is often an iterative process since there are many scheduling possibilities including timing of lunch periods, breaks, off-phone time, start and end time, and so on. Finding a balance between the customer needs and service objectives with those of the staff and their schedule preferences is the biggest challenge in the scheduling process. If there are not enough people to handle all of the workload, then the system must figure out how to best utilize the staff available and minimize the impacts of understaffing and overstaffing.

The scheduling process is an iterative one in which all the schedule possibilities and combinations are evaluated.

Once the schedule is in place, staffing and service is tracked on an intra-day basis. Agents call in sick, calls arrive differently than planned, and calls may take longer to handle than planned. The workforce management system tracks the forecast against the actual situation and can re-forecast within the day based on new information. The resulting information can help the workforce team make decisions about calling in extra people, authorizing overtime, scheduling a team meeting, or offering time off.

Because of the delicate nature of the scheduling process and the difficulties in managing daily service, everyone in the call center should be aware of what any single change to the plan can make. As a supervisor, you should always check with the workforce team before making any change to team member schedules. The whole center's situation must be considered in these changes, not just your team. If each supervisor decides to take one person off the phones for a coaching session in the same hour, you can image what the service impact would be.

It is critical for a supervisor to check with the WFM team before making any change to the schedule.

In addition to the basic functions of a workforce management system just described, a range of optional functions can be added to manage real-time agent adherence to schedules, plan and manage non-phone contacts such as email, and administer vacation time. Some systems even allow the agents to do schedule trades online and view the current schedule, while others will support a vacation bidding process customized to your company's rules.

The WFM system is often linked to other systems in the center that benefit from a scheduling component or just share common information like the list of employees. For example, a quality monitoring system will need to record calls when an agent is actually logged into the system, so the quality monitoring system uses the data link to read information determine the agent's schedule rather than requiring the user to manually enter this data.

Advanced workforce management functions provide for real-time adherence monitoring, online schedule trades, and vacation administration.

A learning management system may need to push a 15-minute training module to each agent during low volume periods to ensure everyone gets the latest updates. This learning management system can also be linked to the workforce management system to track the agent schedules and to find the best times to schedule these training modules.

87. How are outbound calls placed to customers?

Placing outgoing telephone calls is commonplace in most call centers, even in those that are primarily dedicated to inbound call handling. Callbacks on follow-up requests, contact with other departments for research, and many other requirements can generate these calls. There are also some centers that have many outbound calls to make for telemarketing, surveys, debt collection, and other purposes.

Where there is a quantity of calls to generate, an automated dialer may be appropriate. A list of numbers to be called is loaded into the dialer's database and the system generates the calls automatically. The purpose of these systems is to automate the look-up and dialing process as much as possible, resulting in better productivity for the agents and improved list management. If there is a live answer, the call is completed as planned. If no one answers or there is a busy signal, the dialer will disconnect the call and place that number back into the database for another try later. If an answering machine is reached, the dialer can either disconnect or the agent can leave a message. In either case, the called number will generally be put into the database for another try.

There are many different types of dialers and they can operate in a variety of modes. One dialing mode is preview dialing, which is primarily used in situations where an agent may want to prepare for each call separately, such as a debt collections application. The dialer locates the next number in sequence, pulls up the account information and presents it to the agent's desktop. When the agent has all the information and is ready for the call, the agent presses a button that tells the dialer to dial the call.

The purpose of dialer systems is to automate the dialing process as much as possible, resulting in better productivity for the agents and improved list management.

In a predictive mode, the dialer also has a list of numbers to call, but the calls are essentially all alike so that agent does not need to prepare separately prior to each call. In this case, the dialer will place the calls without an agent on the line. If a busy signal or no answer is reached, the call will be disconnected and the number stored for another try later. If the call reaches a live person, the dialer will look for an idle agent in the center to connect to the call, hopefully instantaneously. If the call reaches an answering machine, it can be programmed to disconnect or to connect an agent to leave a message as appropriate. The predictive dialer works on a sophisticated mathematical algorithm that dials at a speed that will maximize utilization of the agents without dialing too fast so that answered calls find no agent available.

The benefit of this kind of dialer is clearly in the automation of the dialing process as well as the list management. The improvement in productivity can be as much as 300% with the use of such systems since the agents are only involved in calls that successfully reach the called party. The drawback of predictive dialers is that they can dial too fast, resulting in calls that reach a live answer, but there is no agent in the center to take the call. Customers find it highly annoying to have the phone ring, answer it, and have only silence greet them.

88. What are the options for monitoring and recording calls?

In order to supervise and coach employees, it is important for you to be able to hear both sides of an interaction with the customer. That is the only way to tell for sure if the agent is listening effectively, answering the customer's questions correctly, and entering the right information into the system and process forms. There are several ways that this call monitoring function can be provided.

Nearly every ACD is equipped with the capability to support silent monitoring of calls by a third party. This allows you to access a call currently in progress, listening to both sides of the conversation between the caller and agent without either of them knowing you are observing. The drawback of this approach is that it requires you to access these conversations in real-time. While centers typically set a goal of listening to several calls per agent per month, when silent monitoring in real time is the only option, the goal is often missed.

Silent monitoring allows monitoring of a live call in progress, without the caller or agent being aware they that are being observed.

Automated recording of the calls is the role of the quality monitoring system. While some organizations record every call for business purposes, most do not. The quality monitoring system typically is set to record randomly, sampling each agent at different times of day throughout the sample period. Some systems may also record the data screens so that you can see exactly what the agents saw on the screen and what keystrokes they entered as they processed the call.

With call recording, you can review the calls whenever you have time, since most systems allow remote access to the recordings. One of the additional benefits is that you can listen to the recording together with your agent in a coaching session.

There are legal issues involved in the recording of calls and these must be considered in the use of these systems. Agents must be informed that their calls may be recorded and it is a good idea for them to sign a notice indicating that awareness. In addition, it is good practice (and required in some places) to provide notification to the callers that the call may be monitored. This is generally done through a recorded announcement when the call first enters the ACD.

There are legal issues involved in the recording of calls and these must be considered in the use of quality monitoring and recording systems.

Whether you do the monitoring yourself, or whether you have a team of quality specialists that do the recording and scoring, it is important to provide meaningful information back to the agent as quickly as possible that will result in improved performance.

89. How can customer contacts be tracked and managed?

In your call center, you may hear repeatedly from the same customers. Tracking the ongoing interactions with individual customers is essential to manage the relationship and to ensure that the customer does not think that "the right hand doesn't know what the left is doing."

Whether the contract being tracked is a trouble ticket reported to your help desk, a sales lead, or a customer interaction requesting some service, a contact management system can assist. This type of system tracks interactions by customers but also provides the databases and analytical tools to look for trends. For example, if a customer reports a technical problem with his product, a trouble ticket number may be assigned to the report and all of the relevant data about the request and the solution are recorded in the system. If the customer calls in later with the same problem telling the agent that the suggested solution did not work, using the ticket number and customer ID, the agent can find the record of the prior interaction. This allows the agent to see what has already been tried unsuccessfully in order to suggest something else, or transfer the caller to the higher skilled agents.

A contact management system tracks interactions by customers and also provides the databases and analytical tools to review and analyze trends.

A sales contact system can allow a sales rep to track interactions with a prospect including time of call, specific contacts, and next steps. The system can be flagged to notify the sales person when the next step is scheduled so that it is not forgotten. Management can review the pipeline of sales prospects and the interactions to make better-informed decisions about what the sales forecast should be and which sales people may need some coaching on their techniques or level of activity.

In a call center, the contact management system can provide a record of all the prior interactions with the customer. Repeat callers don't have to tell their whole history to the agent, and the agent can see what has been done or promised by others that may need to be addressed. As the agent converses with the caller, a variety of personal information may be revealed such as hobbies, interests, additional contacts, and so on. This information can be recorded in the system for later analysis by marketing. Another analysis might reveal customers who prefer to do business via the web rather than by phone and these can be targeted via email rather than through telemarketing.

The contact management system can provide a record of all the prior interactions with the customer whether they took place by phone, email, IVR, or in person in the branch or store.

90. How can employee knowledge be accumulated and accessed?

One of the most valuable assets your organization has is the knowledge of your employees. However, capturing this knowledge and making it available to everyone who needs it is not an easy task. Knowledge management systems are designed to fit this need because they are essentially data storage and retrieval systems. They organize the data in such a way that it can easily be searched to find the answer to questions.

Knowledge management systems organize data in such a way that it can easily be searched to find the answer to questions.

Technical support help desks are heavy users of knowledge management systems. For example, perhaps a customer calls and wants to know if the computer system he has is compatible with a specific printer. The agent would type the computer model and the printer name into the search window, and the knowledge management system would find all the data on the specified model and then search for the printer type. When the information has been located, the data about compatibility, known issues, where to go to download the appropriate printer drivers, etc. will be displayed for the agent to answer the customer's question. Even though this agent may never have heard of the printer, the information that was stored by someone else is there to solve the problem.

Knowledge management systems enable an agent to sound knowledgeable about a subject about which they know little or nothing.

It is important to note that while these tools can improve service in highly complex environments, they require a great deal of maintenance. Each time a new issue or problem is identified, or the company makes a new product, all of the relevant data must be entered into the system so that those who need it can access it. In many organizations, this updating process requires that the most experienced agents or others test the solution to ensure its accuracy before it can be entered in the system. This prevents erroneous or incomplete data from being entered and proliferating. The initial data entry to set up the system is generally a huge task, and the ongoing maintenance is essential to ensure that the system stays up to date and as effective as possible.

91. How are email transactions tracked and managed?

Email has become a major communications tool over the last few years. You and your team members probably use it widely to communicate with each other and perhaps customers or contacts outside the company. But the primary issue for call centers is the management of incoming emails from customers and prospects. These often are emails generated to ***info@company.com*** or ***service@company.com*** or ***sales@company.com***, rather than addressed to a specific person.

Management of emails is a function of automatic receipt, placing them into a queue, distributing them to agents to process, and tracking the progress for reporting purposes.

While the number of emails is low today in comparison to the number of calls, the number is growing rapidly and requires the orderly handling that the call center processes can provide in many cases. Management of the emails themselves is a function of automatic receipt, placing them into a queue, distributing them to agents to process, and tracking the progress for reporting purposes.

Emails to a central mailbox that will be handled by a group of individuals must be managed differently from those individual emails that are received by a single person. With a group of people sharing responsibility for responding, it is important to ensure handling in the desired order, distribution of work in a fair manner, and information to manage the process.

In a sense, the email management system is like an ACD for electronic contacts. The receipt of the email is often acknowledged by an automated message sent within a few minutes telling the sender when a full reply is likely. The message callers see is like the announcement that a caller hears when going into queue on the ACD. Emails are held in a centralized queue much like the queues in an ACD, and may be sorted by type based on the reference line or other content, just like the ACD has different queues for different skill requirements. The emails are distributed to the agents for processing in a way that replicates the ACD. Reporting is provided, although this is somewhat different, primarily due to the longer response time that is acceptable for emails (hours rather than seconds for calls typically).

The email management system works much like an ACD does with telephone calls.

One popular feature of email management systems is the automated reply. When an email is received, the system immediately sends out a canned reply that acknowledges receipt and lets the sender know the anticipated response time. This is reassuring to the sender. Since the response time the sender anticipated and the actual time that the company is likely to respond may be quite different, this automated acknowledgement can prevent another email or call from the sender.

Some of the more sophisticated email management systems may also have an element of artificial intelligence that looks for key words and phrases in the email and selects probable replies. These probable replies are then sent to the agent with the original email for approval and editing. This can increase productivity when the system selects the right choices, but can be risky if the agents are not carefully reading both inquiry and response to ensure that there is a good match.

Another tool that can support online transactions is the "call me" button on your web site. Customers click on that button when they want someone at the company to call them, filling in time and telephone number. This sends a message to the company to schedule the outbound call. This can be highly automated with a dialer function to schedule and make the calls, or may simply send an email to the company for follow-up manually.

Web chats are a cross between the real-time interaction of a phone call and the delayed response technology of the email. A message is sent to the call center that a customer is in queue and as soon as an idle agent is available that agent will open an interactive session with the customer and send a written reply such as "My name is George, how can I help you?" These questions and answers go back and forth until the customer is satisfied and ends the chat session.

The benefits of the interactive web chat to customers include having a near real-time conversation with an agent who can answer their questions. It does not have the inherent delays associated with emails in which the reply may come in a few hours and the risk that the reply will be incomplete or generate another question and another round of emails. It may not be quite as fast as the phone call, but a written record of the instructions in the reply can be preferable over a verbal interchange that is not recorded.

> The benefits of the interactive web chat to customers include having a near real-time conversation with agents who can answer their questions.

For the call center, the web chat can typically be handled at a lower cost than a call. Part of that savings is in the cost of the toll-free telephone call that is replaced by an Internet exchange. Another savings may be in the cost of the labor to accomplish the tasks. While the customer is typing in his question, time would be wasted for the agent just waiting for that to happen, so it is common for web chat agents to handle more than one transaction at the same time. The overlapping nature of this kind of work also minimizes the opportunity for the agent to ever get a rest between transactions like they sometimes have between calls.

Quality control for web chats is a challenge in that these are real-time interactions rather than responses that can be reviewed prior to sending like an email. So the supervisor would need to be online during the interaction to observe or there would need to be a recording of the session that could be printed and/or reviewed on-line later. The responses may already in the hands of the customer by then and are written and printable, so it is difficult to fix them after the fact.

92. What technologies support customer relationships?

There are several systems and tools in today's call center that are designed to assist frontline staff in managing customer relationships. For example, a technical support help desk may need to track the trouble request to solve an individual customer problem, but also to identify trends of technical issues that need to be addressed. Sales people need to track the multiple steps of interaction with a prospect to maximize the potential to close the sale. Nearly every company wants to know more about its customers including their demographics, interests, hobbies, product likes and dislikes, etc., so it can better target marketing efforts and improve customer retention. Some of these functions are performed by contact management systems (described earlier in this chapter), and some fall under the heading of customer relationship management (CRM) tools.

Data Warehousing & Analytics

Analysis of customer data requires a central storehouse of all of the information a company has on its customers. This data is often housed in departmental systems that do not communicate or share information because they were designed to handle very specific and separate processes. Data warehouse systems are essentially central repositories of all of this data in databases that can be effectively searched, sorted, and analyzed.

Data warehouse systems are essentially central repositories of data in a database format that can be effectively searched, sorted, and analyzed.

There are major challenges in implementing these central repositories, not the least of which is getting the departments to deposit their data. Most organizations have provided incentives and competitive pressures between departments so that each wants to "own" the customer relationship and keep the others out. Breaking down this barrier takes a directive from the top of the organization and a great deal of patience. It may even require a change in the compensation plan to change the rewards from competitive product or departmental goals to those that focus on the entire relationship with the enterprise.

The next challenge is scrubbing the data so that Jack Jones, J. Jones, John R. Jones and J. R. Jones are all united into one record if they are in fact the same person. Addresses and other information conflicts must be reconciled, as some systems may have been updated while others have not been changed over time. Little of this scrubbing can be done on an automated basis, requiring a massive effort by the implementation team. And with new data coming in all the time, the process never really ends.

The technical requirements of data warehousing include huge storage capacity, of course, but also the processing power to access and sort the data, and a network that is robust enough to support the high levels of interaction with the system anticipated by the centralization process. This places a significant load on the Information Technology department that can drastically slow these implementations.

When all the data has been centralized and scrubbed, the analytical tools (sometimes referred to as data mining) can sort and summarize the information in a variety of ways that support market segmentation, sales initiatives, and customer retention strategies. The key capabilities of these systems are to quantify the value of the customer interaction, set thresholds that trigger rules and events for automation, and help qualify customer information. Many of the analytical tools available are designed to meet the needs of a specific industry. This simplifies the implementation and shortens the time it takes to get valuable management information out of the data. There are a number of general analytical tools that can be configured to meet nearly any company's needs, but they take more time and knowledge of what is desired at the outset to be successful.

Web assistance tools allow a customer to access a live agent to assist while browsing on the company website.

It is well known that a significant percentage of items placed in electronic shopping carts on the web are abandoned. Many customers become confused on the web site and would be delighted to be able to access live assistance. These are the issues addressed by web collaboration tools.

A simple form of tool is to place a "call me" button on the web site. The customer who selects that button enters a telephone number to call, a time to call, and a brief description of the question on the web page that pops up. That generates a message to the call center to make an outbound call to the customer at the time designated, and it can be managed by a dialer or manually.

A more sophisticated version of this tool is the "help me" button on the web site. When the customer selects that button, a message is sent to the call center immediately and a response is generated while the customer is still on the system. This could take the form of a web chat in which a message box pops up on the customer's computer with typed messages from the agent and a place for the customer to type in responses in real-time. It could also take the form of a phone call from the agent to the customer. If the customer has a second phone line so both call and web session can be handled, the call could be separate. But for the client with only one line, the voice portion can be handled via Voice over Internet Protocol (VoIP).

Web collaboration tools make it possible for both the agent and the customer to be on the web site together with the agent pushing pages to the customer and directing the interaction.

Web collaboration makes it possible for both the agent and the customer to be on the web site together with the agent pushing pages to the customer and directing the interaction. This makes it easy for the agent to ensure that customers can find just what they are looking for and train them on how to better utilize the site in the future as well.

These real-time interaction tools to aid customers using the web promise to increase customer self-service and to reduce the number of items abandoned in electronic shopping carts.

93. What systems help manage the training curriculum?

Training is a constant need for all call center staff. Some programs will be offered in classrooms, others via the web, and others through self-study workbooks and other media. Managing the plan for individual employees and tracking progress through that plan is part of the role of the learning management system.

The advent of e-learning has changed the face of employee training. While classroom instruction is essential for many kinds of training, self-paced computer-based training can be an effective tool for disseminating information and knowledge. A learning management system (LMS) is designed to serve as a repository of these self-paced modules and to provide scheduling and tracking of all educational modules that employees have completed. In addition, some of the learning management systems for call centers include the capability to "push" a module of e-learning to an agent's desktop at a scheduled time, or to allow the agent to access it on demand. Knowledge tests can be included in the content to ensure that the student has completed the course with the appropriate learning, or is directed back to those modules that need more review.

A learning management system (LMS) is designed to serve as repository of self-paced training modules and to provide scheduling and tracking of all educational modules that employees have completed.

Some of these tools include the functions that support the development of e-learning programs in addition to storing and managing the processes. The system provides the basic layout and page advancing functions, allowing the instructional designer to develop the text and graphics within the basic framework. The systems can be used to deliver "tip of the day" or small amounts of information that do not need all of the functions found in a full course. The common length of a learning module is about 15-minutes, with multiple modules linked together to create a full course. This allows a module to be completed by an agent in a reasonable period that can be scheduled off the phones during a shift. Games and interactive instructional tools are common and needed to maintain the student's interest in the programs, but the quality of the actual course materials vary widely. The recent emergence of technical standards should make it easier to transport a program written for one platform to another, but much of the existing material is somewhat limited in terms of platform portability.

There are learning management tools that have been designed specifically for the contact center, primarily available from various quality monitoring vendors), but there are also a number that are designed for broader application throughout an organization. The former can typically be linked to the workforce management or quality monitoring system, and do the "push" of modules to the agent, while the latter may not include those capabilities. When the LMS is linked to the quality monitoring system, for example, when an agent receives a low score on a particular skill on the monitoring, the LMS may automatically schedule that agent for a module of training to improve that skill, working with the workforce management system to find the best time to push that module to the desktop.

94. What are the steps of technology needs assessment and acquisition?

If your call center is considering the acquisition and implementation of a new technology, it is likely that a business case has or will be developed that evaluates and proves the need for such a technology in the call center. A business case is an analysis, evaluation, and presentation of data to support a specific business need and its proposed solution. A business case is developed to demonstrate that a technology or new service is financially justified, will be well managed, and will benefit the organization.

> A business case is an evaluation and presentation of data to support a specific business need and its proposed solution.

There are many reasons that a business case may be developed when considering a new technology for the call center. Some of these reasons include:

- Justification of the technology requirement
- Verification of the need to the business
- Identification of all potential solutions to the problem
- Communication of the objectives and possible solutions to others
- Coordination of implementation activities
- Basis to measure actual versus expected results
- Vehicle for achieving buy-in from all affected parties

There are many steps to performing a thorough business case. These steps include:

Step 1: Define and Obtain Approval

This step defines the specific objectives of the business case and the resources required to develop it. Since developing a business case can be a time-consuming project, you may need to get approval from senior management to proceed with the business case analysis.

Step 2: Recruit the Team

Team members should be identified in this early stage. Necessary skill sets (technical, financial, human resources, etc) should be defined and project members recruited. Responsibilities of each team member should be defined up front.

Step 3: Assess Current Situation

In this step, all the relevant data is gathered, sorted, and organized. This phase is designed to answer the question of "what is happening now?" in many different areas. It should evaluate the current internal and external environment, customer and employee status, and current financial impact.

Step 4: Prepare SWOT Analysis

SWOT is an acronym that stands for strengths, weaknesses, opportunities, and threats. The SWOT analysis is used to fully understand a need or situation in terms of current environment (strengths and weaknesses) and future situation (opportunities and threats).

Step 5: Define Objectives

The objectives should define the direction or what you want to happen as a result of the SWOT analysis. The objectives should outline the specific problem to be addressed and what the overall desired outcome will be of the business case.

Step 6: Identify Potential Solutions

The next step is to identify potential solutions. The objective in Step 5 is the "what" and the solutions are the "how" of the case. All solutions should be considered and prioritized relative to the impact each would have on the situation at hand.

Step 7: Identify Assumptions and Methodology

This step is necessary to record all assumptions. Include methods used to perform calculations and how conclusions were reached. Estimates of savings or improvements should include all the assumptions and methods used to arrive at the numbers.

Step 8: Identify Metrics

The team should agree on the metrics to be used to measure the before and after results. Determine the data and calculations to be used and decide on the performance criteria that will be used to define whether the project is a success or not.

Step 9: Quantify Costs

Outline all the costs of the solution, including start-up costs, trials, implementation, and ongoing use. This step will include a thorough financial analysis such as the calculation of return on investment or estimated payback period of the recommended solution.

Step 10: Identify Risks

Risks are identified in Step 4 as current weaknesses and future threats. In this phase, all risks of implementing the solution should be outlined. This risk assessment should rank the risks with those most likely to happen and having the biggest impact at the top.

Step 11: Quantify Benefits

The benefits of the proposed solution in the call center should be grouped as financial benefits and non-financial benefits. The final recommendation will be based on weighing the costs, risks, and benefits of the proposed solution.

Step 12: Develop Implementation/Contingency Plan

The implementation plan is a blueprint for actual execution. It should be specific, identify key personnel, and outline the process from start to finish, including the risks and possible recovery steps in the event that something does go wrong.

Step 13: Prepare Presentation

The final presentation begins with an executive summary, and follows with a situation assessment, solution overview, conclusion, and detailed recommendations. Appendices should include all the details that support your analysis and findings.

Once a decision has been made to move forward to acquire a new technology or service based on the business case, the acquisition process can include a variety of options.

Acquisition Process

When a technology or new service is to be acquired from outside vendors, it is common to use the Request for Information (RFI) or Request for Proposal (RFP) process. The RFI is a document that can assist you in exploring the options available in the marketplace without requesting a firm bid for a specific system. It can be helpful in understanding options and the tradeoffs of various options prior to a formal RFP process.

The RFP is more common than the RFI. The RFP carefully defines your company's needs and expectations. It requires a legally binding price quote and answers to questions about the offerings that can become part of a contract between you and the vendor. The RFP process is designed to be a fair and equal process that allows all vendors to compete equally, but it helps you assess the differences in vendor offerings at a very detailed level.

An RFI can be helpful at an initial stage to simply understand the various options available in the marketplace.

An RFP should provide the specifications of requirements and the desired capabilities that you are trying to acquire. It ensures that all vendors will be bidding on a similar set of specifications so that bids are comparable. The RFP contains various sections with questions each vendor must answer in order to be considered for further review. Typical sections of the RFP include vendor qualifications, technical specifications of the service or technology being proposed, and a financial analysis of the proposed solution.

Typical sections of an RFP include vendor qualifications, technical specifications of the service or technology being proposed, and a financial analysis of the proposed solution.

Once proposals have been submitted in response to your RFP, your management team should employ a systematic decision process in narrowing options and making a final decision. The selection criteria are first based on the "must-haves." These are the capabilities the vendor must provide to be considered for further review. If vendors are missing any of the "must-haves" they should be eliminated from the review cycle.

The next step is to assign a fixed number of points to each of the RFP selection criteria categories. A committee should agree upon how many points each category should be assigned based on its relative importance. For example, if the most important factor is the cost of the solution, more points will be assigned to the "cost" or financial category. If the technical capabilities are more important, more points will be assigned to the technology section.

Once the major categories have been assigned points, the "line items" in each category (those desirable characteristics, not the "must-haves") will need to be assigned a portion of the section's points, again based on the relative importance of the item. These points represent the weight that is given to each item and the total should equal 100 percent of the decision value. The proposals can then simply be scored to determine a winner.

Learning Activities

1. Make a list of all the call center technologies discussed in this chapter that you employ in your call center. Draw a diagram of the system showing how they are linked together and exchange data with one another.

2. Call into your IVR (if you have one) and listen to each menu option and go down each tree of choices. Analyze it from a caller's perspective. Is there industry jargon that needs to removed? Is it logical and does the flow makes sense? If there are changes you would recommend, document your findings and share them with your manager.

3. If a workforce management system is used in your call center, ask the workforce planning team to provide a demonstration to you of its capabilities. Ask how they analyze the requests from agents and supervisors for changes and make decisions to recommend they be approved or not.

4. Think about a technology described in this chapter that you do not currently have in place. Would it be beneficial to your call center? If you think so, develop a business case to prove its financial and non-financial benefits to the call center.

Chapter 13 – Legal and Personnel Issues

With the increasing number of new workforce regulations and legislation, it is crucial for call center managers and supervisors to be familiar with the wide range of employment and labor laws and how they impact daily decisions. The call center management team should maintain frequent contact with the human resource department and legal counsel and become familiar with the legalities that impact conduct in the center.

The legal complexities involved can be daunting. It is important to stress that the human resource environment is a constantly evolving situation and maintaining awareness of the changes is essential. Every day, new statutes and regulations are passed and adopted by the state and federal agencies. Failure to comply with these statutes and regulations could result in severe penalties to an organization.

Some of the particular labor challenges that affect the call center are related to the Family Medical Leave Act (FMLA). Other laws that affect the hiring and ongoing supervisory process have to do with discrimination issues as outlined by the Equal Employment Opportunity (EEO) legislation.

In addition to legal issues, there are privacy and diversity concerns that impact every call center, perhaps much more so today than even ten years ago.

This chapter discusses many of these labor issues and provides suggestions for remaining within the law and providing employees with a fair and respectful workplace.

95. What personnel legislation should you know about?
96. What is FMLA and how does it affect call center staffing?
97. How does EEOC and discrimination law affect staffing?
98. What are the biggest concerns about privacy in the call center?
99. What should you know about diversity in the workplace?
100. What steps should you use for discipline and termination?

95. What personnel legislation should you know about?

As a supervisor, you should be aware of the most common labor laws, particularly those with implications in the call center workplace. Some of these labor regulations include:

- OSHA regulations related to the physical workplace
- FMLA regarding family leave rights
- EEOC regarding discrimination issues
- ADA pertaining to accommodation of disabilities
- IRCA regarding immigration policies
- NLRA pertaining to union activity
- FLSA regarding compensation policies
- COBRA and HIPAA regarding health care coverage

All these will be discussed briefly below to provide you with an overview and familiarity with the legislation and how it applies in the call center workplace. FMLA and EEOC are two areas of particular concern and they will be discussed as more detailed topics later in this chapter.

The goal of OSHA is to ensure safe and healthful working conditions for employees.

Occupational Safety and Health Act (OSHA)

The goal of the Occupational Safety and Health Act (OSHA) is to ensure safe and healthful working conditions for employees. OSHA outlines requirements such as keeping walkways, doorways, and fire exits clear. It also defines safety requirements like availability of fire extinguishers and sprinklers, and actions to be taken for unsafe conditions like slippery floors, frayed electrical wires, burned out lights, and so on. Supervisors should be familiar with all OSHA requirements and be on the lookout for violations in the workplace to report immediately.

OSHA penalties vary depending on the violation level and enforcement is affected by the gravity of the violation, the company's history of previous violations, and size of the company.

OSHA defines a violation that has a direct relationship to job safety and health, but probably would not cause death or serious physical harm as an "other-than-serious" violation. A "serious" violation is defined as a violation where there is substantial probability of death or serious physical harm. A willful violation is a violation when the employer either knows that what the company is doing constitutes a violation, or is aware that a hazardous condition exists and has made no reasonable effort to eliminate it.

The penalties for these types of violations can be as low as $5,000 or as high as $70,000, depending on the level of violation. Penalties may be adjusted downward, based on the gravity of the alleged violation, the employer's good faith, history of previous violations, and the size of the organization.

Effective ergonomics policy is part of OSHA's overall strategy for reducing workplace injuries and illnesses. OSHA is currently developing industry and task-specific guidelines to reduce and prevent ergonomic injuries and musculoskeletal disorders (MSDs). Until these guidelines are released, OSHA has encouraged businesses and industries to develop internal guidelines for prevention of these injuries.

Americans with Disabilities Act (ADA)

The Americans with Disabilities Act (ADA) prohibits employment discrimination against qualified individuals with disabilities in the private sector, and in state and local governments. You should understand several important ADA definitions to know what constitutes illegal discrimination.

The ADA prohibits employment discrimination against qualified individuals with disabilities in the private sector, and in state and local governments.

An individual with a disability under the ADA is a person who has a physical or mental impairment that substantially limits one or more major life activities. Major life activities are activities that an average person can perform with little or no difficulty such as walking, breathing, seeing, hearing, speaking, learning, and working. A qualified employee or applicant with a disability is someone "who satisfies skill, experience, education, and other job-related requirements of the position, and who, with or without reasonable accommodation, can perform the essential functions of that position."

Reasonable accommodation for disabled persons may include making facilities readily accessible to and usable by persons with disabilities; job restructuring; modification of work schedules; providing additional unpaid leave; acquiring or modifying equipment or devices; adjusting or modifying examinations, training materials, or policies; and providing qualified readers or interpreters. Reasonable accommodation may be necessary to apply for a job, to perform job functions, or to enjoy the benefits and privileges of employment that are enjoyed by people without disabilities.

An employer is required to make a reasonable accommodation to a qualified individual with a disability unless doing so would impose an undue hardship on the operation of the employer's business. Undue hardship means an action that requires significant difficulty or expense when considered in relation to factors such as the size of the business and financial resources.

An employer is required to make a reasonable accommodation to a qualified individual with a disability unless doing so would impose an undue hardship on the operation of the business.

Employees and applicants currently engaging in the illegal use of drugs are not protected by the ADA when an employer acts on the basis of such use. Tests for illegal use of drugs are not considered medical examinations and, therefore, are not subject to the ADA's restrictions on medical examinations. Employers may hold individuals who are illegally using drugs and individuals with alcoholism to the same standards of performance as other employees.

There are five sections of the ADA. Title 1 prohibits employment discrimination against individuals with disabilities for employers with 15 or more employees. Title II prohibits discrimination against individuals with disabilities from participating in services, programs, or activities of "public entities" (state and local governments). All fixed bus routes and commuter rail services must be accessible to passengers with disabilities. Title III requires that places of public accommodation and commercial facilities be accessible to individuals with disabilities. Any area of a business or organization open to the public is classified as a "public accommodation." Office buildings, warehouses, factories, and nonresidential buildings are covered if the operation affects commerce. Title IV requires that telecommunications for hearing and speech-impaired individuals be provided and Title V contains administration and enforcement provisions and lists individuals who are not considered disabled under the Act.

Title III of the ADA is the portion that contains regulations related to the design and accessibility of public workspaces such as a call center.

For call centers to comply with the Title III requirement to provide access to commercial facilities for individuals with disabilities, it is often necessary to redesign or remodel the cubicle layout for those individuals who have wheelchair requirements. Instead of redesigning the call center layout, some call centers have implemented procedures to accommodate individuals with disabilities through remote agent programs. The technology available to enable telecommuting has enabled many individuals with disabilities who prefer to remain at home to work remotely.

Immigration Reform and Control Act (IRCA)

The Immigration Reform and Control Act (IRCA) makes it illegal for an employer to discriminate in recruiting, hiring, or termination based on an individual's national origin or citizenship.

The IRCA defines penalties for employers who knowingly hire illegal immigrants.

The IRCA also defines the penalties for employers who knowingly hire illegal immigrants. Employers are required to examine potential employee's identification documents. The employer must ask for proof of identity such as a driver's license, Social Security card, birth certificate, immigration permit, or other documents. New employees must sign verification forms about their eligibility to work legally in the United States.

National Labor Relations Act (NLRA)

The National Labor Relations Act (NLRA), enacted by Congress in 1935, prohibits discrimination on the basis of union activities and guarantees workers the right to join unions without fear of management reprisal. It created the National Labor Relations Board (NLRB) to enforce this right and prohibits employers from committing unfair labor practices that might discourage organizing or prevent workers from negotiating a union contract. Revisions made in the 1950s and 1960s protect employees who take part in grievances, picketing, and strikes. It also outlines provisions for how to vote on union representation.

The NLRA guarantees workers the right to join unions and prevents labor practices that might prevent workers from negotiating a union contract.

Fair Labor Standards Act (FLSA)

The Fair Labor Standards Act (FLSA) sets minimum wage standards, overtime rates, and other salary-related regulations for any. company that engages in interstate commerce. The FLSA was designed to protect employees from unfair wage and compensation practices. The most significant topic of the FLSA related to call centers is the definition of exempt versus non-exempt employees. An exempt employee can work any number of hours, without being paid overtime. The exempt employee must regularly receive the same amount of pay, regardless of the number of hours worked. A non-exempt employee is entitled to overtime pay at one-and-one-half times the regular rate of pay for all hours over 40 in a week.

The FLSA defines the difference between exempt and non-exempt workers.

The FLSA exempts executive, administrative, professional, and outside sales employees from the minimum wage and overtime requirements of the FLSA, provided they meet certain tests regarding job duties and responsibilities and are compensated "on a salary basis" at not less than stated amounts.

COBRA

Consolidated Omnibus Budget Reconciliation Act (COBRA) of 1986 requires employers with 20 or more employees to offer continuing health coverage for certain former employees, retirees, spouses, former spouses, and dependent children and the right to temporary continuation of health coverage at group rates. Prior to COBRA, when employees left the company, they and any covered family members lost their health insurance. With the COBRA legislation, employers now offer the ex-employee and/or the covered dependents the opportunity to buy the employer's health insurance back from the employer, even though the employee is no longer working at the company.

COBRA legislation enables employees who have left the company to continue health care insurance at group rates.

In general, the health coverage for COBRA participants is usually more expensive than health coverage for active employees, since the employer usually pays a part of the premium for active employees while COBRA participants generally pay the entire premium themselves. Even though COBRA participants pay more than active employees, it is typically less expensive than individual health coverage.

Even though life insurance is not covered under COBRA, the medical benefits provided under the terms of the plan and available to COBRA beneficiaries may include inpatient and outpatient hospital care, physician care, surgery and other major medical benefits, prescription drugs, and any other medical benefits, such as dental and vision care.

Health Insurance Portability and Accountability Act (HIPAA)

The Health Insurance Portability and Accountability Act (HIPAA) provides protection for workers in danger of losing health care coverage. The act allows employees to purchase insurance on their own – provided some conditions are met. These conditions include guaranteed availability, portability, continuation of coverage, creditable coverage, restrictions on limitation period, and premiums. The HIPAA act includes requirements such as guaranteed availability, preexisting conditions, portability, and premiums.

96. What is FMLA and how does it affect call center staffing ?

The Family Medical Leave Act (FMLA) is designed to help employees balance work responsibilities with family and medical needs.

The Family and Medical Leave Act (FMLA) of 1993 is a federal law designed to help employees balance their work responsibilities with their family and medical needs. The Act sets national standards for employers when providing leave for such purposes.

FMLA leave may be taken intermittently, or your employees may work a reduced leave schedule when such arrangements meet their medical necessity. For employees to be eligible, they must have been employed 12 months, worked 1,250 hours before the leave, and must work at a site where there are 50 or more employees within a 75-mile radius of the site.

To be eligible for FMLA, employees must have been employed 12 months, worked 1,250 hours before the leave, and must work at a site where there are 50 or more employees.

Under FMLA, eligible employees must be provided with up to 12 weeks of unpaid, job-protected leave in a 12 month period for specified family and medical reasons. FMLA leave applies equally to both male and female employees. The annual period can be a calendar or fiscal year, or it can be based on the employee's anniversary date of hire. Whichever method the employer chooses must be applied consistently to all employees. The leave can be taken for:

- Birth of a child
- Adoption of a child or initiation of foster care
- Care for a family member who has a serious health condition
- Employee's own serious health condition

Care for a family member is typically related to the family member being unable to care for her/his own basic medical, hygienic, or nutritional needs or safety, or is unable to travel to the doctor. The care may also include providing psychological comfort and reassurance, which would be beneficial to a child, spouse or parent with a serious health condition who is receiving inpatient care.

FMLA can be used to care for a family member such as a spouse, parent, or child, as covered by FMLA official definitions.

The terms for spouse, parent, or child needs to be defined when applied to FMLA. The definition for a spouse is a husband or wife, as defined under state law, including common law marriage in states that recognize this type of union. A parent is defined as a biological parent or an individual who has day-to-day responsibilities to care for and financially support a child, or those who had responsibilities for the employee when the employee was a child. This does not include parents-in-law. A son or daughter is defined as a biological, adopted, foster child, stepchild, legal ward, or a child who is either under age 18, or age 18 or older and incapable of self-care due to mental or physical disability.

The definition for a serious health condition means an illness, injury, impairment, or physical or mental condition that involves inpatient care such as an overnight stay in a medical care facility (hospital, hospice, or residential facility), or continuing treatment by a health care provider for a period of incapacity of more than three consecutive calendar days. This treatment includes the period of incapacity due to pregnancy, or for prenatal care. It also includes the treatment for a chronic serious health condition that requires periodic visits for treatment by a health care provider, continues over an extended period, and may cause episodic incapacity.

Unless complications arise, common colds, upset stomachs, minor headaches, minor ulcers, or routine dental problems do not meet the definition of a serious health condition and do not qualify for FMLA leave.

Leave can be taken in one extended period, or can be taken intermittently. Intermittent leave may reduce an employee's working hours per day or week.

Intermittent leave is time taken in separate blocks of time due to a single illness or injury and may include leave periods from an hour or more to several weeks. An example of this is leave taken several days at a time spread over a period of six months for chemotherapy. A reduced leave schedule may reduce your employee's usual number of working hours per workweek or hours per workday.

Employers are not required to provide paid leave for a situation in which the employer would not normally provide paid leave. The Act allows an employee to use paid leave such as paid vacation time to cover FMLA absences in some circumstances.

If the need for FMLA leave is foreseeable, the employee may be required to provide you with 30 days advance notice of the leave request.

If the need for leave is foreseeable, an employee must provide you at least 30 days advance notice before the FMLA leave is to begin. Notification should be provided by the employee either in person or by telephone, or with other electronic means such as email. If 30 days notice is not practical due to the lack of knowledge as to when leave will be required to begin, notice must be given as soon as possible. The employee should give notification at least verbally within one or two business days of when the need for leave becomes known to the employee. If the employee is unable to provide notice personally, the employee's family member may provide notification.

Employers must notify employees of FMLA designation in writing and explain the specific expectations and obligations of the employee.

Once an employee requests leave based on the FMLA guidelines, you must notify the employee within two business days of whether the leave counts against the twelve-week allotment, and whether any accrued paid time should run concurrently with the FMLA leave. You may notify the employee of the FMLA designation verbally, but it must be confirmed in writing no later than two business days. The written notification should be used to confirm the FMLA leave and to explain the specific expectations and obligations of the employee and any consequence of failure to meet these obligations. Employees retain any benefits accrued before the leave.

97. How does EEOC and discrimination law affect staffing?

Equal employment opportunity is a broad concept that states that all individuals should have equal treatment in all employment related actions. The primary reason for an organization to practice equal employment practices is to embrace the fact that all people have knowledge, skills, and abilities that can be used by the organization, regardless of their race, color, religion, sex, or national origin. The goal is to tap into the potential of all individuals to hire the best person to achieve organizational goals and objectives. The second reason for your company to practice equal opportunity practices is to follow local, state, and federal laws and regulations to avoid penalties for failure to comply with the regulations.

Equal opportunity employment practices are laws that prevent discrimination and help ensure the company hires the best potential candidate for the job based on knowledge and skills and not race, color, sex, or religion.

The Equal Employment Opportunity Commission (EEOC) is an independent federal agency that promotes equal opportunity in employment through administrative and judicial enforcement of the federal civil rights laws and through education and technical assistance. The EEOC enforces all of the following laws:

- Title VII of the Civil Rights Act
- Equal Pay Act (EPA)
- Age Discrimination in Employment Act (ADEA)
- The Civil Rights Act

Title VII of the Civil Rights Act

This act prohibits employment discrimination based on race, color, religion, sex, or national origin. It is illegal to discriminate against an individual because of birthplace, ancestry, culture, or linguistic characteristics common to a specific ethnic group.

It is illegal to discriminate against an individual because of birthplace, culture, or linguistic characteristics common to a specific ethnic group.

For example, if your call center has a rule requiring that employees speak only English in the workplace, it may violate Title VII unless your company can show that the requirement is necessary for conducting business. If your company believes such a rule is necessary, employees must be informed when English is required and what the consequences are for violating the rule.

Equal Pay Act (EPA)

This act protects men and women who perform substantially equal work from sex-based wage discrimination. The Equal Pay Act (EPA) prohibits discrimination on the basis of sex in the payment of wages or benefits, where men and women perform work of similar skill, effort, and responsibility for the same employer under similar working conditions.

Under this law, employers may not reduce wages of either sex to equalize pay between men and women. A violation of the EPA may occur where a different wage is paid to a person who works in the same job before or after an employee of the opposite sex.

The Equal Pay Act prevents an employer from paying a different wage based on gender for performing the same work.

The EPA provides flexibility for companies to provide different pay for the same position based on merit, productivity, seniority, and other job responsibilities. One employee can be compensated more than another employee if the employee is performing better than the other. The EPA also permits the company to compensate employees based on the length of time an employee has worked at the company. Other job responsibilities that may be compensated differently include shift differentials and cost-of-living difference in different geographic regions.

Age Discrimination in Employment Act (ADEA)

This act protects individuals who are 40 years of age or older. The ADEA's broad ban against age discrimination also specifically prohibits statements or specifications in job notices or advertisements of age preference and limitations. An age limit may only be specified in the rare circumstance where age has been proven to be a bona fide occupational qualification. (BFOQ).

The ADEA prohibits job and wage discrimination for individuals over 40 years of age.

The ADEA also prevents denial of benefits to older employees. An employer may reduce benefits based on age only if the cost of providing the reduced benefits to older workers is the same as the cost of providing benefits to younger workers.

The Civil Rights Act

This act made major changes in the federal laws against employment discrimination enforced by the EEOC. The Act was enacted in part to reverse several Supreme Court decisions that limited the rights of persons protected by these laws, and also provides monetary damages in cases of intentional employment discrimination. This legislation authorizes compensatory and punitive damages in cases of intentional discrimination.

Title VII, the ADA, and the ADEA, also make it illegal to discriminate in any aspect of employment, including the hiring, firing, transfer, promotion, layoff, or recall of employees. These laws also provide guidelines for compensation, assignment, classification of employees, pay, retirement plans, disability leave, and other terms and conditions of employment.

The EEO Employer Information survey is conducted annually in accordance with the Equal Employment Opportunity Act of 1972. All employers with 15 or more employees are required to keep employment records as specified by EEOC regulations. This report must be filed on an annual basis based on the number of employees and federal contract activities.

98. What are the biggest concerns about privacy in the call center?

Privacy and confidentiality issues should be addressed in every call center. The first type of privacy issue is the question of privacy and confidentiality related to personal information. Employees expect that confidential or personal information disclosed in private will not be shared in a public setting. The federal Electronic Communications Privacy Act (ECPA) makes it unlawful to intercept messages in transmission or access stored information on electronic communication services. The ECPA provides protection to employees regarding private telephone conversations and prohibits employers from deliberately listening to an employee's personal conversation on the telephone.

The ECPA prohibits employers from listening to private telephone conversations. However, with informed consent, job-related customer communications may be monitored and recorded.

An exception to ECPA guidelines permits your company to monitor your employees' use of telephone and electronic communications media, as long as one or both of the communicating parties has given prior consent. Your call center probably complies with this requirement by having a recorded greeting that includes a phrase such as, "Your call may be monitored or recorded for quality control purposes." Your employees probably sign a consent form upon hiring that allows you to monitor their calls for job-related purposes. These forms may also include verbiage indicating that email and other electronic communications are company property, should be used for business purposes only, and that electronic messages are subject to monitoring at the company's discretion.

The second category of privacy issues is the privacy related to electronic communications such as email, voice mail, and Internet communication. Since your employees are given passwords to access these systems, they may assume that their communications are private and confidential. In reality, these electronic communications may be monitored to ensure the quality of the customer's interaction with the call center.

To ensure compliance with harassment and anti-discrimination policies, some call centers are monitoring not only the voice and email transactions, but also the employee's Internet use. Some centers block employee access to undesirable and discriminatory Internet sites to help avoid or successfully defend against claims of harassment and discrimination.

With the ease with which employees can send documentation using e-mail, the call center is also faced with the risk of allowing confidential and proprietary information to be disclosed. To avoid these violations, call centers have implemented policies stating that no confidential or proprietary information should be shared without management's expressed written approval.

It is important to recognize that electronic communications can be used to support a variety of claims against a company during litigation. With the continued growth of electronic communication media in the call center, management should proactively implement policies regarding the proper usage of the media, establish the right to monitor communications, provide guidelines to prohibit harassment and discrimination, and to avoid dissemination of confidential and proprietary information. Consequences should be clearly identified for violation of the policies.

99. What should you know about diversity in the workplace?

Today's call center is comprised of a multi-cultural workforce, and effectively managing workplace issues is paramount to the call center's success. In most call centers, people from a variety of cultures are working side-by-side each day. To lead your team effectively, you will want to work with your team members to embrace diversity, see unique traits as an advantage, and work together to focus on the goals of the team.

To lead a team effectively, encourage your team members to embrace differences and work together to focus on the goals of the group.

Many call centers celebrate the diversity of their workforce in special ways. When there are potluck events, you may encourage people to bring food that demonstrates their unique culture and background. Art and decorations should follow a variety of styles and recognize events and holidays that may not be well known by most of your team.

The contemporary workplace is characterized by a great variety of human experiences and backgrounds. This is why diversity awareness is an increasingly important part of the call center environment. Diversity is about celebrating and capitalizing on the ways in which people who share a common humanity are also different and unique.

With the globalization of the labor market, diversity is a source of both innovation and conflict. Managers and employees need to cope with different styles and cultures including differences in age, physical appearance, attire, language, interaction styles, culture, race, and heritage.

With the globalization of the labor market, diversity is a source of both innovation and a source of conflict.

The first step in managing a diverse workforce is to recognize the value of differences by going beyond stereotypes and looking for the individuality of each person. Even if employees find it difficult working with those who are different, they must learn to accept them in order to be valuable to the organization. It is not a job requirement to like co-workers, but it is a requirement to get the job done without causing problems for others or for the organization.

In order to accept differences, employees must look at their own stereotypes and prejudices. Stereotypes and prejudices are most frequently based on past experiences and backgrounds, and employees must be aware of them. Diversity training can raise people's awareness of stereotypes, but it generally cannot overcome long-held prejudices.

Diversity training can raise people's awareness of stereotypes, but it generally cannot overcome long-held prejudices.

Prejudices are simply negative beliefs that have been learned. You may not be able to erase an individual's prejudices, but you can ensure that these prejudices are not exhibited in behaviors and actions towards those who are different. Despite negative feelings that an employee may have about those who are different, the actions of that employee should not in any way be harassing or demeaning to others.

Your role as a supervisor is to focus on programs that facilitate learning, encourage sharing, demonstrate appreciation, and increase opportunities to work together. The management team needs to communicate diversity issues and publicize the call center's efforts to increase diversity awareness.

A diversity training program needs to find ways for diverse individuals to interact and work with one another. Policies, systems, and practices can be designed to support workplace diversity and encourage flexibility. For example, the call center's ability to help employees develop the careers they want, adjust job descriptions, work hours to suit employee needs, and implement a strategic plan to hire retired or "seasoned" and temporary workers are strategies that support a diverse and flexible workplace.

The call center management team should focus on the following perspectives:

- Be flexible and stay attuned to individual differences and needs.
- Find ways to celebrate and utilize differences effectively rather than just focusing on accommodating them.
- Encourage collaboration, cooperation, and teamwork.
- Be prepared to challenge the status quo and take risks.

Find ways to celebrate and utilize differences effectively rather than just trying to accommodate them.

Age is one of the differences that may be found in call center employees. There are three typical age groups represented in the call center workforce: Baby Boomers (born between 1946 and 1964), Generation X employees (born between 1964 and 1982), and Generation Y employees (born after 1982).

These groups of employees will have different lifestyles, interests, and work perspectives. It is interesting to compare the characteristics of these three groups because what motivates an individual in one group is vastly different than what motivates an individual in another group.

Baby-Boomers, Generation X, and Generation Y employees will have different interests and motivational needs based on age.

Baby-boomers may be more interested in monetary compensation and security, while the younger Generation X and Y workers may care more about benefits and time-off policies. The implications suggest that workers in the Generation X and Generation Y group will be more motivated by personal fulfillment opportunities on the job than by traditional monetary rewards. Managing these workers will require different motivational programs than those designed for your more mature workers.

100. What steps should you use for discipline or termination?

Having a formal disciplinary process in place ensures that your employees are treated fairly, consistently, and systematically when their performance falls short of expectations. Your formal disciplinary procedure is usually defined by the human resources department to make sure that each step in the process is implemented properly and that all internal and external guidelines and legalities are being followed.

Many call centers use a process of progressive discipline to deal with unacceptable performance.

Most call centers use a process called progressive discipline to deal with unacceptable employee performance. Since progressive discipline is based on performance expectations and workplace conduct, you must first ensure that all employees are aware of the expectations and standards for their particular job. It is impossible to justify discipline or termination for an employee for violating expectations or standards that were not made clear in the first place.

As employee performance is monitored, policies and practices must be applied consistently so that there is no favoritism or discrimination for individual employees. It is critical to document interactions with all employees, including details of the infraction or problem, along with the steps taken to remedy the behavior. If disciplinary action is required, you must make sure the discipline is appropriate for the severity of the offense.

Apply praise and discipline consistently so there is no perception of favoritism or discrimination.

Progressive discipline generally includes the following four stages:

- ***Preliminary notification.*** During this phase, you will notify the employee that job performance or workplace conduct does not meet the standards and expectations. You will typically deliver the news in a one-on-one meeting with the employee.
- ***Second notification.*** During this second phase, you will notify employees that problems identified during the preliminary notification stage have not been resolved or performance has worsened. This notification is again accomplished with a one-on-one meeting with the employee, but in addition to verbal notification, you will include a written warning. You may require the employee to sign the document to acknowledge understanding of problem and the steps required to improve.
- ***Final notification.*** This stage is the most formal phase of the disciplinary process. Employees receive notification that if the performance problems continue, the employee will be subject to further disciplinary action, up to and including termination. Documentation provides specific steps that must be followed along with associated disciplinary actions such as suspension, leave, or demotion.

- ***Termination.*** The final phase in the disciplinary process is termination. This step is taken when all other steps have failed to resolve the problem.

The steps of progressive discipline will be different for each organization. Check with your human resources team to ensure you follow the mandatory steps for your company.

It is expensive to hire and train new agents, so every attempt should be made to address performance problems early on. All employees have the opportunity to improve performance through coaching and training. However, you have a responsibility to the organization, and a responsibility to the employees who are performing well, to terminate employees who are not performing up to the standard after repeated attempts at coaching.

Firing or terminating employees is never easy – either for you or the employee. Termination is the last action to be considered, and it should be used only when other options are exhausted. In most cases, you don't have the flexibility to restructure the job, and reassignment to a different position may not be a viable option. In other words, you may have no recourse but to terminate employment. When the decision to terminate an employee is made, the termination should not come as a surprise if the steps of progressive discipline have been followed consistently.

Termination should not come as a surprise to an employee if the steps of progressive discipline have been followed.

When it is time to deliver the termination message, it is best to choose a time when there will be few interruptions, possibly before or after the normal work day. To allow for privacy, an office out of the view of the regular workplace traffic should be selected. If the termination meeting is expected to be contentious, it may be a good idea to have someone from human resources or perhaps even security staff standing by to assist.

Your message to the employee should be well prepared. If possible, rehearse your delivery of the message prior to the actual meeting with the employee. A written outline or checklist will help you make sure you cover all the important points. You may want to have a human resource representative included in the meeting to assist with note-taking and to act as a witness to any comments or questions that occur at the session.

Take time to prepare the termination message and rehearse it if possible to make actual delivery of it easier. Use an outline to cover all the required points.

As the termination message is delivered, it is important to state the facts clearly without making excuses or minimizing the basis of the decision. Personal attacks or derogatory generalizations should not be made. It is critical to make sure the employee understands that his or her employment has been terminated.

You should explain the status of employee benefits, including any documentation that must be completed and the timetable in which it must be done. The type of employment reference the company will provide (if any) should be described to the employee. All company property should be returned at this time or immediately following the meeting. A checklist should be prepared to include items such as a corporate credit card, access card, identification badge, employee manual, and other company confidential documents.

If the employee raises any concerns or questions, they should be answered honestly and as completely as possible. Fairness and professionalism should be exhibited at all times during the meeting. Once all questions have been answered, the employee should be escorted back to the work area to remove personal belongings and then escorted from the premises. If additional information is required to answer a question completely, state the expectation of when the answer will be provided.

Unfortunately, another type of termination may have to happen that is not a result of poor performance by the employee. Many companies today are implementing different staffing strategies to improve the bottom line and a reduction in workforce may be one of those strategies. While some companies are large enough to redeploy staff to other areas of the company, there may still be staff that will be forced to leave the company.

Some terminations will be due to an overall reduction in workforce, requiring a different set of termination steps.

There are various ways to accomplish a reduction in force. Some companies just wait for people to leave or retire on their own through a natural attrition process. Another strategy is to offer voluntary retirement or early retirement incentives to eligible employees. Another option is to offer a leave of absence with full benefits for a specified period of time. These employees are promised a job upon their return from the leave, but it may not be the same job or at the same pay level.

In some cases, a staff lay-off is unavoidable. Such a reduction in force is different than terminating an employee since the employees who are being let go haven't done anything to warrant the termination. Reductions in force will generally involve some sort of severance package. While there are usually no legal requirements for a company to provide severance pay, your company may provide some package to bridge the gap between this job and the employee's next one.

While there is no legal requirement to do so, most companies will provide some sort of severance package if a reduction in force is required.

If a severance package is offered, it generally includes a continuance of pay, with a common amount being one to two weeks pay for every year of service. Outplacement services may also be provided to help employees market their skills, analyze career options, and find a suitable job. Medical insurance may be paid for a certain length of time by your company, with the employee eligible to take over payments as part of COBRA legislation. Vacation pay that has been accrued may be paid out as well. If the employee has vested stock options, those may be exercised before they are lost.

Your company may ask departing employees to sign a waiver and release statement. This type of agreement usually states that the employee has accepted the terms of the severance package and that by accepting the severance check agrees not to sue the company for any type of wrongful termination.

Learning Activities

1. Schedule a meeting with your human resources department to discuss how the company meets OSHA and EEOC rules and regulations. Outline what you should do as a supervisor to ensure you are complying with all guidelines.

2. Research the use of FMLA leave used by the staff in your call center. What percentage of frontline employees have used this leave option within the last year? Review the cases to see if all employees had legitimate FMLA circumstances or whether the policy is being abused by call center staff.

3. Research your company's and your call center's privacy policy. What information is shared with employees and what privacy statements are communicated to customers? Are all aspects of customer interactions covered by existing policy or does the policy need to be expanded or upgraded?

4. Review the steps of progressive discipline with your human resources department. Are you and your fellow supervisors adhering to all components of the progressive discipline policy when addressing ongoing performance problems with employees, particularly the written documenta tion? How are the steps communicated to staff? Outline a 10-minute presentation that explains the process to staff so they understand the process and implications of the progressive discipline process.